First World War
and Army of Occupation
War Diary
France, Belgium and Germany

30 DIVISION
Divisional Troops
Royal Army Veterinary Corps
40 Mobile Veterinary Section,
Divisional Train (186,187,188,189, Companies A.S.C.)
4 September 1915 - 27 May 1919

WO95/2326/1-2

The Naval & Military Press Ltd
www.nmarchive.com
Published in association with The National Archives

Published by

The Naval & Military Press Ltd

Unit 10 Ridgewood Industrial Park,

Uckfield, East Sussex,

TN22 5QE England

Tel: +44 (0) 1825 749494

www.naval-military-press.com

www.nmarchive.com

This diary has been reprinted in facsimile from the original. Any imperfections are inevitably reproduced and the quality may fall short of modern type and cartographic standards.

© **Crown Copyright**
Images reproduced by permission of The National Archives, London, England, 2015.

Contents

Document type	Place/Title	Date From	Date To
Miscellaneous	WO95/2326/1		
Heading	30th Division Divl Troops 40th Mobile Vety Section Sept 1915-Apr 1919		
War Diary	Larkhill	20/09/1915	30/10/1915
Heading	30th Division 40th Map. Vet. Sect. Vol. 1 Nov 15 Apr 19		
War Diary	Larkhill	01/11/1915	09/11/1915
War Diary	Amesbury	09/11/1915	09/11/1915
War Diary	Southampton	09/11/1915	10/11/1915
War Diary	Le Havre	10/11/1915	11/11/1915
War Diary	Pont Remy	11/11/1915	11/11/1915
War Diary	Ailly Le Haut Clocher	11/11/1915	18/11/1915
War Diary	Flesselles	19/11/1915	28/11/1915
War Diary	Vacquerie	29/11/1915	30/11/1915
Heading	30th Division 40th Map. Vet Sect Vol 2		
War Diary	Vacquerie	01/12/1915	31/12/1915
Heading	Volume 2 No. 40 Mobile Vety Section DR Williamson Lt AVC		
War Diary	Wargnies	20/01/1916	20/01/1916
War Diary	Pont Noyelles	21/01/1916	21/01/1916
War Diary	Chipilly	22/01/1916	22/01/1916
War Diary	Etinehem	23/01/1916	31/01/1916
War Diary	Vacquerie	01/01/1916	09/01/1916
War Diary	Halloy Les Pernois	10/01/1916	19/01/1916
Heading	40th Mob. Vet. Sect Vol 4		
War Diary	Etinehem	01/02/1916	07/02/1916
War Diary	Chipilly	09/02/1916	29/02/1916
Heading	40th Mobile Vety Section Vol IV July 1916 DR Williamson Capt AVC		
Heading	40 M Vol Sec Vol 5		
War Diary	Daours	27/03/1916	28/03/1916
War Diary	St. Saveur	28/03/1916	31/03/1916
Heading	War Diary 40th Mobile Vety Section Vol 5. March 1916		
War Diary	Chipilly	19/03/1916	22/03/1916
War Diary	Daours	23/03/1916	26/03/1916
War Diary	Chipilly	01/03/1916	18/03/1916
War Diary	St. Sauveur	01/04/1916	30/04/1916
Heading	War Diary 40th Mobile Vety Section Vol VI April 1916 DR Williamson		
War Diary	St Sauveur	01/05/1916	06/05/1916
War Diary	Corbie	07/05/1916	07/05/1916
War Diary	Sailly Laurette	08/05/1916	31/05/1916
Heading	War Diary Vol VII 40th Mobile Vety Section		
War Diary	Sailly-Laurette	01/06/1916	17/06/1916
War Diary	Bois Des Tailles	18/06/1916	31/07/1916
Heading	War Diary Of 40 Mobile Veterinary Section For The Month Of August 1916 Volume X		
War Diary	Bois Des Tailles	01/08/1916	01/08/1916
War Diary	Allonville	02/08/1916	02/08/1916

War Diary	Picquigny Soues	02/08/1916	06/08/1916
War Diary	St. Floris	07/08/1916	11/08/1916
War Diary	Locon	12/08/1916	18/09/1916
War Diary	Doullens	19/09/1916	19/09/1916
War Diary	Hem	20/09/1916	21/09/1916
War Diary	Vignacourt	22/09/1916	30/09/1916
War Diary	War Diary 40th Mobile Vety Section A.V.C. Vol XI DR Williamson Capt AVC OC 40 MVS.		
Heading	War Diary 40th Mobile Veterinary Section Vol XI DR Williamson Capt AVC OC 40 MVS.		
War Diary	Vignacourt	01/10/1916	03/10/1916
War Diary	Allonville	04/10/1916	04/10/1916
War Diary	Ribemont	04/10/1916	10/10/1916
War Diary	Mametz	11/10/1916	27/10/1916
War Diary	Halloy	28/10/1916	31/10/1916
War Diary	Larbret	31/10/1916	31/10/1916
Heading	War Diary Vol XII Nov 1916		
Heading	War Diary Of 40th Mobile Vet Section For The Month Of October 1916 Volume 12		
Heading	40th Mob. Vet. Sect. Vol. 3		
War Diary	Larbret	01/11/1916	30/11/1916
Heading	War Diary 40th Mobile Vety Section Volume XIII November 1916		
Heading	War Diary December 1916 Vol. XIV 40th Mobile Vety. Section. Vol 14		
War Diary	Larbret	01/12/1916	31/12/1916
Heading	War Diary December 1916 Vol XIV 40th Mobile Vety Section		
War Diary	Larbret	01/01/1917	16/01/1917
War Diary	Grouches	16/01/1917	31/01/1917
Heading	40th Mobile Veterinary Section January-1917 Vol. XV		
Heading	40th Mobile Veterinary Section Jany. 1917 Vol XV		
Heading	War Diary 40th Mobile Veterinary Section. February 1917 Vol XVI		
War Diary	L'Arbret	13/02/1917	28/02/1917
War Diary	Grouches	01/02/1917	06/02/1917
War Diary	L'Arbret	07/02/1917	31/03/1917
Heading	40th Mobile Vety Section Vol XVII March 1917		
Heading	40th Mobile Veterinary Section Vol XVII March 1917		
War Diary	L'Arbret	01/04/1917	21/04/1917
War Diary	Agny	22/04/1917	29/04/1917
War Diary	Roellecourt	30/04/1917	30/04/1917
Heading	40th M.V.S Vol. XVIII April 1917 War Diary.		
Heading	War Diary. 40th Mobile Veterinary Section. Vol. XIX May 1917		
War Diary	Rocourt St Laurent	01/05/1917	04/05/1917
War Diary	Oeuf	05/05/1917	15/05/1917
War Diary	Poperinghe	01/06/1917	14/06/1917
War Diary	Watou	27/05/1917	30/05/1917
War Diary	Poperinge	31/05/1917	31/05/1917
Heading	War Diary 40th Mobile Vety Section Vol XIX May 1917		
War Diary	Poperinghe	15/06/1917	25/06/1917
War Diary	Reninghelst	26/06/1917	30/06/1917
Heading	War Diary. 40th Mobile Vety Section Vol XX June 1917		

War Diary	Reninghelst	01/07/1917	31/07/1917
Heading	War Diary. July 1917 Volume XXI 40th Mobile Vety. Section. H.U. Metiner Capt A.V.C O.C 40th M.V.S		
Heading	War Diary August 1917 Volume XXII 40th Mobile Veterinary Section.		
War Diary	Reninghelst	01/08/1917	05/08/1917
War Diary	Godewaersvelde	06/08/1917	07/08/1917
War Diary	Merris	08/08/1917	11/08/1917
War Diary	St Jans Cappel	12/08/1917	23/08/1917
War Diary	Dranoutre	24/08/1917	31/08/1917
Heading	War Diary August 1917 Volume XXII 40th Mobile Vety Section		
War Diary	Dranoutre	01/09/1917	30/09/1917
Heading	War Diary September 1917 Vol XXIII 40th Mobile Veterinary Sect. H.U. Metiner Capt. O.C. 40th M.V.S.		
Heading	War Diary Of 40th Mobile Vety Section For The Month Of September 1917 Volume XXIII		
War Diary	Dranoutre	01/10/1917	31/10/1917
Heading	War Diary Of 40th Mob. Vety Sect. For The Month Of October 1917 Volume 24		
Heading	War Diary November 1917 Vol. XXV 40th Mobile Veterinary Section.		
War Diary	Dranoutre	01/11/1917	15/11/1917
War Diary	Steenvoorde	16/11/1917	27/11/1917
War Diary	Devises Camp	28/11/1917	30/11/1917
Heading	War Diary November 1917 Vol XXV 40th Mobile Vety Sect. H.U.M.		
Heading	War Diary December 1917 Vol. XXVI 40th Mobile Vety. Section.		
War Diary	Aragon Camp	01/12/1917	13/12/1917
War Diary	Conqueror Camp	14/12/1917	31/12/1917
Heading	War Diary December 1917 Vol XXVI 40th M.B.V Section		
Heading	January 1918 War Diary Vol XXVII 40th Mobile Veterinary Section Vol 27		
War Diary	(Westoutre) Conqueror Camp	01/01/1918	05/01/1918
War Diary	Meteren	06/01/1918	06/01/1918
War Diary	Racquinghem	07/01/1918	11/01/1918
War Diary	Corbie	12/01/1918	13/01/1918
War Diary	Reserve	14/01/1918	14/01/1918
War Diary	Nesle	15/01/1918	18/01/1918
War Diary	Echeux	19/01/1918	26/01/1918
War Diary	Dampcourt	27/01/1918	31/01/1918
Heading	War Diary Of 40th Mobile Veterinary Section February 1918 Vol XXVIII		
War Diary	Dampcourt	01/02/1918	09/02/1918
War Diary	Bouchon	10/02/1918	10/02/1918
War Diary	Ercheu.	11/02/1918	22/02/1918
War Diary	St Sulpice	23/02/1918	28/02/1918
Heading	War Diary of 40th Mobile Vety Section February 1918 Vol XXVIII		
War Diary	St Sulpice	01/03/1918	21/03/1918
War Diary	Ercheu.	22/03/1918	22/03/1918
War Diary	Roye	23/03/1918	25/03/1918
War Diary	La Neuville & Ailly. S. Noye	26/03/1918	26/03/1918
War Diary	Ailly S. Noye	27/03/1918	27/03/1918

War Diary	Fouzen Camp & Estree en Amenois	28/03/1918	28/03/1918
War Diary	Estree-En Amenois	29/03/1918	29/03/1918
War Diary	Estree en Amenois & Pissy	30/03/1918	30/03/1918
War Diary	Mareuil	31/03/1918	31/03/1918
Heading	War Diary 40th Mobile Veterinary Section. March 1918 Vol. XXIX		
Heading	War Diary Of 40th Mobile Vety Section For The Month Of March 1918 Volume XXIX		
Heading	War Diary 40th Mobile Veterinary Section Vol XXX April 1918		
War Diary	St Valerie Area Somme	01/04/1918	05/04/1918
War Diary	Elverdinghe Road Standings	06/04/1918	20/04/1918
War Diary	Buysscheure	21/04/1918	30/04/1918
Heading	War Diary. 40th Mobile Veterinary Section Vol XXX April 1918		
Heading	War Diary 40th M.V.S Month Of May 1918 Vol. XXXI		
War Diary	Buysscheure	01/05/1918	15/05/1918
War Diary	St. Quentin Lamotte	16/05/1918	31/05/1918
Heading	War Diary. 40th Mobile Vetery Section May 1918 Vol XXXI		
Heading	40th Mobile Veterinary Section. War Diary June 1918 Vol XXXII		
War Diary	St. Quentin Lamotte	01/06/1918	20/09/1918
War Diary	Rue	21/06/1918	26/06/1918
War Diary	Eperleques	27/06/1918	30/06/1918
Heading	40th M.V.S War Diary Vol XXXIII July 1918		
War Diary	Eperlecques	01/07/1918	07/07/1918
War Diary	St Momelin	08/07/1918	08/07/1918
War Diary	St Marie Cappel Sheet 27 P.13.b. 3.5	09/07/1918	11/07/1918
War Diary	Sheet 27 P 13b 3.5 St Morris Cappel	12/07/1918	31/07/1918
Heading	40th M.V.S. War Diary August 1918 Vol. XXXIV Vol 34		
War Diary	Sheet 27 P 13b. 3.5 St Marie Cappel	01/08/1918	12/08/1918
War Diary	Terdinghem	12/08/1918	31/08/1918
Heading	40th Mobile Veterinary Sect War Diary September 1918 Vol. XXXV H.U Metiner Captain A.V.C O.C 40th M.V.S		
War Diary	Terdinghem	01/09/1918	01/09/1918
War Diary	Boeschepe	02/09/1918	12/09/1918
War Diary	Sheet 27 R 15b 8.7	13/09/1918	30/09/1918
Heading	40th Mobile Vetery Section. War Diary. Vol. XXXVI October 1918		
War Diary	Sheet 27 R 15.b. 8.7	01/10/1918	02/10/1918
War Diary	Sheet 28 M 17b 3.3	03/10/1918	19/10/1918
War Diary	Houthem	20/10/1918	20/10/1918
War Diary	Bousbecque	21/10/1918	21/10/1918
War Diary	Aelbeke	22/10/1918	09/11/1918
War Diary	Aelbeke	23/10/1918	09/11/1918
War Diary	Aelbeke Poltes	10/11/1918	10/11/1918
War Diary	Escanaffles	11/11/1918	16/11/1918
War Diary	Belleghem	16/11/1918	30/11/1918
Heading	War Diary Of 40th Mob. Vety Sec. For Month Of November 1918 Volume XXXVII		
Heading	War Diary 40th M.V.S. December 1918 Vol. XXXVIII Vol 39		

War Diary	Belleghem	01/12/1918	01/12/1918
War Diary	Croix au Bois	02/12/1918	02/12/1918
War Diary	Ebblinghem	03/12/1918	03/12/1918
War Diary	Renescure	04/12/1918	31/12/1918
Heading	40th M.V.S War Diary For January 1919 Vol. XXXXIX		
War Diary	Renescure	01/01/1919	09/01/1919
War Diary	Aire	10/01/1919	31/01/1919
Heading	War Diary 40th M.V.S February 1919 Vol. XL		
War Diary	Aire	01/02/1919	07/02/1919
War Diary	Steenvoorde	08/02/1919	28/02/1919
Heading	War Diary 40th Mobile Vety Section For Month Of March 1919 Vol XLI Vol 42		
War Diary	Steenvoorde	01/03/1919	31/03/1919
Heading	War Diary 40th M.V.S. Vol. XLII April 1919 Vol 43		
War Diary	Steenwoorde	01/04/1919	27/04/1919
War Diary	Dannes	28/04/1919	30/04/1919
War Diary	Dunkerque	06/08/1919	06/08/1919
Miscellaneous	WO95/2326/2		
Heading	30th Division Divl Troops 30th Divl Train ASC Sept 1915-May 1919 186-Coys ASC 189		
War Diary	Havre	04/09/1915	04/09/1915
War Diary	In Train	05/09/1915	05/09/1915
War Diary	Flessels	06/09/1915	17/09/1915
War Diary	Guillaucourt	18/09/1915	20/09/1915
War Diary	Weincourt	21/09/1915	21/10/1915
War Diary	Villers Bretonneux	22/10/1915	31/10/1915
Heading	30th Div Train Vol I Nov 15		
Heading	War Diary Of Lt Col C.M. Ainslie Cmdg 30th Divnl Train From 1st Nov To 30th Nov 15 Volume 3		
War Diary	Villers Bretonneux	01/11/1915	04/11/1915
War Diary	Daours	05/11/1915	06/11/1915
War Diary	Ailly Le Haut Clocher	07/11/1915	17/11/1915
War Diary	Flessels	18/11/1915	27/11/1915
War Diary	Fienvillers	28/11/1915	30/11/1915
Heading	30th Division Train Vol. 2 Decr 15		
Heading	War Diary of Lt Col C.M. Ainslie 30th Divnl Train From 1 Dec 1915 To 31st Dec 1915 Volume I		
War Diary	Fienvillers	01/12/1915	04/12/1915
War Diary	Lemeillard	05/12/1915	31/12/1915
Heading	30th Divl Train Vol. 3		
Heading	War Diary of Lt Col. C.M Ainslie Cmdg 30th Divnl Train From 1 Jan 16 To 31 Jan 16 Volume I		
War Diary	Le Meillard	01/01/1916	07/01/1916
War Diary	Pont Noyelles	08/01/1916	11/01/1916
War Diary	Etinehem	12/01/1916	31/01/1916
Heading	30th Div Train Vol 4 War Diary Of Lt Col C.M Division CM 30th DW Train From 1st Feb 1916 To 29th Feb 1916 (Volume IV)		
War Diary	Etinehem	01/02/1916	29/02/1916
Heading	War Diary Of Lt Col. C.M. Ainslie A.S.C 30th Div Train From 1st March To 31st March Vol 6		
War Diary	Etinehem	01/03/1916	19/03/1916
War Diary	Montigny	20/03/1916	23/03/1916
War Diary	Daours	24/03/1916	27/03/1916
War Diary	Ailly Sur Somme	28/03/1916	31/03/1916

Heading	War Diary Of Lt Col C.M Ainslie A.S.C Commanding. 30th Leave Train From April 1st 1916 To April 30th 1916 Vol 6		
War Diary	Ailly Sur Somme	01/04/1916	30/04/1916
Heading	War Diary of Lieut Col: C.M Ainslie. Commdg 39th Divisional Train From May 1st 1916 To May 31st 1916 30 Div Train Vol 7		
War Diary	Ailly Sur Somme	01/05/1916	04/05/1916
War Diary	Ecluse Mericourt	05/05/1916	17/05/1916
War Diary	Ecluse Mericourt Sur Somme	17/05/1916	31/05/1916
Heading	War Diary of Lieut. Col. C.M Ainslie. A.S.C Commdg 30th Divl. Train. From June 1st To June 30th		
War Diary	Ecluse Mericourt	01/06/1916	12/06/1916
War Diary	Ecluse Mericourt Sur Somme	13/06/1916	30/06/1916
Heading	War Diary of Lieut Col C.M Ainslie. A.S.C Commanding 30th Div Train From July 1st 1916 To July 31st 1916 30 July Div Train Vol 9		
War Diary	Ecluse	01/07/1916	03/07/1916
War Diary	Sailly Laurette	04/07/1916	21/07/1916
War Diary	Dernancourt	22/07/1916	23/07/1916
War Diary	Bray Albert Rd	24/07/1916	31/07/1916
Heading	War Diary Of Lieut Col CM Ainslie A.S.C Commdg 30th Div Train. From August 1st To August 31st 1916 Vol 10		
War Diary	Bray Albert Road	01/08/1916	01/08/1916
War Diary	Poulainville	02/08/1916	02/08/1916
War Diary	Hallencourt	02/08/1916	03/08/1916
War Diary	St Floris	04/08/1916	11/08/1916
War Diary	Locon	12/08/1916	31/08/1916
Heading	War Diary of Lieut. Col. C.M. Ainslie A.S.C Commanding 30th Divisional Train From:- September 1st 1916 To:- September 30th 1916 Vol 11		
War Diary	Locon	01/09/1916	16/09/1916
War Diary	Bethune	17/09/1916	17/09/1916
War Diary	Doullens	18/09/1916	20/09/1916
War Diary	Vignacourt	21/09/1916	30/09/1916
Miscellaneous	D.A.G., 3rd Echelon. 30 Div Train Vol 8	01/07/1916	01/07/1916
Heading	War Diary of Lieut. Colonel C.M. Ainslie A.S.C Commanding 30th Div. Train From:- October 1st 1916 To.- October 31st 1916 Vol 12		
War Diary	Vignacourt	01/10/1916	04/10/1916
War Diary	Rebemont	04/10/1916	10/10/1916
War Diary	Ell Central	11/10/1916	21/10/1916
War Diary	Ribemont	22/10/1916	25/10/1916
War Diary	Lucheux	26/10/1916	30/10/1916
War Diary	Bavincourt	31/10/1916	31/10/1916
Heading	War Diary Of Lieut Col C.M Ainslie A.S.C Commanding 30th Divisional Train. From November 1st 1916 To November 30th 1916 Vol 13		
War Diary	Bavincourt	01/11/1916	30/11/1916
Heading	War Diary Of Lieut Col C.M Ainslie D.S.O. Commanding 30th Divisional Train From:- December 1st 1916 To:- December 31st 1916 Vol 14		
War Diary	Bavincourt	01/12/1916	31/12/1916

Heading	War Diary Of Lieut Col C.M Ainslie D.S.O. Commanding 30th Divisional Train. From:- January 1st 1917 To:- January 31st 1917 Vol 15		
War Diary	Bavincourt	01/01/1917	06/01/1917
War Diary	Neuvillette	07/01/1917	10/01/1917
War Diary	Ivergny	11/01/1917	23/01/1917
War Diary	Bouquemaison	24/01/1917	28/01/1917
War Diary	La Souich	29/01/1917	31/01/1917
Heading	War Diary of Lieut. Col. C.M. Ainslie D.S.O. Period. From:- 1st. February 1917. To:- 28th February 1917 30 Div Train Vol 16		
War Diary	Le Souich	01/02/1917	05/02/1917
War Diary	Labret	06/02/1917	28/02/1917
Heading	War Diary of Officer Commanding 30th. Divl. Train. Period. From:- 1st March 1917 To:- 31st March 1917 Vol 17		
War Diary	Labret	01/03/1917	31/03/1917
Heading	War Diary of Lieut. Col. C.M Ainslie. D.S.O. Period. From:- 1st April 1917 To:- 30th April 1917 30th D Train Vol 18		
War Diary	Labret	31/03/1917	07/04/1917
War Diary	Bellacourt	08/04/1917	10/04/1917
War Diary	Boisleux-Au-Mont	11/04/1917	12/04/1917
War Diary	Larbret	13/04/1917	19/04/1917
War Diary	Achicourt	20/04/1917	30/04/1917
Heading	War Diary Of Lieut. C.M. Ainslie D.S.O. Comdg. 30th. Divl. Train Period. From:- 1st May 1917. To:- 31st May 1917 Vol 19		
War Diary	Roellecourt	01/05/1917	02/05/1917
War Diary	Oeuf	03/05/1917	14/05/1917
War Diary	Wail	15/05/1917	20/05/1917
War Diary	Pernes	21/05/1917	21/05/1917
War Diary	Norrent Fontes	22/05/1917	23/05/1917
War Diary	Steenbecque	24/05/1917	24/05/1917
War Diary	Caestre	25/05/1917	25/05/1917
War Diary	Watou	26/05/1917	31/05/1917
Heading	War Diary. of Lieut. Col. C.M Ainslie D.S.O. Comdg. 30th. Divl. Train. Period. From:- 1st June 1917. To:- 30th June 1917 Vol 20		
War Diary	Buseboom	01/06/1917	30/06/1917
Heading	War Diary Of Lieut. Col. C.M. Ainslie D.S.O. Comdg. 30th Divl. Train. Vol 21 From 1st July 1917 To 31st July 1917 Vol 21		
War Diary	Buseboom	01/07/1917	06/07/1917
War Diary	Wolphus	07/07/1917	18/07/1917
War Diary	Steenvoorde	19/07/1917	23/07/1917
War Diary	G 22 D. 04	24/07/1917	31/07/1917
Heading	War Diary Lieut Col C.M Ainslie D.S.O. Commdg 30th Divl. Train From August 1st 1917 To August 31st 1917 Vol 22		
War Diary	Q 22 D 0.4	01/08/1917	04/08/1917
War Diary	Godwaersvelde	05/08/1917	06/08/1917
War Diary	Merris	07/08/1917	10/08/1917
War Diary	St. Jans Capel	11/08/1917	31/08/1917

Heading	War Diary Of Lieut. Col. C.M Ainslie D.S.O. Commanding 30th Divisional Train. Period 1st To 30th September 1917 Vol 23		
War Diary	Danoutre	01/09/1917	30/09/1917
Heading	War Diary Of Lieut Col C.M. Ainslie D.S.O. From:- October 1st 1917 To:- October 8th 1917. and of Major L. Knapman A.S.C From:- October 9th 1917 To:- October 31st 1917 30 D Train Vol 24		
War Diary	Danoutre	01/10/1917	31/10/1917
Heading	War Diary Of Lieutenant Colonel C.M. Ainslie D.S.O. 30th Divisional Train. Period:- From 1st November 1917 To 30th November 1917 Vol 25		
War Diary	Danoutre	01/11/1917	16/11/1917
War Diary	Steenvoorde	17/11/1917	26/11/1917
War Diary	Westoutre	27/11/1917	30/11/1917
Heading	War Diary. Of Lieutenant Colonel C.M. Ainslie D.S.O. Commanding 30th Divisional Train. Period from 1st December 1917 to 31st December 1917 Vol 26		
War Diary	Westoutre	01/12/1917	31/12/1917
Heading	War Diary Of Lieutenant Colonel C.M. Ainslie D.S.O. Commdg. 30th Divisional Train. Period January 1st 1918 31st January 1918 Vol 27		
War Diary	Westoutre	01/01/1918	06/01/1918
War Diary	Blaringham	07/01/1918	07/01/1918
War Diary	Corbie	08/01/1918	14/01/1918
War Diary	Nesle	15/01/1918	18/01/1918
War Diary	Ercheu	19/01/1918	27/01/1918
War Diary	Chauny	28/01/1918	30/01/1918
War Diary	Appilly	31/01/1918	31/01/1918
Heading	Cover for Documents. Nature of Enclosures. War Diary of Lieut Col C.M Ainslie D.S.O. Comdg. 30th Divl Train Period. Feby 1st to Feby 28th 1918 30 D Train Vol 28		
War Diary	Appilly	01/02/1918	07/02/1918
War Diary	Ercheu.	08/02/1918	22/02/1918
War Diary	Pithon	23/02/1918	28/02/1918
Heading	War Diary Of Lieut. Col. C.M Ainslie D.S.O. Commanding 30th Divisional Train. March 1st 1918 To March 31st 1918 Vol 29		
War Diary	Pithon	01/03/1918	20/03/1918
War Diary	Ercheu	21/03/1918	22/03/1918
War Diary	Roieglise	23/03/1918	24/03/1918
War Diary	Hangest	25/03/1918	25/03/1918
War Diary	Braches	26/03/1918	26/03/1918
War Diary	Ailly Sur Noye	27/03/1918	27/03/1918
War Diary	Estrees	28/03/1918	30/03/1918
War Diary	St Valerie	31/03/1918	31/03/1918
Heading	War Diary Of Lieutenant. Colonel. C.M. Ainslie D.S.O. Commanding 30th Divnl. Train. April 1st 1918-April 30th 1918 Vol 30		
War Diary	St Valery	01/04/1918	03/04/1918
War Diary	Proven	04/04/1918	07/04/1918
War Diary	Elverdinghe	08/04/1918	12/04/1918
War Diary	St Sixty	13/04/1918	20/04/1918
War Diary	G 11 d 04 Busseboom	21/04/1918	24/04/1918
War Diary	St Sixte	25/04/1918	30/04/1918

Miscellaneous	List of Units Fed of Other Formations by 30th Division.	21/03/1918	21/03/1918
Heading	War Diary of Lieutenant. Colonel. C.M. Ainslie D.S.O. Commanding 30th Divisional Train. Period. May 1st 1918-May 31st 1918 Vol 31		
War Diary	Broxeele	01/05/1918	14/05/1918
War Diary	Eu	15/05/1918	31/05/1918
Heading	War Diary. Of Lieutenant. Colonel. C.M. Ainslie D.S.O. Commanding 30th Divisional Train A.S.C Period June 1st 1918 to 30th June 1918 Vol 32		
War Diary	Eu	01/06/1918	26/06/1918
War Diary	Eperlecques	27/06/1918	30/06/1918
Heading	War Diary. Of Lieutenant Colonel. C.M. Ainslie D.S.O. Commdg. 30th Divn'l Train Period. July 1st To 31st 1918 Vol 33		
War Diary	Eperleque	01/07/1918	08/07/1918
War Diary	Cassel	09/07/1918	31/07/1918
Heading	War Diary Of Lt Col. C.M Ainslie D.S.O. Comdg. 30th Divisional Train Period Aug 1st Aug 31st 1918 Vol 34		
War Diary	Cassel	01/08/1918	09/08/1918
War Diary	Terdeghem	10/08/1918	31/08/1918
Heading	War Diary of Lt. Col. C.M. Ainslie D.S.O. Comdg. 30th Divisional Train. Period. September 1st To September 30th 1918 Vol 35		
War Diary	Godewaersvelde	01/09/1918	21/09/1918
War Diary	Mont Des Cates	22/09/1918	30/09/1918
Heading	War Diary Of Lieut. Col. C.M. Ainslie D.S.O. Commanding. 30th Divisional Train. Period. Oct 1st To 31st Oct. 1918 Vol 36		
War Diary	Mont Des Cates	01/10/1918	01/10/1918
War Diary	Locre	02/10/1918	16/10/1918
War Diary	Wytschaete	17/10/1918	18/10/1918
War Diary	Roncq	19/10/1918	19/10/1918
War Diary	Croise	20/10/1918	20/10/1918
War Diary	Aelbeke	21/10/1918	31/10/1918
Heading	War Diary. Of Lt. Col. C.M. Ainslie. D.S.O. Commanding. 30th Divisional Train. Period 1st November To 30th November 1918 Vol 37		
War Diary	Aelbeke	01/11/1918	03/11/1918
War Diary	Rolleghem	04/11/1918	05/11/1918
War Diary	Aelbeke	06/11/1918	09/11/1918
War Diary	Heestert	10/11/1918	15/11/1918
War Diary	Mouscron	16/11/1918	30/11/1918
Heading	War Diary Of Lieutenant. Colonel. C.M. Ainslie D.S.O. Commanding 30th Divisional Train R.A.S.C. Period. 1st December 1918 31st December 1918 Vol 38		
War Diary	Eblinghem	01/12/1918	31/12/1918
Heading	War Diary Of Lieut. Col. C.M. Ainslie. D.S.O. Commanding 30th. Divisional Train. Vol 39 For The Month Of January 1919		
War Diary	Ebblinghem	01/01/1919	14/01/1919
War Diary	Blaringhem	15/01/1919	31/01/1919
Heading	War Diary. Of Lieut. Colonel C.M Ainslie D.S.O. Commanding 30th Divisional Train. February 1919 Vol 40		
War Diary	Blaringhem	01/02/1919	28/02/1919

Heading	War Diary. Of Lieut. Col. C.M Ainslie D.S.O. Commanding 30th Divisional Train. March 1919 Vol 41		
War Diary	Blaringhem	01/03/1919	30/03/1919
Miscellaneous	Headquarters, 30th Division.	04/05/1919	04/05/1919
War Diary	Condette	01/04/1919	30/04/1919
Miscellaneous	Headquarters. 30th Division.	27/05/1919	27/05/1919
Heading	War Diary Of Lieut. Colonel C.M. Ainslie D.S.O. For The Month Of May 1919 Vol 43		
War Diary	Condette	01/05/1919	27/05/1919

00905/2326/1

30TH DIVISION
DIVL TROOPS

40TH MOBILE VETY SECTION
~~NOV~~ 1915-APR 1919
SEPT

WAR DIARY
or
INTELLIGENCE SUMMARY.
(Erase heading not required.)

Army Form C. 2118

Instructions regarding War Diaries and Intelligence Summaries are contained in F. S. Regs., Part II. and the Staff Manual respectively. Title pages will be prepared in manuscript.

Place	Date	Hour	Summary of Events and Information	Remarks and references to Appendices
Corbie	20/4/18	9 a.m.	Demonstration by M.O. to the R.F.A.	
		10.30 a.m.	Lecture by C.O. on map reading, for N.C.O.s	
		11.15 a.m.	Inoculation parade. (Men excused all duty 24 hrs by M.O.)	
	21/4/18	2.15 p.m.	Lecture by C.O. to all ranks on Grooming, taking functions of skin, Grooming Kit & the use of, detail of grooming, handwashing & massage. Grooming & care of not unhealthy animals, care of the feet.	
		4 p.m.	Stables	
	22/4/18	6 a.m.	Stables	
		9 a.m.	Demonstration by C.O. for all ranks on Casco in Sick Lines (Exigusem Caris & wounds)	
		11 a.m.	Stables	
		2.15 p.m.	Lecture by C.O. (all ranks) on Grooming in Stable & tents, at work & sick, hygiene of stall, management of litter & ventilation, clothing & bandages for warmth	
		4 p.m.	Stables	
	23/4/18	6 a.m.	Stables	
		9 a.m.	Demonstration by C.O. on Bandaging & the use of the thermometer, taking of pulse & respiration.	
		11 a.m.	Stables	
		2.15 p.m.	Lecture by C.O. (all ranks). Clipping & use of & proper time, Hospital clipping, Exercise and equipment, how to regulate, leaving on general health, methods of securing - saddle & cart, bleeding & dealing with sickness.	
		4 p.m.	Stables	

Army Form C. 2118.

WAR DIARY
or
INTELLIGENCE SUMMARY.
(Erase heading not required.)

Instructions regarding War Diaries and Intelligence Summaries are contained in F. S. Regs., Part II and the Staff Manual respectively. Title pages will be prepared in manuscript.

Place	Date	Hour	Summary of Events and Information	Remarks and references to Appendices
Larkhill	24 & 7/5	6 a.m.	Morning drill	
		9 a.m.	Demonstration by Capt Davidson on use of thermometer, taking of pulse & respiration, Capt Quilbridge on bandaging.	
		11 a.m.	Stables	
		2.15 p.m.	Lecture by C.O. on dangers of dipping process, various kinds of food, plants, fats that forming, relation of kid of food to the work being done, making of bran mashes &c.	
		4 p.m.	Stables	
	25/7/5	6 a.m.	Morning drill	
		9 a.m.	Demonstration by C.O. on teeth, kinds of food & various grasses.	
		11 a.m.	Inspection by A.D.V.S.	
		2-15 p.m.	Recapitulating Lecture by Capt Davidson on work already done	

Army Form C. 2118.

WAR DIARY
or
INTELLIGENCE SUMMARY.
(Erase heading not required.)

Instructions regarding War Diaries and Intelligence Summaries are contained in F. S. Regs, Part II. and the Staff Manual respectively. Title pages will be prepared in manuscript.

Place	Date	Hour	Summary of Events and Information	Remarks and references to Appendices
Lulworth	1915 26.9	6am 10.30am	Stables. Church parade.	
	27.9	6am	Marching drill.	
		9am	Demonstration by C.O. Clinical observation, use of thermometer, taking pulse & respiration.	
		10am -12.30pm	Stables cleaning of lines & keeping tidying yard	
		2pm	Lecture by C.O. Feeding. Cooking of linseed, making mashes, use of chaff, crushed oats & maize. Feeding of long hay. Times of feeding & quantities	
		3-5pm	Fatigues	
	28.9	6am	Marching drill	
		9am	Demonstration by C.O. management of horses. Various grasses, good & bad in hay. Appearance of good & bad oats, hay, straw	
		10am -12.30pm	Fatigues	
		2pm	Lecture by C.O. management of horses in the stables. Feeding, exercise, grooming; on the march, halts, looking round, feeding, watering, covering.	
		3-5pm	Fatigues	

Army Form C. 2118.

WAR DIARY
or
INTELLIGENCE SUMMARY.
(Erase heading not required.)

Instructions regarding War Diaries and Intelligence Summaries are contained in F.S. Regs., Part II and the Staff Manual respectively. Title pages will be prepared in manuscript.

Place	Date	Hour	Summary of Events and Information	Remarks and references to Appendices
Tackley	1915			
	29.10	6 a.m. -7 a.m.	Marching drill	
		9 a.m. -10 a.m.	Demonstration by C.O. Saddles & their parts, names of hitching gear & camp utensils & their use.	
		10 a.m. -12:30 p.m.	Fatigues	
		2 p.m. -3 p.m.	Lecture by C.O. Pickating of horses, mucking, fodding, grazing, sanitation of lines.	
		3-5 p.m.	Fatigues	
	30.9	6-7 a.m.	Marching drill	
		9-10 a.m.	Demonstration by C.O. Lotting of bad horse, use of oedema, kicking up foot; evening twitch; knee halter.	
		10 a.m. -12:30 p.m.	Fatigues	
		2 p.m. -3 p.m.	Lecture by C.O. Appearance & health of horse, mule, nursing :- fomenting, Poulticing, Drenching, Backing, giving enemata, blistering.	
		3-5 p.m.	Fatigues	
	1.10	6-7 a.m.	Marching drill	
		9-10 a.m.	Demonstration by C.O. Points of horse, how to describe horse, washing out sheath, Drenching.	
		10-12:30 p.m.	Fatigues	
		2-3 p.m.	Lecture by C.O. Disinfection, Destruction of animals; Manzy Diseases - Fevers, Colds, etc.	
		3-5 p.m.	Fatigues	

Army Form C. 2118.

WAR DIARY
or
INTELLIGENCE SUMMARY.

(Erase heading not required.)

Instructions regarding War Diaries and Intelligence Summaries are contained in F. S. Regs., Part II. and the Staff Manual respectively. Title pages will be prepared in manuscript.

Place	Date	Hour	Summary of Events and Information	Remarks and references to Appendices
Lonteuil	4/15 2-10	6 a.m. -7 a.m.	Stables	
		9-9.45 a.m.	Demonstration by CO. Fomenting, Poulticing, bandaging, turning of horses in camp.	
		10-11 a.m.	Inspection by A.D.V.S.	
		11.30-12.30	Latrines	
		2-3 pm.	Lecture by CO. Pneumonia, Influenza.	
		3-5 pm.	Latrines	

2/10/15

S.R. Williman Lt. A.V.C.
O.C. No 40 mobile Vety Section

Army Form C. 2118.

WAR DIARY
or
INTELLIGENCE SUMMARY.
(Erase heading not required.)

Instructions regarding War Diaries and Intelligence Summaries are contained in F. S. Regs., Part II. and the Staff Manual respectively. Title pages will be prepared in manuscript.

Place	Date	Hour	Summary of Events and Information	Remarks and references to Appendices
Lahore	4.10.15	6 a.m.	Stable manoeuvres	
		9 a.m.	Demonstration. Instruments their names & uses	
		10 a.m.	Fatigue & dressing	
		11.30 a.m.	Stables	
		2 p.m.	Lecture — Pneumonia, Influenza.	
		3 p.m.	Fatigue	
		4 p.m.	Stables	
	5.10.15	6 a.m.	Stables	
		9 a.m.	Demonstration. Clinical observation of cases in hosp.	
		10 a.m.	Dressing	
		11.30 a.m.	Stables	
		2 p.m.	Lecture. Strangles, mange.	
		3 p.m.	Private hands to maintain workers.	
		4 p.m.	Stables	
	6.10.15	6 a.m.	Stables	
		9 a.m.	Demonstration. Giving of mouth, balling, drenching.	
		10 a.m.	Dressing	
		11.30 a.m.	Stables	
		2 p.m.	Lecture. Ringworm, lice, Letabres	
		3 p.m.	Fatigue	
		4 p.m.	Stables	

Army Form C. 2118.

WAR DIARY
or
INTELLIGENCE SUMMARY.
(Erase heading not required.)

Instructions regarding War Diaries and Intelligence Summaries are contained in F. S. Regs., Part II. and the Staff Manual respectively. Title pages will be prepared in manuscript.

Place	Date	Hour	Summary of Events and Information	Remarks and references to Appendices
Bethune	7/10/15	6 a.m.	Stables	
		9 a.m.	Demonstration. Clinical observation of cases in lines.	
		10 a.m.	Dressing	
		11.30 a.m.	Stables	
		2 p.m.	Lecture :— Colic, Constipation, Diarrhoea	
		3 p.m.	Rifle drill	
		4 p.m.	Stables	
	8/10/15	6 a.m.	Stables	
		9 a.m.	Demonstration. Examination of teeth, rasping of teeth, taking off shoes & dressing hoof.	
		10 a.m.	Dressing & neutering drill	
		11.30 a.m.	Stables	
		2 p.m.	Lecture :— Lymphangitis, Laminitis, Glanders.	
		3 p.m.	Rifle drill	
		4 p.m.	Stables	
	9/10/15	6 a.m.	Stables	
		9 a.m.	Demonstration :- Clinical observation of cases in lines.	
		10 a.m.	Inspection by A.D.V.S.	
		11.30 a.m.	Stables	
		2 p.m.	Lecture :— Wounds & treatment, detail of dressing.	
		3 p.m.	Rifle drill	
		4 p.m.	Stables	

R. M. Wilkinson M.R.C.V.S.
O.C. V.O. Hosp.

Army Form C. 2118.

WAR DIARY
or
INTELLIGENCE SUMMARY.
(*Erase heading not required.*)

Instructions regarding War Diaries and Intelligence Summaries are contained in F. S. Regs., Part II. and the Staff Manual respectively. Title pages will be prepared in manuscript.

Place	Date	Hour	Summary of Events and Information	Remarks and references to Appendices

Army Form C. 2118.

WAR DIARY
or
INTELLIGENCE SUMMARY.
(Erase heading not required.)

4 o.c. mobile vety section
30th Division
2nd A.O.P.

Instructions regarding War Diaries and Intelligence Summaries are contained in F.S. Regs., Part II and the Staff Manual respectively. Title pages will be prepared in manuscript.

Place	Date	Hour	Summary of Events and Information	Remarks and references to Appendices
Lachlie	21-10	6 a.m.	Stables, Exercise & Riding drill	
		9 a.m.	Demonstration Cattle dressing	
		10 a.m.	Dressing & Fatigues	
		11:30 a.m.	Stables	
		2 p.m.	Lecture on Jigsaw organs - the head	
		5 p.m.	Marching drill	
		4 p.m.	Stables	
	22-10	6 a.m.	Stables Exercise & Riding drill	
		9 a.m.	Demonstration, Care in lines & cast hindlegs	
		10 a.m.	Dressing & Fatigues	
		11:30 a.m.	Stables	
		2 p.m.	Lecture on the Body, limbs	
		3 p.m.	Marching drill	
		4 p.m.	Stables	
	23-10	6 a.m.	Stables & Exercise	
		9:30 a.m.	Inspection by A.D.V.S.	
		10:30 a.m.	Dressing	
		11:30 a.m.	Stables	
		2 p.m.	Lecture on Structure & function of foot	
		3 p.m.	Fatigues	
		4 p.m.	Stables	

Lachlie
23/10/15

John Wilkinson Lieut
O.C.

Army Form C. 2118.

WAR DIARY
or
INTELLIGENCE SUMMARY.
(Erase heading not required.)

Instructions regarding War Diaries and Intelligence
Summaries are contained in F.S. Regs., Part II.
and the Staff Manual respectively. Title pages
will be prepared in manuscript.

No 40 Mobile Vety Section
30 L N Division

Place	Date 1915	Hour	Summary of Events and Information	Remarks and references to Appendices
Wikku	17-10	6 am	Stables, Exercise	
		9.15 am	Church Parade	
		11.30 am	Stables	
		4 pm	Stables	
	18-10	6 am	Stables & Exercise	
		7.30 am	Parade for musketry	
		9 am	Remainder to swimming & stables till 12.30	
		2 pm	Musketry	
		4 pm	Remainder Stables	
	19-10	6 am	Stables & Exercise	
		7.30	Parade for musketry	
		9 am	Remainder to swimming	
		10 am	Fatigues - lines for all	
		11.30	Stables	
		2 pm	Parade for musketry	
		4.30 pm	Stables	
	20-10	6 am	Stables & Exercise. Riding drill for half section	
		9 am	Demonstration & remainder	
		10 am	& exercise of horses in lines	
		11.30 am	Stables	
		2 pm	Lecture on Elementary studies of medicines & treatment of injury & wounds of gunshot wounds	
		3 pm	Watering order	
		4 pm	Stables	

Army Form C. 2118.

WAR DIARY
or
INTELLIGENCE SUMMARY.
(Erase heading not required.)

Instructions regarding War Diaries and Intelligence Summaries are contained in F.S. Regs., Part II. and the Staff Manual respectively. Title pages will be prepared in manuscript.

No. 40 Mobile Section A.S.C.

Place	Date	Hour	Summary of Events and Information	Remarks and references to Appendices

40th Infy. Vet: Seet:
Vol: I

121/7708

Army Form C. 2118.

WAR DIARY
or
INTELLIGENCE SUMMARY.
(Erase heading not required.)

40th Mobile Section A.V.C.

Instructions regarding War Diaries and Intelligence Summaries are contained in F.S. Regs., Part II. and the Staff Manual respectively. Title pages will be prepared in manuscript.

Place	Date 1915.	Hour	Summary of Events and Information	Remarks and references to Appendices
Larkhill	1.XI.	10.30 a.m.	Received orders to recall all leaves. Complied with	
	2.XI.		Received 5 Horses	
	3.XI.		Received 20 Horses evacuated 4.	
	4.XI.		Received 4 Horses evacuated 9. Received orders as to Embarkation & disembarkation	
	5.XI.		Received 3 Horses evacuated 27. Received 1 Horse evacuated nil.	
	6.XI.	8.30 a.m.	Wired for Veterinary antitoxin. Received details into entrainment and entraining. Parade in marching order. Returned surplus wheeled stores to Tidworth & medicines to Bradford Vety Stores.	
	7.XI.	2 p.m.	Inspected picketing of wagons. Two more Vety Stores arrived.	
	8.XI.	2 p.m.	Handed our surplus Vety Stores to O.C. 46 14 S.R. F.A. Packed in wagons	
	9.XI.	10.30 a.m.	Received outstanding details from advance. Packed remaining wagon ready for loading.	
Amesbury.		11.45 a.m.	Moved off for Amesbury	
Loutaulu		12.55 h.	Entrained at Amesbury Train started	
		2.45 h.	Arrived Southampton	
		3.15 h.	Started to embark watering horses en route	
		4.5 h.	Complete embarkation of Horses	
		4.35 h.	Cast off moorings	
		8 p.m.	2nd Horse	
Le Havre.	10.XI.	6 a.m.	Watered fed horses & cleared up stalls, being outside Havre, very rough weather	
		10.30 a.m.	Moved into dock.	
		11.15 a.m.	Began to disembark	
		12 noon	Completed disembarkation, enclosed / with horse (?)	

Army Form C. 2118.

WAR DIARY
or
INTELLIGENCE SUMMARY.
(Erase heading not required.)

Instructions regarding War Diaries and Intelligence Summaries are contained in F. S. Regs., Part II. and the Staff Manual respectively. Title pages will be prepared in manuscript.

40 M.V.

Place	Date 1915	Hour	Summary of Events and Information	Remarks and references to Appendices
Le Havre	10.XI.	2 a.m.	sent horses for exercise	
"	"	7 a.m.	fed horses	
"	"	8 a.m.	moved off for station	
"	"	9 a.m.	began entraining	
"	"	9.30	completed "	
"	"	12 noon	Train started	
	11.XI.	7 a.m.	Train stopped 10 minutes, just managed to get dismounted, in time for tea the men no warning given.	
PONT. REMY		10.30 a.m.	Arrived Pont. Remy, detrained, marched to AILLY. LE HAUT. CLOCHER. arrived 3 p.m., weather very wet.	
AILLY. LE HAUT. CLOCHER.		3.30 p.m.	Took over billets in farm, horses in open, men had tea at 3.50, stables at 4. Rolly Soup at 5.15 p.m.	
	12.XI.		Received 4 horses. continuous rain	
	13.XI.		Received 3 horses. very heavy rain. moved horses into	
	14.XI.		Received 4 horses and 1 horse to days of Pitiable by road	
	15.VI.		Cold bending day. Received two horses sent in 6 troops by road, moved horse lines	
	16.XI.		two ours, two horses in tram curtains. Received 15, two returned	
	17.XI.		Hosp., received two horses transferred 17 to Hospital	
	18.XI.		moved to Flexelles, very bad billets no proper division had no means of sent	
Flexelles	19.XI.		Received 6 horses, put in open, no accommodation afternoon sent chasing horses loft by 2.5 D. Am.	
	20.XI.		Received 10 horses, all day collecting horses of 26 D am from road & harness. Appearance	
	21.XI.		moved into billets vacated by 36 m.d	
	22.XI.		Received ten horses.	
			Received 12 horses 3 ambulance carts	

Army Form C. 2118.

WAR DIARY
or
INTELLIGENCE SUMMARY.

(Erase heading not required.)

Instructions regarding War Diaries and Intelligence
Summaries are contained in F. S. Regs., Part II.
and the Staff Manual respectively. Title pages
will be prepared in manuscript.

A.D.M.S.

Place	Date 1915	Hour	Summary of Events and Information	Remarks and references to Appendices
Thiembles	23.XI		Received 7 horses 3 ambulance cars	
	24.XI		Received 2 horses ambulance transport 22 to Hospital	
	25.XI		Received 3 horses transferred two ambulance cars to Hospital & left two more at rankhead, returned with German	
	26.XI		Received 6 horses transferred to be kept intending to left at rankhead night before	
	27.XI		Received 5 horses. left one at army Troops R.E. with name of regiment.	
	28.XI		Moved to Vacquerie very frosty, left two cars with name of Thieulloy, found very good billets, empty farmhouse, cover for 100 horses good billets for men	
Vacquerie	29.XI		Busy cleaning up & got ourselves	
	30.XI		Fitted up temporary dressing shed & watering arrangements, made different bivouacs, will to be known by ticket.	
			Received two horses fit to 19 to Manchester	

J. R. M. Shuman Lt Col
A.D.M.S.

2353 Wt. W2544/1454 700,000 5/15 D. D. & L. A.D.S.S./Forms/C. 2118.

40e huh: Vet, Deel.
Vol: 2

131/7911

30 H Kroon

Army Form C. 2118.

WAR DIARY
or
INTELLIGENCE SUMMARY.
(Erase heading not required.)

40th mobile vety section. 3rd 2 Div.

Place	Date 1915	Hour	Summary of Events and Information	Remarks and references to Appendices
VACQUERIE	1.VII	—	Received 1 horse.	
	2.VII	—	Received 2 horses.	
	4.VII	"	1 horse	
	5.VII	"	2 horses	
	6.VII	"	3 horses	
	7.VII	"	Admitted 7 horses discharged cured 1 horse.	
	8.VII	"	6 horses (Unit unknown) from HOUDENCOURT)	
	9.VII	"	3 horses; discharged cured 1 horse, 1 mule. one horse of 2nd London RFA collected from HAVERNAS 2 mules	
	10.VII	"	5 horses; evacuated to Receiving Vety Sectn 9 horses; discharged cured 2 animals	
	11.VII	"	6 animals (including 1 2nd London RFA from CANAPLES.)	
	12.VII	"	3 animals	
	13.VII	"	5 animals	
	14.VII	"	10 animals; discharged cured 1	
	15.VII	"	4 animals	
	16.VII	"	10 animals	
	17.VII	"	3 animals; evacuated to Receiving Vety Hospl 27 horses 7 mules including 5 remout cases. discharged cured = 4	
	18.VII	"	11 animals; discharged cured = 4	

Army Form C. 2118.

WAR DIARY
or
INTELLIGENCE SUMMARY.
(Erase heading not required.)

Instructions regarding War Diaries and Intelligence Summaries are contained in F. S. Regs., Part II. and the Staff Manual respectively. Title pages will be prepared in manuscript.

A&A Mobile Vety Section, 30th Divn

Place	Date 1915	Hour	Summary of Events and Information	Remarks and references to Appendices
VACQUERIE	19·VII		Admitted 6 animals	
	20·VII		Admitted 13 animals (including 1 suspected mange from Amnl Train)	
	21·VII		Admitted 3 animals; Evacuated to Receiving Vety dept 26 horses 4 mules	
	22·VII		Admitted 4 animals	
	23·VII		Admitted 3 animals; destroyed =1 (one); discharged cured =1	
	24·VII		Admitted 4 animals (suspected mange from 24th Yorks Regt); discharged cured =1	
	25·VII		Admitted 2 animals	
	26·VII		Admitted 1 animal	
	27·VII		Admitted 9 animals; discharged cured =2	
	28·VII		" 5 animals; evacuated to Receiving Vety dept 23 horses 4 mules discharged cured=1	
	29·VII		" 6 animals; discharged cured =6	
	30·VII		" 5 animals; evacuated to Receiving Vety dept 4 horses 4 mules	
	31·VII		" 11 animals	

J.W. Wilkinson Lt A.V.C.
O.C. + Comd.

Volume. 2.
No. 40 Mobile City Section

D R Williamson to MSC
O C 40 m S

Army Form C. 2118.

WAR DIARY
or
INTELLIGENCE SUMMARY.
(Erase heading not required.)

40th Mobile Vety Section Vol III

Place	Date	Hour	Summary of Events and Information	Remarks and references to Appendices
WARGNIES	20-7-16		Moved to PONT NOYELLES; Picked up two animals en route	
PONT NOYELLES	21-7-16		Moved to CHIPILLY; Left two cases PONT NOYELLES. Picked up two PONT NOYELLES, one admitted PONT NOYELLES.	
CHIPILLY	22-7-16		Picked up two cases SAILLY LE SEC	
ETINEHEM	23-7-16		Moved to ETINEHEM. Received two animals (one shell wd one other disease), Returned to unit to duty.	
	24-7-16		Received 12 animals	
	25-7-16		Received 17 animals; two ambulance cases.	
	26-7-16		Received 9 animals (1 shell wd); Evacuated 28 animals (two amb cases) collected 3 at PONT NOYELLES, (2 amb cases)	
	27-7-16		Received 9 animals (1 amb case)	
	28-7-16		Received 3 animals (1 amb case) (one shell wd)	
	29-7-16		Received 13 animals, Evacuated 29 animals (3 amb cases)	
	30-7-16		Received 19 animals (2 shell wds)(4 Ambulance cases)	
	31-7-16		Received 21 animals (5 shell wds), (2 amb cases)	
			Received 12 animals, Evacuated 38 animals (5 amb cases)	

L.R. Thomson Capt AVC
O.C. 40 M.V.S

Army Form C. 2118.

WAR DIARY
or
INTELLIGENCE SUMMARY.
(Erase heading not required.)

40th mobile Vety Section vol III

Place	Date	Hour	Summary of Events and Information	Remarks and references to Appendices
VACQUERIE	1.1.16		Received 6 animals	
	2.1.16		Received 10 animals	
	3.1.16		Received 13 animals, evacuated 28 animals	
	4.1.16		Received 7 animals	
	5.1.16		Received 7 animals; evacuated 15 animals	
	6.1.16		Received 5 animals	
	7.1.16		Received 3 animals	
	8.1.16		Received 4 animals; evacuated 15 animals	
	9.1.16		Moved to HALLOY LÈS PERNOIS. Received two animals	
HALLOY LÈS PERNOIS.	10.1.16		Received 3 animals	
	11.1.16		Received 7 animals	
	12.1.16		Received 3 animals	
	13.1.16		Received 1 animal. evacuated 16 animals	
	14.1.16		Received 19 animals; Horse Ambulance arrived from ABBEVILLE	
	15.1.16		Received 3 animals; two for Ambulance	
	16.1.16		Received 4 animals, two for ambulance	
	17.1.16		Received 3 animals; evacuated 24 animals, 4 foot cases	
	18.1.16		Received 5 animals; two ambulance cases	
	19.1.16		Received 2 animals, evacuated 9 animals. 3 ambulance cases moved to WARGNIES	

30

40.th Inst: Feb: Sech:
Vol: 4

WAR DIARY
or
INTELLIGENCE SUMMARY.

(Erase heading not required.)

Army Form C. 2118.

Instructions regarding War Diaries and Intelligence Summaries are contained in F. S. Regs., Part II. and the Staff Manual respectively. Title pages will be prepared in manuscript.

Place	Date	Hour	Summary of Events and Information	Remarks and references to Appendices
ETINEHEM	1916 1.11		Received 6 horses	
	2.11		Received 11 horses (2 old rate)	
	3.11		Received 11 horses. Returned 31 horses.	
	4.11		Received 12 horses (Drafts to [?]). Received 300 horses to [?]	
	5.11		Received 1 horse. [illegible]	
	6.11		At rest. In order battled.	
	7.11		Moved to CHIPILLY	
CHIPILLY	9.11		[illegible]	
	13.11		Received 21 animals in draft ([illegible])	
	14.11		Received 13 animals	
	15.11		Received 37 animals [illegible]	
	16.11		Received 3 animals	
	17.11		Received 5 animals (Cold [?] draft of 30 animals)	
	18.11		Received 11 animals. Returned [?]	
	19.11		Received 10 animals	
	20.11		Received 3 animals	

Army Form C. 2118.

WAR DIARY
or
INTELLIGENCE SUMMARY.
(Erase heading not required.)

Instructions regarding War Diaries and Intelligence Summaries are contained in F.S. Regs., Part II. and the Staff Manual respectively. Title pages will be prepared in manuscript.

449th Mobile Vety Section Vol. IV

Place	Date	Hour	Summary of Events and Information	Remarks and references to Appendices
CHIPILLY	1916 21.VI		Received 4 animals, evacuated 27 sick & 4 removed cases.	
	22.VI		Received 7 animals. Majority of cases received last 4 days are itchy.	
	23.VI		Received 12 animals, including 4 doubtful mailers from A Hy R.F.A.	
	24.VI		Received 2 animals, a3.Q, wind raw.	
	25.VI		Received 10 animals, evacuated 23 animals walked & well & back into the lynes.	
	26.VI		Received 4 animals. Tested Leban horses in contacts.	
	27.VI		Received 6 animals	
	28.VI		One debin horse now isolated & 1 doubtful variola gave positive reaction. Isolated & an almost intensive outbreak of Variola especially marked in doubtful reactor	
	29.VI		Received 3 horses.	

J.L. Silkman Capt.
S.L. 4 Army

40th mobile Vety Section
Vol IV. Feby 1916.

D.H.Williamson Capt A.V.C.
O.C. Unit

40 M veder
vol 5

Army Form C. 2118.

WAR DIARY
or
INTELLIGENCE SUMMARY.
(Erase heading not required.)

Instructions regarding War Diaries and Intelligence Summaries are contained in F. S. Regs., Part II. and the Staff Manual respectively. Title pages will be prepared in manuscript.

Place	Date	Hour	Summary of Events and Information	Remarks and references to Appendices
Davros	27/3/16		Capt Williamson went away on leave. Capt F.L. Clunies Ross was LO N v S. Received 2 cases, for Ronquieres & observed rattles of Caron 3 milles to the N.W. today	
"	28/3/16		Received our Car. Col Hunt DDVS called, took our allowance P. M. Crompton of Landon & S... oben... destroyed, only observed chancellor Dudley at end of hospital (Neath), no blackdown on Mount Sophie, p. enlarged mounted of several several of them in Low, Trouble on all roads, No Lumps in all 3 been observed. Small ny shells exploded to 12 N. 12 Cours	
St. Saviour	28/3/16		Moved from Davros at 2 p.m. for St Sauveurs. Arrived here 5.30 P.M. found bullets for men, Officers also the one LO belong to 21st M.V.S. developed a problem when near Camien, at... after at Domville transferred to Camien, so left him just outside town. Traveled for by them and becoming much more complete. Continued on leave Operations were delayed to obtain, but on the 31st	
"	29/3/16		Received 6 cases	
"	30/3/16		Rec'd 2 cases	
"	31/3/16		Rec'd 12 cases, discharged one on landed Cose out Purchased nothing of note	F. L. Clunies Capt OC 4O M.V.S.

War Diary

14th Motor Mk Blechin

Vol 5. March 916.

PhShilliver Capt a C
R C Young

Army Form C. 2118.

WAR DIARY
or
INTELLIGENCE SUMMARY.
(Erase heading not required.)

Instructions regarding War Diaries and Intelligence Summaries are contained in F. S. Regs., Part II. and the Staff Manual respectively. Title pages will be prepared in manuscript.

Anti mobile Vety section No 5

Place	Date 1916	Hour	Summary of Events and Information	Remarks and references to Appendices
CHIPILLY	19.III		Admitted 9 animals evacuated 6 shops 33 animals killed in action & in return	
	20.III		Admitted 9 animals including 3 doubtful reactors from 40'' '' R.F.A.	
	21.III		Admitted 10 animals (2 being doubtful reactors 'B' 159 R.F.A.) No Reactor action of doubtful reactor of Rg reached destroyed	
	22.III		moved to DAOURS. Evacuated 12 animals to shops	
DAOURS	23.III		Received 3 animals	
	24.III		Received 7 animals	
	25.III		Received 5 animals evacuated 11 animals to shops.	
	26.III		Received 4 animals. Dickepel con and to units	

R.W.Williamson Capt AVC
J.C.O.S.W.C.

Army Form C. 2118.

WAR DIARY
or
INTELLIGENCE SUMMARY.
(Erase heading not required.)

40th Mobile Vety Section Vol V

Place	Date 1916	Hour	Summary of Events and Information	Remarks and references to Appendices
CHIPILLY	1.III		Admitted 9 animals	
	2.III		Admitted 9 animals, Evacuated 14 animals	
	3.III		Admitted 2 animals	
	4.III		Admitted 10 animals, one skin case died from pneumonia	
	5.III		Admitted 4 animals	
	6.III		Admitted 7 animals	
	7.III		Admitted 3 animals, discharged Damietta Khot.	
	8.III		Admitted 7 animals	
	9.III		Admitted 6 animals, vaccinated 23 animals tetanus	
	10.III		Admitted 2 animals	
	12.III		Admitted 10 animals, destroyed one battery	
	13.III		Admitted 13 animals	
	14.III		Admitted 6 animals, evacuated 27 animals to hospital	
	15.III		Admitted 6 animals, destroyed one cabbatti horses	
	16.III		Admitted 7 animals, destroyed one (hyenesia)	
	17.III		Admitted 1 animals	
	18.III		Admitted 6 animals	

Army Form C. 2118.

Vol 6

WAR DIARY
or
INTELLIGENCE SUMMARY.

(Erase heading not required.)

1st Mobile Vet. Sec.

Place	Date	Hour	Summary of Events and Information	Remarks and references to Appendices
St Sauveur	1.4.16		Ref: from ... have 3 horses (Mule) by Sgt Bison from Kic Hospital 28 of August 1912. ...Capt Dodd 21 November	Sec 2-12 Cpl
	2.4.16		Rec'd 11 Cases. Discharged 13 MMH from Rly Ave Somme 16.	
	3.4.16		Rec'd 2 cases. Incubation 12 B EMH. Amputated Brows Stath. Post mortem on (cow) (3/4/16 — 11/4/16).	
	4.4.16		Rec'd 4 cases.	
	5.4.16		Rec'd 4 cases. Men went to baths	
	6.4.16		Rec'd 2 cases. Rec'd to form 13.9 Div. 11 RFA. Tested mule English Incurable & gave Chavasse's mixture, etc.	
	7.4.16		Rec'd Dreadful Remount from 149. Destroyed such it's one inoculated with B. both had glandular swellings, there was but no abscess in head, lungs or Trachea. Rec'd 5 cases. Evacuated to Hospital. 10 cases.	
	8.4.16		Received 8 cases. Two of which were collected from Byards 17.1 RFA B'station.	
	9.4.16		Rec'd one case. Capt Williamson returned from leave, handed over to him.	

F. L. Clenners Capt. AVC.
40 M.V.S.

Army Form C. 2118.

WAR DIARY
or
INTELLIGENCE SUMMARY.
(Erase heading not required.)

Instructions regarding War Diaries and Intelligence Summaries are contained in F. S. Regs., Part II. and the Staff Manual respectively. Title pages will be prepared in manuscript.

20th Mobile Vety Sectn vol V

Place	Date 1916	Hour	Summary of Events and Information	Remarks and references to Appendices
ST. SAUVEUR.	10.4		Received 8 animals	
	11.4		Received 8 animals, 1 destroyed arthritis	
	12.4		Received 1 colic case 2nd Ld Cavy Divn. Pte Clark returned from leave.	
	13.4		Received 2 animals, evacuated 20 animals	
	14.4		Received 4 animals	
	15.4		Received 7 animals. Pte Ormiston joined from No 7 Vety Hospl. Pte Ward evacuated to Hospl	
	16.4		Received 6 animals, Sgt Onslledge returned from leave. Attempt 2 stays discharges cured & remount	
	17.4		Received 4 animals, evacuated 18 animals	
	18.4		Received 2 animals	
	19.4		Received 3 animals	
	20.4		Received 1 animal, discharged 4 cured	
	21.4		Received 7 animals, 1 discharged cured	
	22.4		Received 7 animals, evacuated 16 animals, 2 discharged cured	
	23.4		Received 1 animal, 1 discharged cured	
	24.4		Received 7 animals	
	25.4		Received 10 animals, 3 discharged cured	
	26.4		Received 42 animals (one died tetanus)	

Army Form C. 2118.

WAR DIARY
or
INTELLIGENCE SUMMARY.
(Erase heading not required.)

Instructions regarding War Diaries and Intelligence Summaries are contained in F. S. Regs., Part II. and the Staff Manual respectively. Title pages will be prepared in manuscript.

Army Form C. 2118.

Place	Date 1916	Hour	Summary of Events and Information	Remarks and references to Appendices
ST. SAUVEUR	27.4		Received 2 animals (Ambulance cases), presented 28 sick & 2 remount cases. ADMS DADVS visited section.	
	28.4		Received 7 animals (one collected by ambulance from VILLE MARGUET.)	
	29.4		Received 9 animals (1 collected by ambulance from ALLONVILLE)	
	30.4		Received 3 animals	

JAS Wilkinson Capt AVC
O.C. 6 M.V.S.

2353 Wt. W2544/1454 700,000 5/15 D. D. & L. A.D.S.S./Forms/C. 2118.

War Diary.

48th mobile vety section.

Vol VI. April 1916.

J.K. Williamson Captain
O C & O in C

WAR DIARY
or
INTELLIGENCE SUMMARY.

(Erase heading not required.)

Army Form C. 2118.

VOL 7

Place	Date	Hour	Summary of Events and Information	Remarks and references to Appendices
ST SAUVEUR	1-5-16		Admitted 2 animals, evacuated 18 animals.	
	2-5-16		Admitted 9 animals	
	3-5-16		Admitted 2 animals.	
	4-5-16		Admitted 3 animals.	
	5-5-16		Admitted 3 animals	
	6-5-16		Moved to Corbie. Evacuated 18 animals.	
CORBIE	7-5-16	7.30am	Advance party arrived 12 noon, left one sick animal with 18th Div. Supply Coln.	
		11.30am	Main body arrived 11 a.m. killed 1 horse 1 mule from water refused & accepted numbers for disposal.	
Aux. Hauling	8-5-16		Admitted 20 animals. took over sick standings & put to use	
	9-5-16		Admitted 4 animals.	
	10-5-16		Admitted 4 animals.	
	11-5-16		Admitted 4 animals. Evacuated 23 animals.	
	12-5-16		Admitted 3 animals, moved into pumped in village	
	13-5-16		Admitted 20 animals, erected hobbling pegs in yard & 65 horses	
	14-5-16		Admitted 1 animal. Evacuated 26 animals	
	15-5-16		Admitted 4 animals, making standings - got stones being used to make	
	16-5-16		Admitted 6 animals. making standings & being now to move	
	17-5-16		Admitted 14 animals making standings utilized to ambulance covers	
	18-5-16		Admitted 15 animals evacuated 3 to animals	
	19-5-16		Admitted 28 animals, erected ladders for shelly warehouse loan	

Army Form C. 2118.

WAR DIARY
or
INTELLIGENCE SUMMARY.
(Erase heading not required.)

Instructions regarding War Diaries and Intelligence Summaries are contained in F.S. Regs., Part II. and the Staff Manual respectively. Title pages will be prepared in manuscript.

4th Mobile Vety Section Vol VII

Place	Date	Hour	Summary of Events and Information	Remarks and references to Appendices
SAILLY LAURETTE	1916 19.5		Received 5 animals evacuated 38 animals. Subways 3 springs 4 attacks 60ty destroyed	
	20.5		7 animals. Cleared out sheds + put disinfected floors in. Evacuated 14 anls.	
	21.5		4 animals dead of wounds. Please it was cold into tarpaulins and given expeditious.	
	22.5		2 animals evacuated, 12 animals 3 ambulances see taken out.	
	23.5		9 animals. Collapsed airplanes ran out to fetch.	
	24.5		8 animals evacuated 16 animals	
	25.5		8 animals coming from no rifles	
	26.5		6 animals	
	27.5		7 animals evacuated 15 animals. Destroyed one (infected splinting wound)	
	28.5		10 animals	
	29.5		9 animals brought out target.	
	30.5		3 animals evacuated 12 animals	
	31.5		11 animals evacuated 3 ambulances sent	

W.H. Williamson Capt RAVC
O.C. 4 M.V.S.

2353 Wt. W2544/1454 700,000 5/15 D.D.&L. A.D.S.S./Forms/C. 2118.

War Diary

Vol XII

H.A. Mobile Arty Autour

Resistance Group
"C Group"

June
Army Form C. 2118.
VOL 8

XXX
~~10th~~ Mobile Vety Section. Vol VIII

WAR DIARY
or
INTELLIGENCE SUMMARY.
(Erase heading not required.)

Place	Date	Hour.	Summary of Events and Information	Remarks and references to Appendices
SAILLY-LAURETTE	1916			
	1-6		G.O.C. Division visited Section & gave permission for animals to be kept in lines if considered necessary	
	2-6		Admitted 3 animals	
	3-6		Admitted 5 animals	
	4-6		Admitted 4 animals. Destroyed one hospital	
	5-6		Admitted 3 animals. Enlarged two open shelter for sick	
	6-6		Evacuated 14 animals	
	7-6		Admitted 5 animals. One returned cured to unit.	
	8-6		Admitted 4 animals	
	9-6		Admitted 8 animals	
	10-6		Admitted two animals	
	11-6		Admitted 7 animals, evacuated 13 animals, one discharged cured, one destroyed destitute	
	12-6		Admitted 6 animals	
	13-6		Admitted 13 animals, cured one animal	
	14-6		Admitted 6 animals, evacuated 21 animals	
	15-6		Admitted 7 animals.	
	16-6		Admitted 7 animals, evacuated 19 animals.	

Army Form C. 2118.

WAR DIARY
or
INTELLIGENCE SUMMARY.
(Erase heading not required.)

4th Mobile Vety Section
Vol VIII

Instructions regarding War Diaries and Intelligence Summaries are contained in F. S. Regs., Part II. and the Staff Manual respectively. Title pages will be prepared in manuscript.

Place	Date	Hour	Summary of Events and Information	Remarks and references to Appendices
	1916.			
SAILLY-LAURETTE	17-6	8 a.m.	Section moved to CORBIE.	
		3 p.m.	Advanced section moved to BOIS DE TAILLES, admitted 3 animals.	
BOIS DE TAILLES	18-6		Admitted 36 animals belonging to 3rd Bdn, 9th Divn, G.S. Divn, 1st A.V. 2nd Hvy Army Tps.	
		6 p.m.	O.C. moved off all the sick in except 6 men to BOIS DE TAILLES, as unsuitable to advanced & shot sick animals.	
	19-6	8 a.m.	Men arrived from CORBIE.	
	19-6		Received 14 animals (wounded) evacuated 29 animals returned to unit 12 animals not service mules for A.P.	
	20-6		Received 8 animals, evacuated 11 animals	
	21-6		Received 10 animals.	
	22-6		Received 6 animals, advanced horse lines under shell fire, two horses wounded, evacuated 18 animals.	
	23-6		Received 7 animals, evacuated 9 animals. (one went old war shot)	
	24-6		Received 5 animals. Returned 2 to duty unit.	
	25-6		Received 3 animals, evacuated 13 animals	
	26-6		Received 2 animals	
	27-6		Received 5 animals	
	28-6		Received 15 animals evacuated 16 animals. (one a shell wd case)	
	29-6		Received 8 animals	
	30-6		Received 16 animals evacuated 15 animals	

J.F. Williamson Captain
O.C. 4th Mobile Vety Section
30th June

Army Form C. 2118.

30 2"9920/16 July

to Intelligence Section GHQ IX

Vol 9

WAR DIARY
or
INTELLIGENCE SUMMARY.
(Erase heading not required.)

Instructions regarding War Diaries and Intelligence Summaries are contained in F. S. Regs., Part II. and the Staff Manual respectively. Title pages will be prepared in manuscript.

Place	Date	Hour	Summary of Events and Information	Remarks and references to Appendices
	1916			
BOIS DES TAILLES	1-7		Received 7 animals. Evacuated 19.	
	2-7		Received 6 animals.	
	3-7		Received 6 animals. Evacuated 16.	
	4-7		Received 7 animals (retained).	
	5-7		Received 12 animals. 1 killed, 1 died.	
	6-7		Received 7 animals (1 died). Evacuated 17.	
	7-7		Received 4 animals (1 died).	
	8-7		Received 2 animals (retained). Evacuated 2. 1 escaped (destroyed)	
	9-7		Received 6 animals (2 died new).	
	10-7		Received 16 animals (1 shot new) (destroyed). Evacuated 11.	
	11-7		Received 4 animals.	
	12-7		Received 8 animals.	
	13-7		Received 9 animals. (2 killed new) Evacuated 15.	
	14-7		Received 10 animals. Evacuated 11.	
	15-7		Received 11 animals (retained) Evacuated 12.	
	16-7		Received 10 animals. (1 killed)	

T2134. Wt. W708—776. 500000. 4/15. Sir J. C. & S.

Army Form C. 2118.

WAR DIARY
or
INTELLIGENCE SUMMARY.
(Erase heading not required.)

Instructions regarding War Diaries and Intelligence Summaries are contained in F. S. Regs., Part II. and the Staff Manual respectively. Title pages will be prepared in manuscript.

40 Mobile Vet. Section Vol. IX

Place	Date	Hour	Summary of Events and Information	Remarks and references to Appendices
	1916			
AUBIGNY DES TAILLES	17.7		Admitted 15 animals. Evacuated 19. Total destin animals 26 AUBIGNY DESTAILLES	
	18.7		Admitted 19 animals (point rel)	
	19.7		Admitted 219 animals (holidays) Evacuated 36	
	20.7		Admitted 9 animals (point rel)	
	21.7		Admitted 8 animals. Evacuated 1 (old mule) Evacuated 19	
	22.7		Revd to Bois des Tailles (W.V.S.) Admitted 25 animals (holidays)	
	23.7		Received 25 animals (holidays)	
	24.7		Received 16 animals (holidays) Evacuated 53	
	25.7		Recd 5 animals (point rel)	
	26.7		Recd 7 animals (old hills) Evacd 19	
	27.7		Recd 3 animals (orf hill)	
	28.7		Admitted 2 animals	
	29.7		Recd 11 animals (holidays) Evacd 10	
	30.7		Recd 12 animals (holidays) Evacd 2 (old mules)	
	31.7		Recd 17 animals (holidays)	

Lt A Wegman Capt RVC
O.C. 40 M.V.S.

SECRET.

40.MVS
Vol 10

War Diary
-of-
40 Mobile Veterinary
Section for the month
-of-
August 1916

Volume X

Army Form C. 2118.

WAR DIARY
or
INTELLIGENCE SUMMARY.
(Erase heading not required.)

Instructions regarding War Diaries and Intelligence Summaries are contained in F. S. Regs., Part II. and the Staff Manual respectively. Title pages will be prepared in manuscript.

40th Mobile Vety Section Vol I

Place	Date	Hour	Summary of Events and Information	Remarks and references to Appendices
	1916.			
BOIS DES TAILLES	1-8	2 a.m.	Recd orders also to move of Transport.	
		9 a.m.	Evacuated 36 animals. Lieut Davidson came from Abbe Park with orders from H.Q.M.S. to move as soon as possible.	
		5.30 pm	Moved off via CORBIE, DAOURS & AILLONVILLE. 23 O.R.'s animals Total 49.	
AILLONVILLE	2-8	2 a.m.	Halt. & bivouacked	
		6 a.m.	moved off via POULAINVILLE, LONGPRE, LACHAUSSEE, PICQUIGNY.	
PICQUIGNY SOUES	3-8	4 pm	Notice of Divisional Transport. M.M.P. Sent ayes to SOUES	
		6.30 pm	Bivouacked out nr camp H.Q.D.S. visiting position	
		5.30 pm	N position from A.D.V.S. but LONGPRÉ LES SAINTE CORPS 4 am to return	
		9 a.m.	Recd LONGPRÉ LES STE CPS R.T.O no information	
		9.30 am	moved its horses out nr camp Hosp stably horses ready for return.	
		5 pm	Recd when A.D.V.S. to return LONGUEAU. 6th at 5 am.	
	4-8		Removed LONGUEAU. Sent KARREVILLE for no plate, waited 24 hr southbound	
	5-8	5 am	Moved off & left horses behind	
		4.0	reached LONGUEAU.	
	6-8	2 am	Entrained train moved off. 4.10 am wired 2nd field ambulance R.T.O. re arrival	

T2134. Wt. W708—776. 500000. 4/15. Sir J. C. & S.

Army Form C. 2118.

WAR DIARY
or
INTELLIGENCE SUMMARY.
(Erase heading not required.)

Instructions regarding War Diaries and Intelligence Summaries are contained in F. S. Regs., Part II. and the Staff Manual respectively. Title pages will be prepared in manuscript.

Place	Date	Hour	Summary of Events and Information	Remarks and references to Appendices
	1916			
	6.8	1pm	Reached THIEMAES. & detrained.	
ST. FLORIS		4.30pm	Reached ST FLORIS.	
	7-8		Recd 12 animals	
	8-8		Recd 32 animals	
	9-8		Recd 5 animals. Evacuated 3?	
	10-8		Received 40 animals. " 10. & 2 Servants	
	11-8		move to LOCON. " 4.	
	12-8		Recd 17 animals. " 16.	
LOCON	13-8		Recd 5 "	
	14-8		10 " Evacuated 8	
	15-8		3 " 12	
	16-8		Recd 24 animals	
	17-8		7 animals Evacuated 22	
	18-8		Received 6 animals - 8	
	19-8		26 animals	
	20-8		4 animals Evacd 9.	

Army Form C. 2118.

WAR DIARY
or
INTELLIGENCE SUMMARY.
(Erase heading not required.)

Instructions regarding War Diaries and Intelligence Summaries are contained in F. S. Regs, Part II. and the Staff Manual respectively. Title pages will be prepared in manuscript.

Place	Date	Hour	Summary of Events and Information	Remarks and references to Appendices
	1916			
LOCON	21.8		Recd 10 animals.	
	22.8		Recd 1 animal. 36 Horses & mules ESTAIRES. 13.134 NW Army relief.	
	23.8		Recd 10 animals.	
	24.8		6 animals. Evacuated 7 horses 1 mule.	
	25.8		Capt Williamson went on leave. Capt F.L. Clemes took charge of Horse Unit.	
		5-30 p.m.	Received 5 animals.	
	26.8		Received 5 horses 8 mules.	
			Recd 1 animal.	
	24.8		Recd 4 animals. "P" Remount reported to start from 20.9.24.	
	29.8		Recd 1 animal. Issue seven. Telegram received re ease of glanders in Horse from I.R.E. 30" Div. P The section visited by D.D.V.S. & A.D.V.S., I relieved all Horses in the section by frand method. 524 animals. Maps & pamphlets of standings. Three men attached for town fatigue.	
	30.8		No re-action. Town arrived for Horse transit, 3 fourneurs. Received 7 animals.	
	31.8		To Rations, Issue of Tounne 5 Hongs. Seven bush bags. Received 13 animals. F. L. Clemes Capt. W & 40 Sp.V.S.	

Army Form C. 2118.

WAR DIARY
or
INTELLIGENCE SUMMARY.

(Erase heading not required.)

Instructions regarding War Diaries and Intelligence Summaries are contained in F. S. Regs., Part II. and the Staff Manual respectively. Title pages will be prepared in manuscript.

Army Vol X

Place	Date	Hour	Summary of Events and Information	Remarks and references to Appendices
Lizson	1/9/16		Received 10 animals.	
	2/9/16		Received 4 animals	
	3-9		Reported by 470M for Fatigue 3 Horses with pie-races sprinkles.	
	4-9		Rec'd 5 animals	
	5-9		Rec'd 2 animals. Issued 11 from Rathuse (Tram) 10 large Batteries	
	6-9		Rec'd 2 animals	
	7-9		Rec'd 2 animals	
	8-9		Rec'd 5 animals evacuated 1st animals	
	9-9		Rec'd 4 animals	
	10-9		Rec'd 2 animals	
	11-9		Rec'd 4 animals	
	12-9		Rec'd 1 animals evacuated 5 animals	
	13-9		Rec'd 4 animals	
	14-9		Rec'd 4 animals evacuated 5 animals by hoof & 1 skin case by rail	
	15-9		Rec'd 3 animals	
	16-9		Rec'd 7 animals	

Army Form C. 2118.

WAR DIARY
or
INTELLIGENCE SUMMARY.

(Erase heading not required.)

*Instructions regarding War Diaries and Intelligence Summaries are contained in F. S. Regs., Part II. and the Staff Manual respectively. Title pages will be prepared in manuscript.

Place	Date	Hour	Summary of Events and Information	Remarks and references to Appendices
	1916			
LOCON	17.9		Received 8 animals	
	18.9		Received 5 animals. Loaded 17 by rail. Rec'd some 6.45. Lv at Lillers 11.51. Left Whylyldh 12 noon with stream to his troops not moving. Left 4 animals with escort. 3:00 9mm on way to St Pol. halted alongside covered in train. Whitet4 ocha road - destroyed - expired by train. P.4 trill built impred. Transport to g4 the rest.	
	19.9		then occurred at 1st bridge in between schs. Several horses ran away & after some time the	
			escta proceeded on its way, being late for train leaving 2.57 but proceeding to 5.40 am.	
DOULLENS.	19.9		arrived 10.30 & proceeded by road & then	
HEM.	20.9		Received 2 destroyed one. escorted in	
	21.9		moved off 8:30 arrived Vignacourt 12.30.	
VIGNACOURT	22.9		Received 4 animals	
	23.9		Received 2 animals destroyed one. evacuated 5".	
	24.9		Rec'd 8 animals.	
	25.9		Rec'd 6 animals - evacuated 8.	
	26.9		Rec'd 3 animals all floated from TALMAS.	
	27.9		Rec'd 2 animals evacuated 8.	
	28.9		Rec'd 2 animals. Two floated from AILLY-SUR-SOMME.	
	29.9		Rec'd 3 animals. Two floated from LONGPRÉ. & SC. Ste.	
	30.9		Rec'd 1 animal. floated at Ed Janvier.	

Vol II

War Diary.

40th Mobile Vty Section
A.I.F

vol XI.

1st-31st November 1918
& 40mf

WAR DIARY
40TH
MOBILE
VETERINARY
SECTION

VOL XI

JS Williunier
Captain

Army Form C. 2118.

VOL 12

40 mob vet...

WAR DIARY
or
INTELLIGENCE SUMMARY.
(Erase heading not required.)

Instructions regarding War Diaries and Intelligence Summaries are contained in F.S. Regs., Part II. and the Staff Manual respectively. Title pages will be prepared in manuscript.

Place	Date	Hour	Summary of Events and Information	Remarks and references to Appendices
	1916			
VIGNACOURT	1-10		At Vignacourt.	
	2-10		Collected two horses from St Sauveur.	
	3-10		Admitted one, evacuated 3.	
		12 noon	Moved off for ALLONVILLE.	
		5 pm	Arrived ALLONVILLE.	
ALLONVILLE	4-10	7.30 am	Moved off for RIBEMONT. Rained all the way, everything wet through.	
RIBEMONT	4-10	11.30 am	Arrived RIBEMONT. found M.V.S. billet occupied by N.Z.M.V.S. M.M.P. + R.E. everything wettest, men slept in mud, without any cover.	
	5-10		Received 2 animals, one from major Mead N.Z.M.M.P. + R.E. moved, got new ground. rats too little shelter.	
	6-10		N.Z. M.V.S. moved off. Off 3 animals, Pvt 1 = fairly comfortable. received 3 animals.	
	7-10		Received 2 animals, men working all day cleaning billet. Took 6 days at Railhead awaiting Remounts train that have unloaded 7 Battalions. sent two Remounts back on a billet made by rate of P.O.O. with a Cover H.D. from R.L.R.	
	8-10		Received 3 animals on a way sent in by V.O. [?] Corps.. sent to M Boulogne. SAILLY-LE-SEC.3715 one of troubled, 7 H.Batt. 13th Regt. Rec'd.	
	9-10		Admitted as animal, evacuated 6. went to MAMETZ. + FRICOURT. Area reconnoitred position for Eastern Char. + MAMETZ.	

Army Form C. 2118.

WAR DIARY
or
INTELLIGENCE SUMMARY.
(Erase heading not required.)

Army Form No. XII

Instructions regarding War Diaries and Intelligence Summaries are contained in F. S. Regs., Part II. and the Staff Manual respectively. Title pages will be prepared in manuscript.

Place	Date	Hour	Summary of Events and Information	Remarks and references to Appendices
	1916			
RIBEMONT	10.10		Moved to MAMETZ. Received Haversacks, cleared up lines, very large dubs & had parade by patents.	
MAMETZ	11.10		Received 29 animals. New about today & yesterday making checks for the colours from new m/c.	
	12.10		Received 20 animals	
	13.10		Received 38 animals. including one stray, evacuated 48.	
	14.10		Received 37 animals. Also one stray one ambulance case from MONTAUBAN. Evacuated 40.	
	15.10		Received 14 animals one amb case TRONES WOOD. Evacuated 56.	
	16.10		Received 10 animals, evacuated 16 animals	
	17.10		Received 9 animals. Conditions very bad, constant rains, whole camp 6 ins deep in mud.	
	18.10		Received 19 animals. Two amb cases MONTAUBAN.	
	19.10		Received 3 animals. Some field guns while fell around the camp during the evening roughly about 29	
	20.10		Received 9 animals	
	21.10		Received 52 animals one amb case MONTAUBAN.	
	22.10		Received 29 animals evacuated 64. Some German shells about 1 km back of camp.	
	23.10		Received 54 animals. Two ambulance cases 1 POMMIER REDOUBT. 1 MONTAUBAN evacuated 24.	
	24.10		Received 43 animals one amb case TRONES WOOD. Sent out with R6-m got talk 4 km Beard SG 1 Midwearts trained.	
	25.10		Received 19 animals approximated Othro at 4 pm A.D.V.S. moved to RIBEMONT a 26 & TALMAS a 27.	

Army Form C. 2118.

WAR DIARY
or
INTELLIGENCE SUMMARY.
(Erase heading not required.)

40 mob MVS XIV

Instructions regarding War Diaries and Intelligence Summaries are contained in F. S. Regs., Part II. and the Staff Manual respectively. Title pages will be prepared in manuscript.

Place	Date	Hour	Summary of Events and Information	Remarks and references to Appendices
MAMETZ	25.10 (al) 25.0 26.0		HALLOY on 28th. wired impossible to move till conducting duty a potter return. no 19 on rail and 3 rem sick. Evacuated HH4. Received 16 animals.	
	27.10	10 am	Moved off from MAMETZ.	
		1 pm	Halted for midday feed nr. HEDAUVILLE.	
		7 pm	Reached HALLOY.	
HALLOY	28.10		Received two animals, one first case DOULLENS.	
	29.10		Received 5 animals.	
	30.10		Collected two animals, one dud case BOUQUEMAISON, one from LESOUICH. Evacuated 8 animals.	
	31.10	9.30am	Moved off for L'ARBRET.	
L'ARBRET		12 noon	Arrived. took over two animals from 41 N Midland M.V.S.	

J S Williamson Captain
O C 40 mob

War Diary

Vol VII Nov 1916.

HQ RA

J.H.Wilkinson Capt RA
D.S.O.M.G

Secret.

War Diary
-of-
40th Mobile Vet Section
for the Month of
October 1916

Volume 1st.

40th Indr: Vet: Ser:
Vol: 3

Army Form C. 2118.

WAR DIARY
or
INTELLIGENCE SUMMARY.
(Erase heading not required.)

Instructions regarding War Diaries and Intelligence Summaries are contained in F. S. Regs., Part II. and the Staff Manual respectively. Title pages will be prepared in manuscript.

26th M.A.C. July 1916

Vol 13

Place	Date	Hour	Summary of Events and Information	Remarks and references to Appendices
	1916			
L'ARBRET	1. XI		Received 1 animal.	
	2. XI		Received 1 animal.	
	3. XI		Received 3 animals, evacuated 16 animals	
	4. XI		Received 4 animals. Estab. shed being disinfected again.	
	5. XI		Received 3 animals, 1 collected from M.G.Coy R.E. ETREE-WAMIN 4/9no. 16 by order R.M.A.	
	6. XI		Received 5 animals, evacuated 24 animals, 1 not delivered from 2 sq.Rn TH 9pm	
	7. XI		Rec'd 3 animals.	
	8. XI		Rec'd 6 animals.	
	9. XI		Rec'd 3 animals, evacuated 26 animals, 1 obtained 93 when rec'd from 620 hm at about	
	10. XI		Rec'd 1 animal. 10 nils 37 mg/g rec'd 4th/16th march damet 335 41 64 62.	
		8pm	Native aeroplane dropped bombs within 20 yards of Lashon lines, Kelled 3 animals and one of R.T.K.L.B. drivers of festion medical first aid, no casualties in esten.	
	11. XI		Rec'd 5 animals one at 6/83 2 admitted 7.11.16, died from pneumonia admitted to stables.	
	12. XI		Rec'd 3 animals, CO visit for exray, harrow demon of will Off section at 5pm to date for battles in 10 days civil Basis.	

J. L. Sullivan Capt A.V.C.
O.C. 4 omd

T2134. Wt. W708-776. 500000. 4/15. Sir J. C. & S.

Army Form C. 2118.

WAR DIARY
or
INTELLIGENCE SUMMARY.
(Erase heading not required.)

Instructions regarding War Diaries and Intelligence Summaries are contained in F. S. Regs., Part II. and the Staff Manual respectively. Title pages will be prepared in manuscript.

Place	Date	Hour	Summary of Events and Information	Remarks and references to Appendices
LaBIET	13/11		Took over charge of 40th M.V.S. 7 p.m. Last evening. Admitted 12 animals and evacuated 32.	
	14/11		Two animals admitted	
	15/11		Three animals admitted. Cpl Willett returned from No 16 Veterinary Hospital. Cpl Dewar posted to Section from No 19 Veterinary Hospital in place of Cpl Wilkins who left this day for No 19 Veterinary Hospital	
	16/11		Three animals admitted; 14 sick animals evacuated.	
	17/11		Four animals admitted	
	18/11		One animal admitted	
	19/11		Eight animals admitted	
	20/11		Four animals admitted	
	21/11		Nine animals admitted and sixteen evacuated	
	22/11		Twenty eight animals admitted; very poor in condition from 30th Divisional Arty 2 animals died	
	23/11		Sixteen animals admitted; forty three evacuated. One N.C.O and five men returned from Australian Division on return of 30th Divisional Gunners to this area. Shrapnel shell from exhaustion; held P.Ms on all three animals	

Army Form C. 2118.

WAR DIARY
or
INTELLIGENCE SUMMARY.
(Erase heading not required.)

Army Vet [Vol VIII]

Place	Date	Hour	Summary of Events and Information	Remarks and references to Appendices
La Bye T	1916 24-11		Fifteen animals admitted. Paraded N.C.O's and men 0.B. Section regarding allotment of leave.	
	25-11		Eighteen animals admitted.	
	26-11		Thirty nine evacuated. Three cases admitted also Remount case float collected on sick case from 149 Brigade C. Batty at Luchus X.	
	27-11		Twenty one cases admitted. Float collected one sick horse from 30 TMTC 2 Section No Doctors. Pt Jackson E.R. ret reported from 14 Vet'y Hospital	
	28-11		Four cases admitted. Twenty three cases gone remount evacuated to Hospital	
	29-11		Nine cases admitted. Float collected one sick horse left behind by 20 4" Middlesex Reg.t. at Warluzel.	
	30-11 Pt		Seven cases admitted. Fifteen evacuated. Pte Wright presented to Cenote.	

H.F. Mc Turves Capt AVC
a/OC 40 TMVS

Kuo Hsiang

Auth. nobilis Vally debim
Volum XIII

November 1916

A.H. Sutherland Upward
A. Upward

Vol 14

War Diary.
December 1916
Vol. XIV.
40th Mobile Vety. Section.

Army Form C. 2118.

WAR DIARY
or
INTELLIGENCE SUMMARY.
(Erase heading not required.)

49th Mobile Vety Section Vol XIV

Place	Date	Hour	Summary of Events and Information	Remarks and references to Appendices
LARBRET	1916 1.XII		Took over from Capt returns on return from leave. Admitted 5 animals	
	2.XII		Admitted 8 animals	
	3.XII		Admitted 4 animals. Evacuated 10.	
	4.XII		Admitted 4 animals	
	5.XII		Admitted 23 animals	
	6.XII		Admitted 14 animals. Evacuated 24.	
	7.XII		Admitted 4 animals	
	8.XII		Admitted 8 animals	
	9.XII		Admitted 4 animals. One float case collected from Beuvrart. Evacuated 26.	
	10.XII		Admitted 12 animals. Standings in Centre yard completed for 40 great cases.	
	11.XII		Admitted 6 animals. Evacuated 24.	
	12.XII		Admitted 6 animals. 2 dogs (1 bank and 1 retrn) were killed from 9.20 km tee	
		9.45.	Section stood to. No casualties, some men escaped in the lines.	
	13.XII		Admitted 30 animals	
		7.40pm.	Enemy commenced bombing village & billets, & the tumult & fire of enemy aircraft the scape gone.	

WAR DIARY or INTELLIGENCE SUMMARY

Army Form C. 2118.

Fifth Mobile Vet. Section Vol XII

Place	Date	Hour	Summary of Events and Information	Remarks and references to Appendices
L'ARBRET	1916.			
	13.XII	8.15	Shelling ceased & returned section here at 8.35 pm. No casualties	
	14.XII		Admitted 14 animals, evacuated 50 animals. No troops westwards of LARBRET going to and fro. Finished to obtain at WARLINCOURT as way the same unless	
		2:45pm	convoy shell fire along ARRAS - DOULLENS road from U 13.C.55 & U 23.C.5.1 strained no heavy shell fallin 43 C.d. at distance of 200 yards unable to obtain truck at WARLINCOURT. R.T.O. opened permission trying to shelfire. Proceeded to MONDICOURT. Looked	
		8.30pm	up there, no casualties & section to acid lorries.	
	15 XII		Admitted 16 animals	
	16 XII		Admitted 10 animals, visited VII Corps DDVS both being used by Division	
	17 XII		Admitted 10 animals, evacuated 32. Visited DDVS of 51st Division the artillery.	
	18 XII		Admitted 12 animals. A Sat L. Shewsbury visited & inspected DDVS of Reshoubterage of 23rd Div Cap Calles no casualties Yorkcart Account	
	19 XII	4.40pm	Village & Railhead again shelled by enemy 23 cattle cap calles no casualties Yorkcart Account	
	20 XII		Admitted 5 animals ambulance cart from BAVINCOURT	
	21 XII		Admitted 2 animals evacuated 25.	
	22 XII 23		No admissions. Section carried on with return of standings disinfection of skin shelling ratly of new road kit.	

Army Form C. 2118.

WAR DIARY
or
INTELLIGENCE SUMMARY.
(Erase heading not required.)

Instructions regarding War Diaries and Intelligence Summaries are contained in F. S. Regs., Part II. and the Staff Manual respectively. Title pages will be prepared in manuscript.

H.Q. Mobile Vety Section Col XIV

Place	Date	Hour	Summary of Events and Information	Remarks and references to Appendices
L'ARBRET.	24.XII		Admitted 2 animals	
	25.XII		Admitted 2 animals destroyed one cast shell sick	
	26.XII		Admitted 28 animals	
	27.XII		Admitted 22 animals evacuated 52 animals	
	28.XII		Admitted 2 animals one an ambulance case from LACOUTURE	
	29.XII		Admitted 16 animals one an ambulance case from LA CAUCIE	
	30.XII		Admitted one animal evacuated 21 animals	
	31.XII		Admitted four animals	
			Carried out duties of A.D.V.S. 49th Division from 24th to 31st during absence on leave of Major H.	

J.R. Skinner Capt.
O.C. 49 M.V.S.

War Diary

December 1916.

vol XIV

40th Mobile Vety Section

A E Silvington
Captain
O Baserif

Army Form C. 2118.

WAR DIARY
or
INTELLIGENCE SUMMARY.
(Erase heading not required.)

Instructions regarding War Diary and Intelligence Summaries are contained in F.S. Regs., Part II. and the Staff Manual respectively. Title pages will be prepared in manuscript.

Place	Date	Hour	Summary of Events and Information	Remarks and references to Appendices
LARBERT.	1917 1-7.			
	2-7.		Admitted 9 animals. 6 with mange. Slow address from Dulrom. Admitted 31 animals. 1 horse from self. 1 from 17 Reserve, 3 from 1/Yorks. 1 from B' Coy, 2 from 'B' Coy, 2 from 301 Res. Batt. Sgt 1000 Yd. A.D.V.S. visited section & inspected horse shoed.	
	3-7.		Admitted 2 animals from 2nd Res. Bn Welsh Regt. Evacuated 39 horses 3 mules	
	4-7		Admitted 1 animal	
	5-7.		Admitted 46 animals mostly 2 train nose D.Train.	
	6-7.		Admitted 6 animals with 2 cow to emp from 2d W.Sh. Evacuated 47 horses 1 mule.	

T2134. Wt. W708-776. 500000. 4/16. Sir J.C. & S.

Army Form C. 2118.

WAR DIARY
or
INTELLIGENCE SUMMARY.
(Erase heading not required.)

Instructions regarding War Diaries and Intelligence Summaries are contained in F.S. Regs., Part II. and the Staff Manual respectively. Title pages will be prepared in manuscript.

4th Mobile Vety Section. 4th [illegible]

Place	Date	Hour	Summary of Events and Information	Remarks and references to Appendices
LA BRETT	1/1/17		2nd block over section by HQMVS. B.O. Lieutenant Thorpy Smith. Bois sent to school of Farriery. Lt Shakeldon admitted 3 animals. Destroyed one horse.	
	5/1/17		Admitted one animal	
	9/1/17		Admitted 47 animals. Evacuated Hospital 53.	
	10/1/17		None admitted	
	11/1/17		Admitted 4. one stray from Tray of Father on way from Guilain. Reserve the veterinary Lieut Officers spoken to HQMVS [illegible] 4 Divn	
	12/1/17		Admitted 27 Animals. Horse Evacuated went on leave to U.K.	
	13/1/17		Admitted 5 animals. Veterinary Lieut 3 B. MVS of army attempted [illegible] the horses gates out [illegible] the HQ OC.	
	14/1/17		Admitted 16 animals.	
	15/1/17		Section packed up ready for moving to rest area on 16/1/7. Capt. Watson [illegible] & arranged for taking over billets at 9 am tomorrow	
	16/1/17		Handed over 20 sick animals & billets to 1/1 West Riding M.V.S. 9.30 a.m. Section moved off to CROUCHES. Billets in very bad condition.	

T2134. Wt. W708—776. 500000. 4/15. Sir J. C. & S.

Army Form C. 2118.

WAR DIARY
or
INTELLIGENCE SUMMARY.
(Erase heading not required.)

Instructions regarding War Diaries and Intelligence Summaries are contained in F. S. Regs., Part II. and the Staff Manual respectively. Title pages will be prepared in manuscript.

A.T. Mobile Vety. Sectn. No 686

Place	Date	Hour	Summary of Events and Information	Remarks and references to Appendices
GROUCHES	17/7	11½	Continued. men up to their knees in mud.	
	17/7		Started clearance of mud from billets, approaches and stanchings. Admitted 15 animals including 6 Stray Mules, one of these animals suffering from Mange	
	18/7		Admitted 5 animals, including 1 Stray mule with Mange & 1 Stray Horse	
	19/7		Admitted 11 animals	
	20/7		Admitted One Stray mule suffering from Fistula Poll. Evacuated 16 horses & 4 mules No SE 70 546 Private Tull A.V.C. reported sick admitted to 96 Field Ambulance.	
	21/7		Admitted 3 animals	
	22/7		Admitted 12 animals including One stray mule suffering with Mange & advanced case of severe Haemorrhage Purpura - entirely due to a wound caused by constriction.	
	23/7		Admitted 31 animals.	
	24/7		Admitted 2 animals. Evacuated 27 horses and 11 mules.	
	25/7		Admitted 2 animals. Operated on a H.D. Mare with Tumour near Shoulder	
	26/7		Admitted 2 animals. D.D.V.S. Third Army visited Section to inspect a case of Ulcerative Cellulitis.	
	27/7		No animals received to day	

Army Form C. 2118.

WAR DIARY
or
INTELLIGENCE SUMMARY.
(Erase heading not required.)

19th Mobile Vety Section Vol XV

Place	Date	Hour	Summary of Events and Information.	Remarks and references to Appendices
GROUCHES. Cont?	28/7		Admitted 5 animals including 1 stray mule suffering from Sarcoptic Mange	
	29/7		Admitted 4 animals including 1 stray mule suffering from Ringworm	
	30/7		Admitted 5 animals	
	31/7		Admitted 1 animal.	

S Williamson Capt
O.C. 19th M.V.S.

— A O ᵗʰ —
Mobile Veterinary Section.
January - 1917
Vol. XV.

SECRET.

40th Mobile Veterinary Section.

Jany - 1917.

Vol. XV.

Vol 16

War Diary.
40th Mobile Veterinary Section.

February 1917.
Vol. XVI

Army Form C. 2118.

WAR DIARY
or
INTELLIGENCE SUMMARY.
(Erase heading not required.)

Instructions regarding War Diaries and Intelligence Summaries are contained in F.S. Regs., Part II. and the Staff Manual respectively. Title pages will be prepared in manuscript.

Place	Date	Hour	Summary of Events and Information	Remarks and references to Appendices
	1917			
LIARBRET.	13.II.		Admitted 11 animals	
	15.II.		Evacuated 23 animals.	
	16.II.		Received 9 animals. Sgt Arey having on detachment from No 5 V.H.	
	17.II.		Received 2 animals. Thriving.	
	18.II.		Admitted 1 animal. Amb. from HUMBERCOURT.	
	19.II.		D.D.V.S. inspected section. Admitted 11 animals 27 Bn PK, mange debility	
	20.II.		Received 2 animals.	
	21.II.		Admitted 6 animals. Floors of stables simply in mud owing to heavy frost like a sponge.	
	22.II.		Admitted one animal. Evacuated 28 animals.	
	23.II.		Enemy shelled neighbourhood of village & billets & previously during past week.	
	24.II.		Admitted 2 animals, one shell went 27 Bn PK hit at station. Repleka & horsepipe	
	27.II.		Admitted 25 animals.	
	28.II.		A.D.V.S. inspected section.	

S.W. Thomson Capt.
26 Horse.

T2134. Wt. W708—776. 500000. 4/15. Sir J. C. & S.

Army Form C. 2118.

WAR DIARY
or
INTELLIGENCE SUMMARY.
(Erase heading not required.)

Instructions regarding War Diaries and Intelligence Summaries are contained in F. S. Regs., Part II. and the Staff Manual respectively. Title pages will be prepared in manuscript.

497 Mobile Vety Section Vol XI

Place	Date	Hour	Summary of Events and Information	Remarks and references to Appendices
	1917.			
GROUCHES	1.II		Admitted 10 animals including 10 tag mules; two ambulance cases from Sus STEER	
	2.II		Admitted 5 animals	
	3.II		Admitted 2 animals	
	4.II		Admitted 3 animals, 1 sent case from BRENIERS. 58th Divn Train	
	5.II		Section inspected by A.D.V.S. Sent N.C.O. 1 man &1 Horse to L'ARBRET for school instruction	
	6.II		Moved to L'ARBRET. very cold day 1 mule very slippery. 49 kms L had not completed march so on own arrival.	
L'ARBRET.	7.II		Completed move. N.C.O. & men billeted. moved to L'ARBRET with two mules and cases	
			Pte Allen reported as reinforcement from 23 V.H. admitted 2 animals	
	8.II		Admitted 3 animals. evacuated 32	
	9.II		2d Lt Mansbridge R.A.V.C. 2 Shyhnold for duty took rent. admitted 3 animals	
	10.II		Admitted 1 animal. Village shelled by enemy at 10 am - one shell fell in front of billets 10 yds from officers mess the other in middle of yd do no casualties no damage except to windows further.	
	11.II		Admitted 5 animals	
	12.II		Admitted 2 animals	

Army Form C. 2118.

WAR DIARY
or
INTELLIGENCE SUMMARY.
(Erase heading not required.)

40th Mobile Vety Section Vol XVIII

Instructions regarding War Diaries and Intelligence Summaries are contained in F. S. Regs., Part II. and the Staff Manual respectively. Title pages will be prepared in manuscript.

Place	Date	Hour	Summary of Events and Information	Remarks and references to Appendices
	1917			
L'ARBRET.	1. III		Admitted 1 animal. Evacuated 28 animals.	
	2. III		Admitted 1 animal. Evacuated 1 animal. Requested for particulars for badges for men.	
	3. III		Village shelled at 11.15 hrs. All men railhorses turned out & proceeded along Beaumont Road, remained out till 12.30 hrs. Then returned to LGH	
	4. III		Received 4 animals	
	5. III			
	6. III		Admitted 15 animals. One Amb. case injured by motor car near 43 Cas	
	7. III		Admitted 5 animals. One amb case BEAUMETZ.	
	8. III		Evacuated 28 animals. Admitted 3. AVS repeated names of men for transfer to 96th Mobile Vet[y] 9 C.M. for milk ration	
	9. III		Admitted 1. Enemy commenced shelling in direction of Railway Station about 7.30 hrs. and again about 9.10 hrs.	
	10. III		Admitted 5 animals. 1 amb case from MINCOURT. 1 Amb case from BEAUMETZ. Enemy fired two large calibre shells about 12 midnight	
	11. III		12.15 hrs. One platoon all men turned out & put on Gas alerts. Alarm off 2 am. Admitted 4 animals. Erited form of Mr DERAMCOURT. Young carcase of heifer Suspected ANTHRAX, notified the Maire of SAULTY, french mayor at KANCOURT. "A.V.S." AVITY COURT. Admitted 2 animals. Carcase of Anthrax case buried & description of premises kept.	
	12. III			
	13. III		Admitted 14 animals. Visited Mr Deramcourts premises & inspected animals Sent report on telegraph form.	

T2134. Wt. W708-776. 500000. 4/15. Sir J. C. & S.

Army Form C. 2118.

WAR DIARY
or
INTELLIGENCE SUMMARY.
(Erase heading not required.)

4/th Mobile Vety Section vol XVII

Instructions regarding War Diaries and Intelligence Summaries are contained in F. S. Regs., Part II. and the Staff Manual respectively. Title pages will be prepared in manuscript.

Place	Date	Hour	Summary of Events and Information	Remarks and references to Appendices
LARBRET.	1917			
	14-iii		Admitted two animals. Inspected animals in Authow farm	
	15-iii		Admitted 2 animals. Do.	
	16-iii		Admitted 6 animals. ADVS inspected Vety Depôt operation.	
	17-iii		Evacuated 28 animals. Inspected animals in Authow farm.	
	18-iii		Admitted 1 animal. Inspected & reported on horse of SSULT7, for which owner claimed compensation for injuries.	
	19-iii		Admitted 10 animals, Inspected animals in Authow farm.	
	20-iii		Admitted 4 animals, visited Authow infected farm with DDVS.	
	21-iii		Further disinfection of premises etc. Disinfectant limed by DDVS. Carried out sundry my supervision also enquiry of stray horses. Inspected animals in Authow farm. Admitted 7 animals, evacuated SOUY.	
	22-iii		Inspected animals in M. Durancourts farm. Visited farm at LAHERLIERE exit animal reported, unknown treatment of it.	
	23-iii		Admitted 22 animals. Tracted report KAD.V.S. on horse observed & reported as infected with F.B.C. 123 Bee R-72 in having his way into the field & eating his animals at tongue of the cart, making my return on return of the food.	
	24-iii		Admitted 9 animals, evacuated 51. Issued Sech animal LAHERLIERE. Inspected animals in M Durancourt.	
	25-iii		Admitted 10 animals, Reported replacements of O.S. Boot.	
	26-iii		Inspected animals on M Durancourts farm.	

Army Form C. 2118.

WAR DIARY
or
INTELLIGENCE SUMMARY.
(Erase heading not required.)

40th Mobile Vety Section Vol XVII

Instructions regarding War Diaries and Intelligence Summaries are contained in F. S. Regs., Part II. and the Staff Manual respectively. Title pages will be prepared in manuscript.

Place	Date	Hour	Summary of Events and Information	Remarks and references to Appendices
L'HARMEL	1917. 27.III		Admitted 10 animals. Chron ScheDuren Reported case of ill treatment of pack horse by typing headrope to saddle of another & dragging it along behind by Cd of Coy 15 Sqadn, R.F.C. 4th Bde R.F.a.	
	28.III		Inspected animals at m. Demonanto farm, all healthy reported anumps 15 days allowed by trench lous have now elapsed there are no fresh cases.	
	29.III		Admitted 3 animals	
	30.III		Admitted 12 animals. Copy of Vety arrangements when operations are contemplated received	
	31.III		Admitted 26 animals, evacuated 56.	

B.W.Wilkinson Capt A.V.C.
O.C. 40 MVS.

WAR DIARY

INDIAN EXPEDITIONARY FORCE "D"

10th mobile Stationery

Vol XVII

March 1917

Lt H. S. Shinnour Cabinet
R.E. Command

40th Mobile Veterinary Section.

Vol. XVII

March 1917.

WAR DIARY or INTELLIGENCE SUMMARY

Army Form C. 2118.

JSL/18 Light Mobile Veterinary Section XSt??

Place	Date	Hour	Summary of Events and Information	Remarks and references to Appendices
L'ARBRET	1917 1.4.		Received 30 animals most from Cav. bdes. the way through from front line, many in a state of extreme exhaustion & all very foot sore. Ambulance collecting them from road sides during most of the night.	
	2.4.		Admitted 12 animals. Orders issued from (Corps?) sent to (unit) but had 30 astray & telephone communication down. Eventually succeeded at 10 pm.	
	3.4.		Evacuated 46 animals. Very snowy & cold day. One bay horse kept way to stable. Held in long halt. Ambulance out and tied too heen after.	
	4.4.		Admitted 17 animals. Evacuated 52. 2 Amb. journeys BELLACOURT v MONCHICOURT. 26 miles	
	5.4.		Admitted 11 animals. Received horse from the front or BLAREVILLE with A.D.V.S. Amb. BELLACOURT v GROSVILLE. over 30 miles	
	6.4.		Admitted 23 animals	
	7.4.		Admitted 10 animals. Evacuated 30 animals	
	8.4.		Admitted 20 animals. Very fall of snow	
	9.4.		Admitted 30 animals. Wet day. Gold G.S. Wagon faulty to turn report to have no means ob? of Railway truck & found that it had been conveyed as unattached into B.P.D. Branch +1½ = 53. Amb. driver reported stated by police between GROSVILLE v BELLACOURT. About the 27 SL.	

T2134. Wt. W708—776. 500000. 4/15. Sir J. C. & S.

Army Form C. 2118.

WAR DIARY
or
INTELLIGENCE SUMMARY.
(Erase heading not required.)

4th Mobile Vety Section B.E.F.

Instructions regarding War Diaries and Intelligence Summaries are contained in F. S. Regs., Part II. and the Staff Manual respectively. Title pages will be prepared in manuscript.

Place	Date	Hour	Summary of Events and Information	Remarks and references to Appendices
	1917			
L'ARBRET.	10.4		D.D.V.S. visited section 6.30 p.m re evacuation from forward areas & arrangements for earthquakes	
	11.4		visited 11.30 p.m. to place sick host for S.A.V.C. Now ready for work.	
			Proceeded with ado hoc [illegible] to little-meurs between hour & evacuated sick ranges in long. Admitted two animals. Evacuated 7.	
	12.4		Heavy snow. Admitted 42 animals	
	13.4		Admitted 63 animals	
	14.4		Admitted 30 animals. Evacuated 99 animals	
	15.4		Admitted 8 animals. Snow during night	
	16.4		Admitted 7 animals. Evacuated 41 animals	
	17.4		Admitted 14 animals	
	18.4		Admitted 6 animals. Evacuated 19 animals	
	19.4		Admitted 6 animals. Snow & sleet	
	20.4		Admitted 11 animals. received orders known to forward area. reorganised from at A.G.N.Y.	
	21.4		Evacuated 9 animals. moved to A.G.N.Y.	
A.G.N.Y.	22.4		Admitted 23 animals. weather fine	
	23.4		Admitted 17 animals. Evacuated 45 from AR.A.S.	

Army Form C. 2118.

WAR DIARY
or
INTELLIGENCE SUMMARY.
(Erase heading not required.)

40th Mobile Vety Section vol XVIII

Instructions regarding War Diaries and Intelligence Summaries are contained in F. S. Regs., Part II. and the Staff Manual respectively. Title pages will be prepared in manuscript.

Place	Date	Hour	Summary of Events and Information	Remarks and references to Appendices
	1917			
AGNY.	24.4		Admitted 12 animals.	
	25.4		Admitted 18 animals.	
	26.4		Admitted 7 animals. Evacuated 33 from ARRAS. Ray keep explosion one killed & shot away no injuries to men or animals	
	27.4		Admitted 24 animals.	
	28.4		Admitted 4 animals evacuated 20.	
	29.4		Moved off to rest area. Bivouacked in BOIS DE HEROUBAL after march of 2 Kilometers	
ROELLECOURT	30.4		Arrived ROELLECOURT. 9.30am found billets not suitable as no water, marched 3 klm. & selected farm at ROCOURT. ST. LAURENT moved there.	

Lt Col Ameron CAMVC

J. Leonard

SECRET.

40th M.V.S.

Vol. XVIII

April 1917.

War Diary.

Vol 19

40TH MOBILE SECTION, ARMY VETERINARY CORPS.
No.
Date 5-6-1917.

War Diary.

40th Mobile Veterinary Section.

Vol. XIX.

May 1917.

Army Form C. 2118.

WAR DIARY
or
INTELLIGENCE SUMMARY.

(Erase heading not required.)

Instructions regarding War Diaries and Intelligence Summaries are contained in F. S. Regs., Part II. and the Staff Manual respectively. Title pages will be prepared in manuscript.

Place	Date	Hour	Summary of Events and Information	Remarks and references to Appendices
	1917			
ACOURT, ST	1.5.		Admitted 12 animals including 1 horse V.O. Third Army Troops.	
LAURENT	2.5.		Arrived R.T.O. ST. POL to evacuate sick animals. Admitted 14 animals.	
	3.5.		Evacuated 14 animals.	
	4.5.		Moved to 9 V.E. Took over duties of A.D.V.S.	
O.E.V.E.	5.5.		Making billets ready for receiving animals & collecting materials &c.	
	6.5.		Received 2 animals. One killed in open in an orchard - heavy full moon.	
	7.5.		Received 5 animals.	
	8.5.		Rec'd two animals.	
	9.5.		Evacuated 12 animals.	
	10.5.		Rec'd 1 animal. Weather very good. men employed cleaning up & equipment.	
	11.5.		Rec'd 3 animals.	
	12.5.		Rec'd 1 animal.	
	13.5.		Rec'd 5 animals.	
	14.5.		Rec'd 1 animal.	
	15.5.		Rec'd 1 animal.	

Army Form C. 2118.

WAR DIARY
or
INTELLIGENCE SUMMARY.
(Erase heading not required.)

10th Mobile Vety Section XX   Vol 20

Instructions regarding War Diaries and Intelligence Summaries are contained in F. S. Regs., Part II. and the Staff Manual respectively. Title pages will be prepared in manuscript.

Place	Date	Hour	Summary of Events and Information	Remarks and references to Appendices
	1917			
POPERINGHE	1-6		Admitted 4 animals.	
	2-6		Admitted 9 animals	
	3-6		Admitted 1 animal, evacuated 20. by road to ST. OMER.	
	4-6		Admitted 1 animal	
	5-6		Admitted 4 animals	
	6-6		Admitted 6 animals.	
	7-6		Admitted 11 animals, 1 died enteric. N.I. Horse.	
	8-6		Admitted 1 animal. evacuated 2 Class B cases to X Corps M.V. Det.	
	9-6		Admitted 6. Established Advanced Post at H.16.a.3.9. 1 Cpl & two men. Evacuated 14 by road to ST. OMER. two others admitted & sent by road to catch up party at first halt.	
	10-6		Two men arrived back having handed over 2 animals to main body.	
	11-6		Admitted 7 animals.	
	12-6		Admitted 1 animal.	
	13-6		Admitted 28 animals.	
	14-6		Admitted 28 animals. & transferred to X Corps M.V. Det.	

Army Form C. 2118.

WAR DIARY
or
INTELLIGENCE SUMMARY.
(Erase heading not required.)

Auth: mobility [illegible] all X/s

Place	Date	Hour	Summary of Events and Information	Remarks and references to Appendices
	1917.			
WATOU	27.5.		Received 3 animals.	
	28.5.		Received 3 animals.	
	30.5.		Received 2 animals, moved to POPERINGHE very good billet.	
POPERINGE	31.5.		Received 5 animals.	

D K Stillman Capt
96 oms

Instructions regarding War Diaries and Intelligence Summaries are contained in F. S. Regs., Part II. and the Staff Manual respectively. Title pages will be prepared in manuscript.

War Diary

4th Middlesex Regt.

Vol VI

May 1917

Westminster Reg 1916

9.6.40 am S

Army Form C. 2118.

WAR DIARY
or
INTELLIGENCE SUMMARY.
(Erase heading not required.)

40th Mobile Vety Section Vol IX

Place	Date 1917	Hour	Summary of Events and Information	Remarks and references to Appendices
POPERINGHE	15.6.		Admitted 10 animals. D.D.V.S. Fifth Army & D.D.R. visited Section. Called in advanced Post & ordered them back. Orr billet vacated by 47th Divl M.V.S.	
	16.6.	9.a.m.	Evacuated 67 by road to ST. OMER.	
		10.45am	Moved KRENINGHELST. & took over stay home river mob. left by 47 Divl M.V.S.	
	17.6.		Admitted 2 animals	
	18.6.		Admitted 1 animal.	
	19.6.		Admitted 10 animals including too sharp	
	19.6.		Admitted 6 animals.	
	20.6.		Established Advanced Post at H.26.A.8.8. Admitted 27 animals nearly all knuckled.	
	21.6		Admitted 41 animals	
	22.6.		Admitted 11 animals. D.D.R. Inspected 14 animals suffering from exhaustion as to disposal.	
	23.6.		Admitted 4 animals, evacuated by road 94 animals to ST. OMER	
	24.6.		Admitted 5 animals, one case Tetanus collected by Advd Post. destroyed. 20 animals conveyed by ambulance to WIPPENHOEK. 6 otherwise B. walked.	
	25.6.		Admitted 3 animals 2 by ambulance from WIPPENHOEK. 2 otherwalking 31 evacuated by rail from WIPPENHOEK.	

Army Form C. 2118.

WAR DIARY
or
INTELLIGENCE SUMMARY.

(Erase heading not required.)

40th Mobile Vety Section Vol IX

Place	Date	Hour	Summary of Events and Information	Remarks and references to Appendices
	1917			
RENINGHELST	26.6		Admitted 8, including two stray afterwards claimed by A/148.	
	27.6		Admitted 6.	
	28.6		Admitted 19 animals, one quadrat and 2nd wife developed gas gangrene more destroyed	
	29.6		Admitted 3 animals. Relieved advanced not horsed animals.	
	30.6		Evacuated 24 by road to ST. OMER.	

Thos S Wiseman Major AVC
O.C. 40 Mr V S

War Diary
——

40th Mobile City Station
——

Vol IX June 1917.
——

Lt R Tillinson RAMC
O.C. 40 mvs.
——

WAR DIARY.

40th MOBILE VETY SECTION.

VOL. XX JUNE 1917.

Army Form C. 2118.

WAR DIARY
or
INTELLIGENCE SUMMARY.
(Erase heading not required.)

40th Mobile Vety Section vol XXI

Vol 21

Place	Date	Hour	Summary of Events and Information	Remarks and references to Appendices
RENINGHELST.	1917 1.7		Admitted 1 animal.	
	2.7.		Admitted 1 animal.	
	3.7.		Admitted 6 animals.	
	4.7.		Admitted 3 animals. Visited advanced Posts.	
	5.7.		Admitted 12 animals. Ambulance shelled, killed animals 3.P. D19K53a204	
	6.7.		Admitted 14 animals.	
	7.7.		Admitted 4 animals. Evacuated 17 animals. Handed over to Capt Blackart.	

RW Thompson Major a/c

Army Form C. 2118.

WAR DIARY
or
INTELLIGENCE SUMMARY.
(Erase heading not required.)

40th Mobile V.A. Sect. Vol XXI

Place	Date	Hour	Summary of Events and Information	Remarks and references to Appendices
Renningfurt	7/17		Took over Command 40 ORs from Major Williamson	
	8		Admitted 1 animal	
	9		Admitted 3 "	
	10		Admitted 4 "	
	11		Admitted 6 including two strays	
	12		9 ORs now here inspected ORs had dismounted. 2 Down of 9	
	13		Admitted 20 animals	
	14		Admitted 1 and evacuated 11 animals to 2nd Armm	
	15		Admitted 4 animals	
	16		Admitted 9 " including stray mules	
			+ evacuated 36 animals to Corps Coll. Stn N.D.	
	17		Admitted 6 animals including two strays	
	18		" 2 " including one stray	
	19		Admitted 10 " including one stray	
	20		Admitted 9	
	21		Admitted 35 animals including 28 of 2nd Australian	

Army Form C. 2118.

WAR DIARY
or
INTELLIGENCE SUMMARY.
(Erase heading not required.)

1st Mobile Vet. Sec. MEF

Place	Date	Hour	Summary of Events and Information	Remarks and references to Appendices
	21		Evacuated 21 animals to 2 Corps Mobile	
	22		Handed over Command of Section to Capt Patterson Colonel Gotham + Col Griffin called & inspected Section	

F Chalk
Capt A.V.C.

Army Form C. 2118.

WAR DIARY
or
INTELLIGENCE SUMMARY.
(Erase heading not required.)

40th Mobile Vet. Sect. Vol XXI

Instructions regarding War Diaries and Intelligence Summaries are contained in F.S. Regs., Part II. and the Staff Manual respectively. Title pages will be prepared in manuscript.

Place	Date	Hour	Summary of Events and Information	Remarks and references to Appendices
Rouinghelst	22		Took over command of this Unit from Captain Chalk. A.V.C. on return of Major Williamson A.D.V.S. from leave: two animals admitted.	
	23		Eight cases admitted: destroyed mare from 148 Bde, R.G.A.	
	24		Seven cases admitted to Section. Sixteen cases including ten mares evacuated to II Corps Mobile V. Detachment.	
	25		Admitted four cases. Seven cases returned evacuated to II Corps Mobile V Detachment.	
	26		Twenty oned cases of Gas Poisoning gined to This Unit: Seventeen sick and wounded animals admitted. D.A.D.V.S visited this Unit.	
	27		Twelve animals admitted: One case of gunshot wound (abdomen) died. D.A.D.V.S visited the Section. Twenty nine cases evacuated to II Corps Mobile Veterinary Detachment: Inspected the Advanced Post with Staff Sergeant.	
	28		Ordered destruction of one animal. Twenty two cases admitted to Section.	
	29		Admitted nine animals. D.A.D.V.S visited the Unit.	
	30		Seventeen animals admitted. Seventeen cases evacuated to II Corps Mobile Veterinary Detachment.	

Army Form C. 2118.

WAR DIARY
or
INTELLIGENCE SUMMARY.
(Erase heading not required.)

48th Mobile Vety Section VCXV

Place	Date	Hour	Summary of Events and Information	Remarks and references to Appendices
Reninghelst	31		Twenty six sick and wounded animals admitted: Seventeen cases evacuated to 11 Corps Mobile Veterinary Detachment.	

War Diary.
July = 1917
Volume XXI
40th Mobile Vety. Section.

H.J. McTurner
Captain
O.C. 40th M.V.S

Vol 22

War Diary

August 1917.

Volume XXII.

40th

Mobile Veterinary Section.

Army Form C. 2118.

WAR DIARY
or
INTELLIGENCE SUMMARY.
(Erase heading not required.)

HQ Mobile Vety Section No XXII

Place	Date	Hour	Summary of Events and Information	Remarks and references to Appendices
Rouchelot	1-8		Six animals admitted. Evacuated 9 # 6 by road to 2-3 Vety Hospitals & one and 14 to 2nd Corps Mobile Vety Detachment by road.	
	2-8		Admitted four animals. A.D.V.S and D ADVS visited section.	
	3-8		Three sick animals admitted.	
	4-8		Admitted fourteen sick animals. Evacuated 19 by road to II Corps M. Vety Detachment.	
	5-8		Handed over to 21st Infantry Brigade 12 animals Fit for duty. Transferred 4 to 16th M.V.S (6th Division) evacuated one to II Corps M.V. Detachment. Moved from Rouen Rodigt to Godewaersvelde DADVS. Marched by road to new billet - with the section.	
Godewaersvelde	6-8		D.A.D.V.S visited Section. Inspected to sick animals of the Infantry Brigades with the D.A.D.V.S. March from Godewaersvelde to Meuris.	
Meuris	7-8			
	8-8		Admitted four sick animals. Visited 21st Infantry Brigade.	
	9-8		Admitted three sick animals. Visited 69th Infantry Brigade.	
	10-8		Admitted three sick animals. Inspected new billet at St Jans Cappel.	

Army Form C. 2118.

WAR DIARY
or
INTELLIGENCE SUMMARY.
(Erase heading not required.)

H⁰ Mobile Vety Section VIII Corps

Place	Date	Hour	Summary of Events and Information	Remarks and references to Appendices
Menis	11-8		Admitted one evalanimal. Moved from Menis to St Jans Cappel.	
St Jans Cappel	12-8		admitted two sick animals a/ADVS IX Corps visited section.	
	13-8		Admitted four animals : Q/f'd all 2 mang's cases at IX Corps Horse Dp̄t	
	14-8		Admitted two sick animals. Seven cases sent to IX Corps mobile vet sect.	
	15-8		Admitted four sick animals. Visited 87 & 89 Syfers Coys (e-e not DADVS	
	16-8		Admitted five sick animals. Visited 2, 3 and 4 Coys of Sig Train	
	19-8		Admitted five sick animals ordly at IX Corps Horseshow during	
			afternoon. 9 animals shown — Seventy Brigade.	
	18-8		Admitted fourteen sick animals; visited 2 13ᵗʰ Syfers Brigade	
	19-8		Admitted four sick animals ; DADVS inspected section. examined	
			twenty four sick animals being sent to 23 Hospital St Omer	
			Q/f'd 2 mang's Cases : visited 213, 4 Coys Syf's Train ADVS IX	
	20-8		Corp's inspected section. wrote a Census.	
	21-8		Admitted two sick animals ; evacuated 4 to IX Corps M. Vet. Detaches.	
			Horst Case transfer infection from 91ˢᵗ Field Ambulance.	

Army Form C. 2118.

WAR DIARY
or
INTELLIGENCE SUMMARY.
(Erase heading not required.)

4th Mob'lg Vety Section Vol XXII

Place	Date	Hour	Summary of Events and Information	Remarks and references to Appendices
St Jans Cappel	22-8		1st Army Motor Horse Ambulance conveyed two cases to 23 Hospital. No sick news billet at Dranoutre; evacuated 1 case to II Corps M. Vety Detachment; admitted six cases.	
	23-8		Moved to Dranoutre. Took over standing from 4th Aust. Division M.V.S.	
Dranoutre	24-8		Admitted two sick cases.	
	25-8		Admitted one sick case.	
	26-8		Admitted one case. A.D.V. Six Corps and D.A.D.V.S visited II Corps section.	
	27-8		Admitted two cases.	
	28-8		Admitted six cases. D.D.V.S II Army & A.D.V.S II Corps visited the section.	
	29-8		A.D.V.S II Corps visited section.	
	30-8		Two cases admitted.	
	31-8		Admitted one case.	

H.V. McTurk Capt. R.C.
O.C. 4th M.V.S.

War Diary

August 1917

Volume XXII

40th Mobile Vety Section
HM Etwal
Capt MRC
OC 40th M.V.S.

Army Form C. 2118.

WAR DIARY
or
INTELLIGENCE SUMMARY.
(Erase heading not required.)

4th Mobile Veterinary Section / XXIII

VM 23

Instructions regarding War Diaries and Intelligence Summaries are contained in F.S. Regs., Part II. and the Staff Manual respectively. Title pages will be prepared in manuscript.

Place	Date	Hour	Summary of Events and Information	Remarks and references to Appendices
Ransart	1-9		Admitted one sick animal. DADVS visited the Section	
	2-9		Twenty-five sick animals sent to 1st (Omer No 23 Hospital) and evacuated over the night IX Corps M.V.D.	
	3-9		Two animals admitted DADVs visited Unit; notified 30th Div Train	
	4-9		One sick animal admitted	
	5-9		Two animals admitted. Three sick animals sent to IX Corps	
	6-9		M.V.D. DADVS visited the Section. Six sick and lame animals admitted	
	7-9		Four cases admitted. Two cases evacuated to IX Corps M.V.D. visited 2/6 Machine Gun Co. 30th Divisional Train.	
	8-9		Nine sick animals admitted; Seventeen evacuated to IX Corps M.V.D. Infected animals of Divisional Transport DADVS	
	9-9		Three Animals admitted.	
	10-9		DADVS visited Section	
	11-9		One sick animal admitted	
	12-9		Four sick animals admitted. DADVS visited to Section	

T2134. Wt. W708—776. 500000. 4/15. Sir J. C. & S.

Army Form C. 2118.

WAR DIARY
or
INTELLIGENCE SUMMARY.
(Erase heading not required.)

H.Q. "M" Mobile Veterinary Section Vol XXIV

Instructions regarding War Diaries and Intelligence Summaries are contained in F.S. Regs., Part II. and the Staff Manual respectively. Title pages will be prepared in manuscript.

Place	Date	Hour	Summary of Events and Information	Remarks and references to Appendices
Armentis	13-9		Two sick animals admitted. Three animals evacuated to IX Corps M.V.D.	
	14-9		Six sick animals admitted	
	15-9		Ten sick and lame animals admitted; evacuated nineteen to 23 H.Hospital and one unmanageable mule to Field Remount Section; one case sent to IX Corps M.V.D.	
	16-9		Admitted two animals. D.A.D.V.S. visited unit. Two footed Divisional Train Horses.	
	17-9		Eight animals admitted including two strays. Visited 2. 6. M. F. Amb and detachment 1st Canadian Reserve Park; one animal sent to IX Corps M.V.D.	
	18-9		D.A.D.V.S. visited unit	
	19-9		Three animals admitted; one sent to IX Corps M.V.D.	
	20-9		Visited 30th Divisional Train; 2. 6. M F. Amb and 1st Canadian Res Park.	
	21-9		Eleven animals admitted; D.A.D.V.S. visited the unit.	
	22-9		Nine animals admitted. Visited 30th Divisional Train	
	23-9		Forty-one sick and lame animals admitted	
	24-9		Sick animals sent to 23 Hospital, evacuated six from IX C.of M.V.D.	

WAR DIARY
or
INTELLIGENCE SUMMARY.
(Erase heading not required.)

Army Form C. 2118.

Instructions regarding War Diaries and Intelligence Summaries are contained in F. S. Regs., Part II. and the Staff Manual respectively. Title pages will be prepared in manuscript.

40th Mobile Veterinary Section

Place	Date	Hour	Summary of Events and Information	Remarks and references to Appendices
Navarin	25-9		Admitted two animals including one stray. Skewing class for 21st Infantry Brigade (horses) formed. D.A.D.V.S. inspected Unit.	
	26-9		Visited 218 M.G. Coy, 30th D.S.V.S and Train and detachment of Canada Reserve Park.	
	27-9		One animal admitted. D.A.D.V.S. visited Section.	
	28-9		Nine animals admitted. Visited 30th Divisional Train, 216 M.G. Coy.	
	29-9		One animal admitted. Evacuated five mang Route Veterinary to 26 M.V.S., to TA Coln M.V.D.	
	30-9		Fifteen animals admitted including one stray. D.A.D.V.S. visited Section. Skewing class for 21st Infantry Brigade closed.	

H.V.McTurk Capt AV C
± M.V.S
OC 40

40TH MOBILE SECTION
3 - OCT 1917
A.V.

War DIARY

September 1917

Vol XXIII

40th Mobile Veterinary Sect.

A.C. McLaurin
Capt.
O.C. 40th M.V.S.

War Diary
—of—
40th Mobile Vety Section
for the month of
September 1917.

Volume XXIII

Army Form C. 2118.

WAR DIARY
or
INTELLIGENCE SUMMARY.
(Erase heading not required.)

HQ the Mobile Veterinary Section XIV
Vol 24

Place	Date	Hour	Summary of Events and Information	Remarks and references to Appendices
Oyanouthe	1-10		Admitted 4 Animals including 3 Stray 2 Stray claimed by B/149 RFA. Evacuated 24 sick animals by road to St Omer. — 23 HQ total	
	2-10		Admitted one solid No 1,2,3,4 Co. 30 Dismounted Trainers and 126 mps.	
	3-10		Admitted 5 including 2 Stray and surplus wallet Detachment 1st Canadian Reserve Park	
	4-10		Admitted two animals, visited demonmal Train	
	5-10		Handed over unit to Major Williams. DADVS during absence on leave 6/7-10/17	
Dranouthe 6/10			Admitted 4 Animals including 1 Stray Mule	
	7-10		Admitted 19 Animals	
	8-10		Evacuated 21 animals by road to St Omer : 23 Hospital	
	9-10		Admitted 3 animals including 2 Stray Mules	
	10-10		Admitted 1 Animal	
	11-10		Admitted 2 Animals	
	12-10		Admitted 2 Animals	
	13-10		Admitted 4 Animals including 2 Stray Mules —	
	14-10		Admitted 4 Animals —	

Army Form C. 2118.

WAR DIARY
or
INTELLIGENCE SUMMARY.
(Erase heading not required.)

Instructions regarding War Diaries and Intelligence Summaries are contained in F. S. Regs., Part II. and the Staff Manual respectively. Title pages will be prepared in manuscript.

Place	Date	Hour	Summary of Events and Information	Remarks and references to Appendices
IRANOUTRE	18 Nov 17		Admitted 3 Animals including One Stray Mule. Evacuated 10 sick animals by road to St. OMER. No 23 Vety Hospital	
		16.10	Admitted 4 Animals	
		17.10	Admitted 5 Animals including 2 Stray Mules.	
		18.10	Handed over Command of Unit to Captain H.V. McKewen on his return from leave.	
			A.J. Wiseman Major	
Granoutre	19.10		Took over Unit from Major Wiseman. admitted three including one Stray, and one Army horse found in possession of civilians by M.P.	
			Admitted our Animals: included (Canadian Reserve Pk. TH/31.1.14.6.) Ois Train	
		20.10	Admitted four animals: horses 21 5.M. 9.6.7.	

T2134. Wt. W708—776. 500000. 4/15. Sir J. C. & S.

Army Form C. 2118.

WAR DIARY
or
INTELLIGENCE SUMMARY.
(Erase heading not required.)

Instructions regarding War Diaries and Intelligence Summaries are contained in F. S. Regs., Part II. and the Staff Manual respectively. Title pages will be prepared in manuscript.

Place	Date	Hour	Summary of Events and Information	Remarks and references to Appendices
Dranoutre	21-10		Sick animals admitted.	
	22-10		Evacuated to No 23 Hospital 5 Ponies 16 sick and lame animals also two evacuated by Bays (3 cases) to vans Hospital Westoutre. Cliffords Refit with DADVS. horses No 1, 2, 3 & 4 Cos 30 Horses seen.	
	23-10		A.A.Q.M.G. and D.A.Q.M.G. with D.A.D.V.S. visited this Unit.	
	24-10		Admitted sick animal.	
	25-10		Admitted 5 animals, evacuated two (3 cases) by Bays 6 No 23 Hospital 5 horses.	
	26-10		G.O.C. two inspected this Unit. D&D.V.S. were present.	
	27-10		Admitted four animals. Visited No 1, 2, 3, 4 Cos 30 Horses seen and	
			1, 6 m. G. Coy.	
	28-10		Admitted ten animals. Casualty 5 Pts Chevalier - kicked.	
	29-10		A.D.V.S. Corps inspected this Unit.	
	30-10		Admitted one animal, evacuated seven (Cos 4 & 5. Cos 10, 2) by Bays to No 3 Hospital 5 Horses.	
	31-10		Admitted two sick animals.	

A.W. McEwan
Capt. A.V.C.
O.C. 4th Arm V.S.

War Diary
— of —
40th Mob. Vety. Sect.
for the month of
October 1917

Volume 34.

H.W.Metiva
Capt AVC
O.C. 40th M.V.S.

Vol 25

War Diary.
November 1917.
Vol. XXV.
40th Mobile Veterinary Section.

Army Form C. 2118.

WAR DIARY
or
INTELLIGENCE SUMMARY.
(Erase heading not required.)

40th Mobile Veterinary Section V LXXX

Instructions regarding War Diaries and Intelligence Summaries are contained in F. S. Regs., Part II. and the Staff Manual respectively. Title pages will be prepared in manuscript.

Place	Date	Hour	Summary of Events and Information	Remarks and references to Appendices
Vignacourt	Nov 1st		Admitted 1 Stray L D mule, 1 L D Stray Mule unmarkable noted Field Remount Section (2 Breed).	
	Nov 2nd		Admitted two animals.	
	Nov 3rd		Admitted three animals.	
	Nov 4th		Admitted thirteen animals: DADVS visited Section	
	Nov 5th		Admitted five animals, including one stay, evacuated twenty seven animals to 23 Vety Hospital.	
	Nov 6th		Admitted four animals, two animals evacuated (Barro) to Barges (Bac St Maur) to 23 Vety Hospital	
	Nov 9th		D.A.D.V.S 4th Australian Division visited Section's Camp with a view to taking it over hitherto in to O.C units and V.O.S. Army.	
	Nov 8th		Admitted seven animals. Arris	
	Nov 4th		Admitted two cases evacuated four animals to 23 Vety Hospital (2 cases) from Bac St Maur (Barge).	
	Nov 10th		Admitted nine animals.	
	Nov 11th		Admitted twenty one animals.	

T2134. Wt. W708-776. 500000. 4/15. Sir J. C. & S.

WAR DIARY
or
INTELLIGENCE SUMMARY.
(Erase heading not required.)

Army Form C. 2118.

40th Mobile Veterinary Section

Place	Date	Hour	Summary of Events and Information	Remarks and references to Appendices
Vanquels	Nov 12th		Admitted six animals including one sick, evacuated thirty nine animals to 23 Vety Hospital. Eight (Boers) by Barge (Boc Steam) to 23 Vety Hosp.	
	Nov 13th		Visited Camp of H.q. 4th Divisional M.V.S. in Steenvorde area with a view to taking it over on move of Divisional from Forward Area.	
	Nov 14th		Admitted one animal. 49th Divisional M.V.S. Camp unsuitable. Visited Steenvorde area and arranged for billets in town.	
	Nov 15th		Divisional Move : M.V.S. moved to Steenvorde.	
Steenvorde	Nov 16th		Admitted one animal from 2nd Australian Division on the move.	
	Nov 17th		Admitted two animals.	
	Nov 18th		Parade of Section — full marching order.	
	Nov 19th		Admitted two animals. D.ADVS	
	Nov 20th		Admitted two animals. Section and Officers Depot paid. D.A.D.V.S. visited Section	
	Nov 21st		Admitted eleven animals from R.G.A. on the move.	
	Nov 22nd		4 00rs: Admitted one animal. D.A.D.V.S visited Section	
	Nov 23rd		Visited forward Area (Westontre G.S.a) arrangts to take over Area on Camp.	
	Nov 24th		Admitted one animal. D.A.D.V.S visited Section; thirteen animals sent	

Army Form C. 2118.

WAR DIARY
or
INTELLIGENCE SUMMARY.
(Erase heading not required.)

40th Mobile Veterinary Section 1/3/17

Instructions regarding War Diaries and Intelligence Summaries are contained in F. S. Regs., Part II. and the Staff Manual respectively. Title pages will be prepared in manuscript.

Place	Date	Hour	Summary of Events and Information	Remarks and references to Appendices
Steenwoods	Mar 2nd		CE to 23 V.H. Hospital by road	
	Mar 5th		Admitted one strayed animal. Evacuance party & section sent to forward area.	
	Mar 16th – Mar 9th		Four animals evacuated by 2nd Army Motor Ambulance to 23 V.H. Hospital.	
			Divisional Move. M.V.S. moved to Dump refilled [horse] by 39th Divisional M.V.S. near Canada Corner (Devry's Camp). Handed over three	
Devry's Camp	Mar 4th		Four animals admitted including one stray.	
	Mar 9th		M.V.S. moved to Aragon Camp. Admitted three animals. P.A.D.V.S. visited unit.	
	Mar 30th		Admitted six animals: one foot case fetched from 11th South Lancs. Wagon Lines.	

H.M. Maturin Captain
5 12/17 OC 40th M.V.S

War Diary

November 1917
VC XXV / 40th Machine Gun
Machine Corps

War Diary.

December 1917.

Vol. XVI

40th Mobile Vety. Section.

F.W.McClure
Captain A.V.C.
O.C. 40

WAR DIARY
or
INTELLIGENCE SUMMARY.

Army Form C. 2118.

(Erase heading not required.)

40th Mobile Veterinary Section Section VI Corps

Place	Date	Hour	Summary of Events and Information	Remarks and references to Appendices
Aragon Camp	Dec 1		Admitted four animals. DADVS visited section	
	Dec 2		Admitted thirty two animals including twenty two purchases.	
	Dec 3		Admitted ten animals evacuated twelve viz. 23 Arty Hospital animals and seven to A Corps M.V.D.; four men sent to Corps M.V. Detachment. ADVS into the field unit.	
	Dec 4		Admitted thirteen animals.	
	Dec 5		Admitted six animals: DAD-VS inspected unit.	
	Dec 6		Admitted five animals; evacuated twenty one animals by rail to 23 Vety Hospital, all others to Corps M.V. Detachment. AA QMG and Dr DVS visited unit.	
	Dec 7		Admitted two animals. ADVS & A/o visited section.	
	Dec 8		Admitted seven animals. Four nr. O.S. from Divisional M.V.s reported for duty with Division. Horse Rest Farm Site was to be inspected with ADVS	
	Dec 9		Admitted one stray; DAD-VS visited section and arranged Rest Farm	
	Dec 10		Four animals admitted to the Section and six animals to "Rest Farm".	
	Dec 11		Admitted seven in duding one stray to M.V.S and eleven to "Rest Farm"	
	Dec 11		Admitted fifteen to the Section and fourteen to Rest Farm; Evacuated	

Army Form C. 2118.

WAR DIARY
or
INTELLIGENCE SUMMARY.
(Erase heading not required.)

4/8th Mobile Veterinary Section W.W.

Instructions regarding War Diaries and Intelligence Summaries are contained in F. S. Regs., Part II. and the Staff Manual respectively. Title pages will be prepared in manuscript.

Place	Date	Hour	Summary of Events and Information	Remarks and references to Appendices
Aragon Camp	Dec 13th		Six animals to Corps M.V.D. Detachment. Two Vettee cases returned to unit to breaking up of Detachment	
	Dec 13		Admitted five animals to Rest Farm. Twenty animals evacuated by road to 23 Vety Hospital; A.D.V.S. Corps and O.D.A.D.V.S. visited unit.	
Conquer Camp	Dec 14th		Move of 40 m.v.s. and Devonshire Rest Farm to Conquer Camp.	
	Dec 15th		Admitted four animals including one stray and M/5 Rest Farm. D.A.D.V.S visited Unit.	
	Dec 16th		Admitted eleven animals. A.D.V.S. Corps visited Unit.	
	Dec 17th		Admitted nine animals to section.	
	Dec 18th		Four men re detachment with Corps M.V.D. Detachment rejoined Unit.	
	Dec 19th		Admitted three to Section and evacuated twenty two to 23 Vety Hospital by road; D.A.D.V.S. visited Section	
	Dec 20th – Dec 25th		Admitted two animals including one stray to Section. Admitted five animals including one stray to Section and one to Rest Farm. D.A.D.V.S visited Unit.	
	Dec 24th		Admitted seven animals including one stray to Section and one to Rest	

Army Form C. 2118.

WAR DIARY
or
INTELLIGENCE SUMMARY.
(Erase heading not required.)

40th Mobile V=by Section BEF

Place	Date	Hour	Summary of Events and Information	Remarks and references to Appendices.
Conques Camp	Dec 11th		Farrier: Two men reported from No 2 Vety Hospital another watch picked joined up together; these men to replace two staying away the visit the Section.	
	Dec 12 Dec 13th		Admitted two animals to the Section: A.D.V.S keep inspected unit. Admitted two animals both Section. Evacuated four to @ 4 Vety Hospital through Huzue @ V.C. Station	
	Dec 15th		Admitted one stray. Sports and Dinner for N.C.O's and men of Section and Rest Farm. D.A.D.V.S inspected stables and presented Prizes.	
	Dec 18th		Admitted one stray. Five men completed to No 2 Vet Hospital Category A: the other man (Cutajar in A) admitted to Field Ambulance. Two animals admitted to Rest Farm.	
	Dec 29th		Two animals admitted to Rechin and two to the Rest Farm. D.A.D.V.S visited unit.	
	Dec 1st Dec 15th Dec 30th		Admitted Tys Animals to the Section. Admitted five animals to the Section. D.D.V.S (Army) A.D.V.S (Corps) and D.A.D.V.S (Division) visited unit.	

Army Form C. 2118.

WAR DIARY
or
INTELLIGENCE SUMMARY.
(Erase heading not required.)

Instructions regarding War Diaries and Intelligence Summaries are contained in F. S. Regs., Part II. and the Staff Manual respectively. Title pages will be prepared in manuscript.

Place	Date	Hour	Summary of Events and Information	Remarks and references to Appendices
Conquer Camp	Dec 30th		See Section and Rest farm. Two animals admitted to Section. Thirteen animals admitted to Section. Pte + Cpl no 10532 Hachan. P. mentioned in dispatches.	L/C 5th Mobile Veterinary Sect 1/12/16
	Dec 31st			

J.V. Magente
Capt AVC
i/c 5 M.V.S

4/1/16

War Diary
December 1917
Vol XXVI
HQ M.G.V Section
H/M.G forp:
DC 405M/15

JM 27

January 1918.

War Diary.

Vol. XXVII

40th Mobile Veterinary Section

Army Form C. 2118.

40th Mobile Vety Section Vol XXVIII

WAR DIARY
or
INTELLIGENCE SUMMARY.
(Erase heading not required.)

Instructions regarding War Diaries and Intelligence Summaries are contained in F.S. Regs., Part II. and the Staff Manual respectively. Title pages will be prepared in manuscript.

Place	Date	Hour	Summary of Events and Information	Remarks and references to Appendices
(Westoutre) Gonquelaubt	July 1st		Admitted seven animals: Animals of Divisional Rest Farm returned to Units owing to Divisional Move	
	Jan 2nd		Admitted three animals: Thirty seven animals evacuated by Rail to Mobile Vety Hospital. DADVS visited Section.	
	Jan 3rd		Admitted six animals: ADVS Corps visited Section.	
	Jan 4th		Admitted three animals:	
	Jan 5th		Evacuated eight animals to 1st Corps V.C.C. Station Oudezeele. DADVS visited Section.	
METEREN	Jan 6th		Section moved to METEREN. (Severe frost)	
RACQUINGHEM	Jan 7th		Section moved to Rue Quinghem. (very frosty weather).	
	Jan 7th		D.A.D.V.S. visited Unit.	
	Jan 8th		Case of Colic admitted from No 2 Coy (Train) and cured to No 2 Coy on Sunday	
	Jan 9th		Admitted one animal: train ready to road to 23 Vety Hospital	
	Jan 10th		Section prepared to move: moved to entraining station (Steenbecque) 11 p.m.	
CORBIE	Jan 11th		Arrived at Steenbecque 2 a.m.: entrained 3 a.m. Train moved off 6 a.m.	
	Jan 12th		Arrived Longeau 2 p.m.: detrained 2:30 p.m.: proceeded to Corbie: arrived Corbie 7 p.m.	
	Jan 13th		D.A.D.V.S. visited Section	
ROSIERES	Jan 14th		Section moved to Rosieres: started 9 a.m.: halted and fed Bayonvillers: arrived Rosieres 1 p.m.	
NESLE	Jan 15th		Section moved to Nesle: started 9 a.m.: arrived Nesle 1:30 p.m.	

Army Form C. 2118.

WAR DIARY
or
INTELLIGENCE SUMMARY.
(Erase heading not required.)

40th Mobile Vety Section Vol XXVII

Place	Date	Hour	Summary of Events and Information	Remarks and references to Appendices
Nesle	Jan 16th		Admitted five animals. D.A.D.V.S visited Section.	
	Jan 17th		Admitted five animals: sold injured animal (96 Field Ambulance) to local butcher.	
	Jan 18th		Admitted ten animals. D.A.D.V.S visited Section.	
Echaux	Jan 19th		Section moved to Echaux. G.O.C. (Division) visited Section on arrival at Echaux.	
	Jan 20th		Admitted four animals: D.A.D.V.S visited Unit.	
	Jan 21st		Admitted one animal: sold two animals to Butcher (Nesle).	
	Jan 22nd		Evacuated fourteen animals from NESLE to No 7 Vety Hospital (Forges)	
	Jan 23rd		Admitted four animals. Received Divisional Rest Farm: Ganimals admitted to D.R. Farm.	
	Jan 24th		Admitted six animals to M.V.S. D.A.D.V.S visited Section and Rest Farm.	
	Jan 25th		Admitted three animals to M.V.S: evacuated six to 7 Vety Hospital: 11 animals admitted to Rest Farm.	
	Jan 26th		A.D.V.S Corps visited Section: Two admitted to M.V.S: Three admitted to D.R. Farm.	
DAMPcourt	Jan 27th		Section moved to DAMPcourt.	
	Jan 28th		D.A.D.V.S visited Section.	
	Jan 29th		Section dismounted Parade.	
	Jan 30th		Admitted three animals Cont- Wounds: Hock-wound out &fm to being wounded animals	
	Jan 31st		Admitted four animals.	

H.J. Melvin
Capt AVC
OC 40th M.V.S.
1-2-18.

War Diary.
of
40th Mobile Veterinary Section

February 1918.

H.O.Welin
Captain A.V.C.

Vol. XXVIII

Army Form C. 2118.

WAR DIARY
or
INTELLIGENCE SUMMARY.

(Erase heading not required.)

40th Mobile Vety Section
Vol XXVIII

Place	Date	Hour	Summary of Events and Information	Remarks and references to Appendices
Dampcourt	1st Feb.		Admitted one Rider from 10th Dragoons (French Cavalry) D.A.D.V.S visited Section	
	2nd Feb.		Admitted nine cases, including Col. MacDonalds charger (flotations) and one case of Volvulus (M.M.P): the last case was admitted at 6 pm and died at 2 am the following morning: admitted one animal for Rest Farm.	
	3rd Feb.		Admitted five animals: called on R.T.O to arrange about Evacuation of animals. One man proceeded on leave.	
	4th Feb.		Seven animals admitted	
	5th Feb.		Evacuated twenty animals to No 7 Vety Hospital, two men proceeded on leave.	
	6th Feb.		Handed over Command of Section to Captain Little, A.V.C. prior to proceeding on leave. (9 2/15 - 21 2/15)	

J.M.Matheson Capt/-
OC 40 M.V.S.

Army Form C. 2118.

WAR DIARY
or
INTELLIGENCE SUMMARY.
(Erase heading not required.)

Instructions regarding War Diaries and Intelligence Summaries are contained in F. S. Regs, Part II. and the Staff Manual respectively. Title pages will be prepared in manuscript.

Place	Date	Hour	Summary of Events and Information	Remarks and references to Appendices
Dunkirk	6/2/18		Took over command of 4 O.M.V.S from C. Keen Prestance, proceeding on leave. Admitted five animals A.D.V.S III Corps visited section	
	7/2/18		Admitted ten animals. D.A.D.V.S. 30 D.I. visited section. Two first came collected at Quarry for	
	8/2/18		Made preparation for move to back area	Red Label
	9/2/18		Handed over to 2/Lt London M.V.S. Fourteen sick animals. Moved to Bouchon	
Bouchon	10/2/18		Moved to Eclen	
Eclen	11/2/18		D.A.D.V.S. visited section	
	12/2/18		Admitted on animal to M.V.S & one moved to Div Rest Farm	
	13/2/18		Admitted four animals to M.V.S.	
	14/2/18		Admitted nine animals to M.V.S excluding two stray mules, 2 few animals to Div Rest Farm	
	15/2/18		Evacuated ten sick animals at No 7 V.Hospital	
	16/2/18		Admitted three sick animals to M.V.S - three to Rest Farm	
	17/2/18		D.A.D.V.S. visited M.V.S & Div R.M Farm	
	18/2/18		Admitted twelve animals & M.V.S including two L.D stay horse. Two animals admitted Rest Farm	
	19/2/18		Admitted five animals to M.V.S & one to Div Rest Farm	
	20/2/18		D.A.D.V.S visited section. Standard Div. Staff Capt. H.T.1. command made on road. Twenty five sold to Butcher 100 Fr.	
	24/2/18		Evacuated 16 sick animals to No 7 V.H. No further Animals owned Capt Parker on	
	27/2/18		reporting from leave of absence.	

[signature] Capt AVC

Army Form C. 2118.

WAR DIARY
or
INTELLIGENCE SUMMARY.
(Erase heading not required.)

40th M.V.S

Vol XXVIII

Place	Date	Hour	Summary of Events and Information	Remarks and references to Appendices
Erchin	22/7/18		On my return from 14 days leave, took over command of MVS from Captain Little.	
St Sulpice	23/7/18		(a) no normal move: M.V.S moved to Camp to St Sulpice (b) A.D.V.S Corps visited Section: Admitted four animals to M.V.S and two to D.W. Rest Farm.	
	24/7/18		Admitted twenty animals (animals) from stray animals, there are claimed by C/232 Bgs A.F.A Reserve Vétérinaire	
	25/7/18		Twenty three animals either evacuated to No 7 Vety Hospital eight animals admitted to M.V.S nineteen Remounts handed over to this Unit from Arme Railhead Indistribution to units	
	26/7/18		in to Divisn.	
	27/7/18		Admitted three including one stray	
	28/7/18		Admitted ten animals.	

HWMcTurk Capt AVC
OC 40 M.V.S

War Diary
of
40th Mobile Vety. Section

February 1918.

H.M.Kinnear
Captain A.V.C.

Vol. XXVIII.

Army Form C. 2118.

WAR DIARY
or
INTELLIGENCE SUMMARY.
(Erase heading not required.)

40th Mobile Vety Section
V. XXIX

Instructions regarding War Diaries and Intelligence Summaries are contained in F. S. Regs., Part II. and the Staff Manual respectively. Title pages will be prepared in manuscript.

Place	Date	Hour	Summary of Events and Information	Remarks and references to Appendices
St Sulpice	1/3/18	—	Admitted four animals: A.D.V.S Corps and D.A.D.V.S No 7 Vety Hospital. Evacuated	
	2/3/18	—	Eighteen animals to No 7 Vety Hospital.	
	3/3/18	—	Admitted one stray animal.	
	3/3/18	—	Admitted two sick animals.	
	4/3/18	—	Admitted thirteen sick animals. D.A.D Visited section.	
	5/3/18		Admitted two animals. Evacuated twenty two animals to No 7 Vety Hospital.	
	6/3/18		Admitted nine animals. A.D.V.S Corps visited M.V.S.	
	7/3/18		Admitted nine animals.	
	8/3/18		Admitted one animal. D.A.D.V.S visited section. Nineteen sick animals evacuated to No 7 Vety Hospital.	
	9/3/18		One stray admitted to section.	
	10/3/18		Sold in Laufeure purposes to civilian at No H.Q.to authority from a Director of Reclin (200 francs).	
	11/3/18		Admitted thirteen sick animals. D.A.D.V.S Corps visited section.	
	12/3/18		Admitted two animals. Evacuated fourteen to No 7 Vety Hospital.	

Army Form C. 2118.

WAR DIARY
or
INTELLIGENCE SUMMARY.
(Erase heading not required.)

HQ Mobile Vety Section   Vol XXIX

Place	Date	Hour	Summary of Events and Information	Remarks and references to Appendices
St Sulpice	13/3/18	-	Orders received to disband and report to 2nd Army V.C.C.S. Issued animals & Rest Farm and be prepared to join 2nd Army V.C.C.S. XVIII Corps.	
	14/3/18		Admitted fourteen sick animals. D. & D.V.S. visited section.	
	15/3/18		Evacuated thirteen animals to No 7 Vety Hospital. Admitted four animals including one stray.	
	16/3/18		Admitted one stray. A.D.V.S. Corps visited section.	
	17/3/18		Admitted nine sick animals	
	18/3/18		Admitted six animals. Evacuated twelve animals to No 7 Vety Hospital	
	19/3/18			
	20/3/18		A.D.V.S. and D.A.D.V.S. visited section. Final arrangements made for 2nd Army Corps V.C.C.S.	
	21/3/18		Section started to function as Corps V.C.C.S. MVC ? Anglesea reported for duty from 46 M.V.S. Similar purpose from 61 Div M.V.S. Admitted twenty seven animals from 61st Div. Twenty seven from 61st Div. M.V.S. Six from 46 M.V.S. & from 32nd M.V.S. A.D.V.S. Corps visited V.C.C.S.	
Erchen	22/3/18		V.C.C.S. ordered to move (orders to stand to) Four animals admitted Admitted enclosed animals. Cleared Erchen at 11 a.m. animals were loaded at 10:30 32 M.V.S. into Horselines. Hostel & No. Section. Transport Mobile Vet Section moved 2 miles to Erchen	

Army Form C. 2118.

WAR DIARY
or
INTELLIGENCE SUMMARY.
(Erase heading not required.)

Army Form C. 2118.

H.Q. 2nd Mobile Vety Section
No. XXIV

Place	Date	Hour	Summary of Events and Information	Remarks and references to Appendices
Roye	23/3/16		Orders received to move to Roye; all wounded as all invalids moved with Train No 1 and was unfit to proceed to Rouel. From Roye, six more wounded animals admitted.	
	24/3/16		Admitted nine animals in charge two strays. Eighty wounded and sick animals evacuated by rail from Roye to Inf'y Hospital.	
	25/3/16		Admitted five animals to Section; Section devoted Section returned to HQ MVS	
La Neuville	26/3/16		Orders to situation. Section prepared to move at 1 a.m. Section marched to Hargest in fifteen minutes at 5-40 a.m.; Received orders to proceed to La Neuville; Arrived La Neuville 7h.m; attached 2nd Cav Bde to proceed to Ailly S. Noye. 6 h.m. Arrived at Ailly S. Noye	
Ailly S. Noye		10 h.m.	Section 'Standing to'	
	27/3/16		Section 'Standing to' Instructed to proceed to Fouencamp; left Ailly Noye 11 a.m. arrived	
Fouencamp Estrée en Amienois	28/3/16		at 1-30 p.m.; instructed to proceed to Estrée en Amienois at 3 p.m.; Arrived at destination 6 p.m.	
Estrée en Amienois	29/3/16		Section Standing to.	

Army Form C. 2118.

WAR DIARY
or
INTELLIGENCE SUMMARY.

(Erase heading not required.)

4o Mobile Vety Sect...
Vol XXIX

Place	Date	Hour	Summary of Events and Information	Remarks and references to Appendices
Estrée Wamin + Rosy	30/3/18		Admitted three sick animals; evacuated three to 34 Vety Hospital Abbeville. Moved to Rosy; O.C. & Section on line of march.	
Marceuil	31/3/18		Moved to Marceuil	

H.W.W. Blair Capt.
O.C. 4o M.V.S.

War Diary.
40th Mobile
Veterinary Section.
March 1918
Vol. XXIX

War Diary
-of-
40th Mobile Vet. Section
for the month of
March 1918.

Volume XXIX.

War Diary.
40th Mobile
Veterinary Section

Vol. XXX

April 1918.

Army Form C. 2118.

WAR DIARY
or
INTELLIGENCE SUMMARY.
(Erase heading not required.)

440th Mobile Vety Section
I Army XXII

Place	Date	Hour	Summary of Events and Information	Remarks and references to Appendices
St Valeris aux Somme	1/4/18	—	M.V.S. moved to St Valeris from Maizieul: Evacuated ten horses and one Mule to 14 Vety Hospital.	
"	2/4/18	—	D.A.D.V.S. visited section: admitted one animal.	
"	3/4/18	—	Admitted five animals including two strays.	
"	4/4/18	—	Evacuated four animals to 14 Vety Hospital	
"	5/4/18	—	Section moved W at 3 a.m to Fresserville-Penguin Station: left two animals at St Valeris with Special Coy R.E (Camouflage Coy) - G.H.Q Troops - the animals are collected by 14 Vety Hospital (Horse Ambulance) in the afternoon: M.V.S entrained at 6 a.m: M.V.S detained at 12 p.m at Rousburg(?) movsd on to new Billet Elverding's Road standing - Sheet 28 A 28 @ 4.9; arrived at the Camp 6 a.m.	
Elverdinges Road Standing	6/4/18	—	Camp cleared up; and standings arranged for receiving sick animals.	
"	7/4/18	—	Six men sent to VIII Corps V.F.S: A.D.V.S VIII Corps visited section.	
"	8/4/18	—	Admitted six animals.	
"	9/4/18	—	Admitted eight animals, including G. OC VIII Corps 2 chargers, who were wounded on Main Poperinghe Road.	

A5834 Wt. W4973/M687 750,000 8/16 D. D. & L. Ltd. Forms/C.2118/13.

Army Form C. 2118.

WAR DIARY
or
INTELLIGENCE SUMMARY.

(Erase heading not required.)

H.O. II Mobile Vety. Section
Vol. XXI

Instructions regarding War Diaries and Intelligence Summaries are contained in F.S. Regs., Part II. and the Staff Manual respectively. Title pages will be prepared in manuscript.

Place	Date	Hour	Summary of Events and Information	Remarks and references to Appendices
Elverdinghe Road Standings	10/4/18	—	D.D.V.S. II Army and A.D.V.S. VIII Corps visited Section. Admitted six sick animals and twelve sick animals evacuated to VIII Corps V.E.S.	
"	11/4/18	—	Admitted one sick animal. D.A.D.V.S. visited Section.	
"	12/4/18	—	Admitted three sick animals. A.D.V.S. II Corps visited Section.	
"	13/4/18	—	Admitted two animals and evacuated seven to VIII Corps V.E.S. Notified D.A.D.V.S. of the arrival of 14 O.R. – (A.V.C) – from 19 Vety Hospital; these men were sent up to this Unit when two Unit was functioning as XVIII Corps V.E.S.	
"	14/4/18	—	A.D.V.S. II Corps visited Section. Admitted one sick animal and evacuated two to VIII Corps V.E.S; station D.R – (A.V.C) from 19 Vety. Hospital sent to VIII Corps V.E.S in accordance with A.D.V.S instructions.	
"	15/4/18	—	Admitted four animals. Warning orders for a move received. Three riding animals lent to VIII Corps V.E.S transit in evacuation (sick by road) to 3 Vety Hospital.	
"	16/4/18	—	Horse Ambulance loaned to VIII Corps V.E.S. to move floating cases to V.E.S. Proven.	
"	17/4/18	—	A.D.V.S. II Corps visited. M.V.S. Evacuated these animals to VIII Corps V.E.S.	

Army Form C. 2118.

WAR DIARY
or
INTELLIGENCE SUMMARY.
(Erase heading not required.)

40th Mobile Vety Section
Vol XXI

Place	Date	Hour	Summary of Events and Information	Remarks and references to Appendices
Edewinghe Road Standing	18/4/18		Admitted four sick animals	
	19/4/18		Attended D.A.D.V.S Conference; instructions received to despatch Pts H/A.V.C Wellaston G.H. to No 2 Base Vety Hospital to proceed as Sergt A.V.C. for field unit.	
	20/4/18		Admitted four animals. 6 p.m. Section moved to LEDERZEELE AREA.	
Buysscheure	21/4/18		M.V.S. arrived at 3 a.m. in new area: Billet at Buysscheure.	
	22/4/18		Standings arranged for receiving sick animals.	
	23/4/18		Four animals admitted. D.A.D.V.S visited Section.	
	24/4/18		Admitted one animal. Evacuated eleven to 23 Vety Hospital. One Sergeant Pte O.R-A.V.C - sent in accordance with D.A.D.V.S instructions to report to V/O i/c 30 D.A.C to form advanced vety detachment with 30 D.A.C.	
	25/4/18		Inspected Divisional Units in the Area for D.A.D.V.S.	
	26/4/18		Attended Conference D.A.D.V.S at Divisional Hdqrs.	
	27/4/18		Admitted one sick animal.	

WAR DIARY
or
INTELLIGENCE SUMMARY.

(Erase heading not required.)

Army Form C. 2118.

40th Mobile Vety Section
V. Hum's XXX

Place	Date	Hour	Summary of Events and Information	Remarks and references to Appendices
Bugsadens	28/9	—	D.A.D.V.S. visited Section.	
	29/9	—	Admitted one animal.	
	30/9	—	Admitted one animal from 183 Tunnelling Coy R.E. suffering from Colic. This animal cured, but returned in Section for Evacuation to Base Vety Hospital in care of orderly on a cold age.	L^t 5/9/18 Montjoie Capture OC 40 M.V.S

War Diary.

40th Mobile Veterinary Section.

Vol. XXX

April 1918.

A.H.Webber
Captain A.V.C.
O.C. no. 40 M.V.S.

Vol 31

War Diary.
40th M.V.S.

Month of
May 1918.

Vol. XXXI

40TH MOBILE SECTION
5 JUN 1918
A.V.C.

WAR DIARY
INTELLIGENCE SUMMARY

Army Form C. 2118.

40th Mobile Veterinary Section Vol XXXI

Place	Date	Hour	Summary of Events and Information	Remarks and references to Appendices
Busseboom	1/8		Admitted three animals	
	2/8		Admitted two animals. Six animals evacuated by rail to No 23 Vety Hospital	
	3/8		Admitted four animals. Inspected surplus animals surplus to establishment of II Army Entrenching Group — New Zealand Infantry.	
	4/8		Three fifteen surplus animals handed over to M.V.S. four of these animals admitted to section for veterinary reasons — cross evacuations — one case detained for treatment renewing ten to stay with M.V.S pending further instructions from D.D.V.S. Second Army.	
	5/8		Nine animals evacuated to No 23 Vety Hospital by rail. DADVS visited Section. Three animals admitted including one stray. Sent ten surplus animals from II Army Entrenching Group to Field Remount Section at Tilques.	
	6/8		Visited by Vet Asst. II Army Commandant — LEEDERKERKE AREA animals belonging to French RE Unit at Wulverdings?	
	7/8		Admitted four animals including one stray mule. Sold LD mule suffering from fracture of Ulna to butcher at St Omer for 120 francs, two hides	

Army Form C. 2118.

WAR DIARY
or
INTELLIGENCE SUMMARY.
(Erase heading not required.)

H.Q. 4th Mobile Vety Section Vol LXXXI

Instructions regarding War Diaries and Intelligence Summaries are contained in F. S. Regs., Part II. and the Staff Manual respectively. Title pages will be prepared in manuscript.

Place	Date	Hour	Summary of Events and Information	Remarks and references to Appendices
Bugochevo	5/8 7		Visited again French R.E. unit at Wislouhinge; Report sent in to D.A.D.V.S. about cases of mange in this unit. LD of L Zettie animals being affected with Mange. Those animals in our working of the area also confused by British Troops.	
	6/8		Admitted three animals; evacuated seven animals by road to No 23 Vety Hospital.	
	7/8		D.A.D.V.S. visited Section; Admitted two animals	
	8/8		Admitted one stray animal. Sent food and forage partie's rejoined section from Advanced Vety Post with Divisional Artillery.	
	9/8		Admitted one animal. Privates Whites and Tucker reported for duty with M.V.S from No 14 Vety Hospital.	
	10/8		Ten animals admitted	
	11/8		Admitted three animals, eighteen animals evacuated to No 23 Vety Hospital	
	12/8		Orad: received instructions from D.H.Q. that M.V.S would entrain at Guest on the 14th for move to a new area; surplus arm n. under treatment for to Field Ambulance Post.	
	13/8		Town Major reported two mules staying in a field Billet No 72 Bugochevo; those animals collected and handed over to 1/3 W. Riding Field Ambulance in this village will instructions as to disposal; entry	

Army Form C. 2118.

INTELLIGENCE SUMMARY.
(Erase heading not required.)

40th Mobile Vety. Section Vol XXXI

Instructions regarding War Diaries and Intelligence Summaries are contained in F. S. Regs., Part II. and the Staff Manual respectively. Title pages will be prepared in manuscript.

Place	Date	Hour	Summary of Events and Information	Remarks and references to Appendices
Busigny	14/5/18	—	D.A.D.V.S. 30th Division; no accommodation there being an accumulation for sick or stray animals at the Time; one animal sent by rail to No 23 Vety Hospital. Horse hospital.	
" "	15/5/18		Following day; Admitted one animal at 9 a.m. from No 3 Cav. Div. Train. Handed over one animal to 90th Brigade Hdqrs. 23 Vety Hospital closed 6 a.m. this animal; Section moved off at 7 a.m. to entrain at Ardouicq.	
" "			Section entrained at 11 a.m. train started at 3 p.m.	
St Quentin Laundry	16/5/18		Arrived at "Wiencourt" at 4 a.m.; detraining completed at 5 a.m.; Proceeded to St Quentin Laundry. Arrived in new billet at 9.30 a.m.	
"	17/5/18		Attended Conference at A.D.V.S. Hd/qts with Returns.	
"	18/5/18		A.D.V.S. Reserve Army with the D.D.R. D.A.D.V.S and Divisional Veterinarian (35th American Division) visited this unit; instructions received from D.A.D.V.S to arrange accommodation for 112 American M.V.S. on their arrival in this area.	
	19/5/18		Admitted one animal; Completed billeting arrangements for American M.V.S.	
	20/5/18		Seven surplus privates sent to No 2 Vety Hospital. Six strong to the reduction of M.V.S establishment; the other, a reinforcement sent in in error.	

Army Form C. 2118.

WAR DIARY
or
INTELLIGENCE SUMMARY.
(Erase heading not required.)

40th Mobile Vety Section Vol XXXI

Instructions regarding War Diaries and Intelligence Summaries are contained in F.S. Regs., Part II. and the Staff Manual respectively. Title pages will be prepared in manuscript.

Place	Date	Hour	Summary of Events and Information	Remarks and references to Appendices
St Quentin La Motte	21/5/18		DADVS and Divisional veterinarian 35st American Division inspected the unit and inspected kit for incoming American M.V.S.	
" "	22/5/18		Admitted one animal.	
" "	23/5/18		Received instructions to send Transport for baggage of 112 American M.V.S. on 24/5/18 to Divisional Hd.Qrs.	
" "	24/5/18		American M.V.S. (No m) arrived.	
" "	25/5/18		DADVS and Divisional veterinarian visited the two units.	
" "	26/5/18		Admitted one animal.	
" "	27/5/18		Demonstration to the two of H.O.N.S. – Anti Gas Masks – to 112 American M.V.S	
" "	28/5/18		Our civilian admitted Veterinary & instruments – Chests, Wallets etc shown to OC 112 American M.V.S. and Instruction with top dressing explained to him.	
" "	29/5/18		Methods of conducting sick animals by road demonstrated to American M.V.S. and inspected by them afterwards.	
" "	30/5/18		Returns made out and explained to O.C. 112 American M.V.S	
" "	31/5/18		Three animals evacuated.	

J.H.S. Mature Capt AVC
4/6/18 OC 40 M.V.S

WAR DIARY.
40th Mobile Vetery. Section.
May 1918.
Vol. XXXI.

Vol 32

9

40th Mobile Veterinary Section.

War Diary

June 1918.

Vol. XXXII

WAR DIARY
or
INTELLIGENCE SUMMARY.
(Erase heading not required.)

Army Form C. 2118.

H.Q. 7th Mobile Vet. Sect. Vol XXII

Place	Date 1915	Hour	Summary of Events and Information	Remarks and references to Appendices
St Quentin Lamotte	1st JUNE		Routine as usual	
"	2		One animal admitted. American Unit instructed in the conducting of Mason's rope Line. Method of	
"	3rd		One animal admitted. Six animals evacuated to the 2nd Base Veterinary Hosp.	
"	4th		Routine as usual. DADVS visited section with ADVS Corps.	
"	5th		Four animals admitted	
"	6th		Routine as usual	
"	7th		Final instruction to American Unit. M.V.S. conducting of Schwoeres to Hospital	
"	8th		One animal admitted. American Unit Left for E.U.	
"	9th		One animal collected by float	
"	10th		Three surplus animals collected from American Units	
"	11th		Section visited by DADVS. Ricks as usual	
"	12th		Two animals admitted. Bilbo arranged for 110th American Mobile Vety Section	
"	13th		One animal collected by float from Gricourt and two from Monchant	
"	14th		110th American Mobile Section assisted for course of instruction	
"	15th		Ten animals evacuated to 14th Base Vety Hospital	

Army Form C. 2118.

WAR DIARY
or
INTELLIGENCE SUMMARY.
(Erase heading not required.)

Instructions regarding War Diaries and Intelligence
Summaries are contained in F. S. Regs., Part II.
and the Staff Manual respectively. Title pages
will be prepared in manuscript.

Place	Date 1918	Hour	Summary of Events and Information	Remarks and references to Appendices
St. Quentin	June 16th		Demonstrations given with Hose Gas Masks to American Div.	
Lamotte	17th		Further demonstrations on the importance of Sick reports	
"	18th		Three animals admitted including one collected by Heet from Garriches	
"			Instructions given to American O.C. on Office Routine of Mobile Section	
"	19th		Warning Order for departure on 26th inst received	
"	20th		Section left Sph Quentin Lamotte for Rue at 9am, arriving at destination at 4pm	
"			Americans left M.F.U.	
Rue	21st		Sick Lines erected. Routine as usual	
"	22nd		Mens bivbs and equipment inspected by O.C. Section inspected by Col. Steele, ADVS, Corps	
"	23rd		One animal admitted collected by Hoar from Noyelles. One animal destroyed	
"	24th		Two animals admitted. Routine as usual	
"	25th		Two animals admitted. Five animals evacuated to 14th Base Vety. Hospital	
"			Warning Order to entrain on 26th inst at Noyelles received	
"	26th		Left Rue for Noyelles at 12pm. Section entrained and left for Andruves	
Ebertieres	27th		Arrived at Ebertieres, detrained and arrived at new billet at 7.30am	
"	"		Sick Lines erected. Routine as usual. Two Section men admitted to Field Ambulance with Influenza	

Army Form C. 2118.

WAR DIARY
or
INTELLIGENCE SUMMARY.

(Erase heading not required.)

N.O. 2ⁿᵈ Mobile Vety. Section. Vol. XXII

Place	Date	Hour	Summary of Events and Information	Remarks and references to Appendices
EPERLEQUES	JUNE 1918 28th		Inspection of Men's billets & equipment. Routine as usual.	
"	29th		Inspection of section by A.D.V.S. VIIᵗʰ Corps. Routine as usual.	
"	30th		Eleven sick animals admitted. Routine as usual.	

H.M.Stewart
Capt. A.V.C.
O.C. 40ᵗʰ M.V.S.

40TH M.V.S.

War Diary

Vol. XXXIII

July 1918.

H.W.Wilson
Captain A.V.C.
O.C. 40 M.V.S.

Army Form C. 2118.

WAR DIARY
or
INTELLIGENCE SUMMARY.
(Erase heading not required.)

40th Mobile Veterinary Section VI/44 W

Place	Date July 1918	Hour	Summary of Events and Information	Remarks and references to Appendices
Ephetleques	1/7		Admitted three sick animals.	
" "	2/7		Admitted eleven sick animals. A.D.V.S VII Corps visited Section.	
" "	3/7		Admitted two sick animals. Evacuated twenty two sick animals to 23 Vety. Hospital. Major G.A. Boxley A.V.C. acquired charge of DADVS and visited Section	
" "	4/7		Horse Ambulance collected sick animal left behind by 41 D.A.C at Runningham. A.D.V.S VII Corps visited Section.	
" "	5/7		Admitted two animals and evacuated two to 23 Vety Hospital A.D.V.S. Corps and DADVS inspected the Section	
" "	6/7		Admitted three animals. Evacuated five animals to 23 Vety. Hospital.	
" "	7/7		Admitted two animals. Warning orders for move on 8th received	
St Mourlin	8/7		Section moved under orders of 95th Infantry Brigade to St Mourlin	
St Marie Cappel 9/7 Shed 27 M 11 P.13. b.3.5.			Mrs. continued under orders of 95th Infantry Brigade to St Marie Cappel (Sheet 27 P.13.b.3.5.) - XV Corps Reserve Area.	
" "	10/7		Standing by for orders. Received sick animals. DADVS visited Section.	
" "	11/7		Admitted four animals.	

Army Form C. 2118.

WAR DIARY
or
INTELLIGENCE SUMMARY
(Erase heading not required.) 40th Mobile Vety Section Vol XXXIV

Instructions regarding War Diaries and Intelligence Summaries are contained in F. S. Regs., Part II. and the Staff Manual respectively. Title pages will be prepared in manuscript.

Place	Date	Hour	Summary of Events and Information	Remarks and references to Appendices
P 13 b 3 5 St Mons Cappel	Feb 1919			
	12		Received instruction from D.A.D.O.S to send Horse Ambulance to I.D.M. (Ethinghem)	
	13	9/18	Greatfields of Condiments. Admitted two animals	
	14	2/18	G.O.C Division Inspected Section. Admitted one animal including mule stray.	
	15	7/18	A.D.V.S (X Corps) Inspected Section. Admitted three including mule stray.	
			Evacuated thirteen animals to X Corps V.E.S	
	16	2/18	Admitted 218 cases including mild lymphangitis from 96 Field Amb. (By General Gorhaman - G.O.C - 21st Infantry Brigade. Evacuated six animals to X Corps V.E.S. Tractor-on-ly Lorry condemned.	
	17	2/18	Admitted seven animals. DADVS visited Section	
	18	2/18	Admitted five animals including two Mules. Bitten by fleet from 1/1 N.M. RFA	
	19	2/18	Evacuated nine animals to X Corps V.E.S.	
	20	2/18	Eight animals to dump on Cassel Poperinghe Road. DADVS	
			as to Removal of natural incubation of Potatoes.	
	21	2/18	Admitted two animals. Evacuated twelve animals to X Corps V.E.S	
	22	2/18	Admitted three animals.	

Army Form C. 2118.

WAR DIARY
or
INTELLIGENCE SUMMARY.
(Erase heading not required.)

HQ - Mobile Veterinary Section. Vol XXXIV

Place	Date	Hour	Summary of Events and Information	Remarks and references to Appendices
Sheet 27 P13 b 3.5 St Marie Cappel	June 1918 23/8			
	24/8		Seven animals admitted. A.D.V.S Corps with D.A.D.V.S Division inspected this Unit. Admitted five Stray animals.	
	25/8		Admitted two animals. Sixteen animals evacuated to X Corps V.E.S. including two strays admitted on the 24/8. New horse ambulance collected.	
	26/8		L.D Mule admitted from 342 Road Con Coy R.E with symptoms of Lymphatics. This animal died P.M. Showed Volvulus:	
	27/8		Admitted m/s: Five Stray animals bought in by M.M.P on the 27th claimed by 36 Machine Gun Corps Bat.	
	28/8		Two animals admitted: Three Strays collected by 36 M G C. Bat.	
	29/8		Admitted four animals including one Stray.	
	30/8		Admitted three animals. D.A.D.V.S visited Section.	
	31/8		Admitted five animals. Thirteen evacuated to X Corps V.E.S. Pte Hive (reinforcement) reported from No 2 Vety Hospital	

H.J.W. Guinie Captain
31/7/8 OC 40 Mobile Vety Section

MOBILE SECTION
31 JUL 1918
A.V.O.

40TH M.V.S.

War Diary.

August 1918.

Vol. XXXIV

Army Form C. 2118.

Vol XXXIV

WAR DIARY
or
INTELLIGENCE SUMMARY.
(Erase heading not required.)

40th Mobile Veterinary Section

Instructions regarding War Diaries and Intelligence Summaries are contained in F. S. Regs., Part II. and the Staff Manual respectively. Title pages will be prepared in manuscript.

Place	Date	Hour	Summary of Events and Information	Remarks and references to Appendices
Sheet 27 St Hilaire Cottes	1/5/18		Admitted four animals.	
" "	2/5/18		Admitted one animal. DADVS visited MVS	
" "	3/5/18		H.Q.s Ambulances collected LD horse (4th Field Army Co) & sent to Cottes	
" "	4/5/18		Admitted three animals, including one animal (LD mare) left behind by Unit (unknown) at St Marie Cottes. Sold to Peterkin to 1st North Rides Heavy Battery & Butchery for 150 francs. Cart Horse.	
" "	5/5/18		Two float cases evacuated.	
" "	6/5/18		D.F. D.V.S. visited Section. Sold 2 animals (L.4 French Fr 275 & Fr 1.30 Fr 575 Francs) Lots included	
" "	7/5/18		Admitted five animals including three sick mules (LD). Two cases Ophthalmia - one case colic. Sent 5 to Corps Vet Sect	
" "	8/5/18		Evacuated eight animals (3) Corps VES	
" "	9/5/18		LD Bay mare admitted as a Stray. Claimant	
" "	10/5/18		Orders received to be prepared to move to 35th Divisional Area	
" "	11/5/18		Visited MVS site in new area. Set notice-board for spare army horse. Line in area. Mans attic Billet available at Terdinghem.	
" "	12/5/18		MVS moved to Terdinghem	

Army Form C. 2118.

WAR DIARY
or
INTELLIGENCE SUMMARY.
(Erase heading not required.)

HD = Mobile Veterinary Sect. Vol XXXIV

Instructions regarding War Diaries and Intelligence Summaries are contained in F. S. Regs., Part II, and the Staff Manual respectively. Title pages will be prepared in manuscript.

Place	Date	Hour	Summary of Events and Information	Remarks and references to Appendices
Tardinghem	12/8		Admitted three animals including one float-case and one LD mule	
	13/8		Inspection by 3D Batty A.F.A. in the latter was left behind by MK (unknown)	
			Six cases admitted - four of these were "Bomb Wounds"	
	14/8		Two float cases evacuated to X Corps V.E.S.	
	15/8		Collected two stray animals, one secured at Westpont & one ownerless	
			Was claimed on the 19th by 7/17 London Regiment. One other	
	16/8		case admitted. Evacuated six animals to X Corps V.E.S.	
	16/8		A.D.V.S. Corps visited Section on account of animals admitted	
	17/8		Gas animal admitted	
	18/8		Authority received to draw Hurdles & R.E. Dump; Harness also etc.	
			and "Bomb Proof" Protection Wire started on lines	
	19/8		Admitted two animals	
	20/8		Admitted two cases - one case of Paraplegia which	
			was collected by horse ambulance	
	21/8		Admitted four animals	
	22/8		Admitted one animal. Evacuated eleven to X Corps V.E.S.	

Army Form C. 2118.

WAR DIARY
or
INTELLIGENCE SUMMARY.
(Erase heading not required.)

40th Mobile Vety Section Vol XXIV

Instructions regarding War Diaries and Intelligence Summaries are contained in F. S. Regs., Part II. and the Staff Manual respectively. Title pages will be prepared in manuscript.

Place	Date	Hour	Summary of Events and Information	Remarks and references to Appendices
Terdeghem	23/8		A.D.V.S Corps inspected Unit.	
	24/8		Admitted two animals.	
	25/8		Admitted two animals.	
	26/8		Two animals admitted	
	27/8		Two animals admitted including one stray. Evacuated seven animals to X Corps V.E.S.	
	28/8		Admitted three animals including one short case.	
	29/8		Four animals (incl) and one stray admitted.	
	30/8		A.D.V.S Corps and D.A.D.V.S visited Section. Admitted two animals. Evacuated forty animals to X Corps V.E.S.	
	31/8		Admitted four animals. Warning order received to move to Busscheep.	

H.M.M.Guire Capt + V.C
OC 40th M.V.S

40th Mobile Veterinary Section
War Diary.
September 1918.
Vol. XXXV.

H.W.M...
Captain A.V.C.
O.C. 40th M.V.S.

Army Form C. 2118.

WAR DIARY
or
INTELLIGENCE SUMMARY.
(Erase heading not required.)

40th Mobile Veterinary Section WRXXIV

Place	Date	Hour	Summary of Events and Information	Remarks and references to Appendices
Terdinghem	1/8	—	Admitted one animal. Advanced Veterinary Post opened at Boescheps. Evacuated six animals to X Corps V.E.S.	
Boescheps	2/8		Mobile Vety Section moved to Boescheps	
" "	3/8		Admitted four animals. DADVS visited Section	
" "	4/8		Admitted five animals. A.D.V.S. Corps visited Section	
" "	5/8		Admitted two animals. Two animals sold to Butcher (Carcase) belonging to 96th A.F.A Brigade for 640 francs less than hides	
" "	6/8		Five animals admitted. Evacuated twelve animals to X Corps V.E.S.	
" "	7/8		Admitted five animals.	
" "	8/8		Admitted three animals	
" "	9/8		Including one 'Stray'. Five animals admitted. Evacuated eleven to X Corps V.E.S.	
" "	10/8		One float case and five actuary cases admitted.	
" "	11/8		Collected one float-case. Nine animals evacuated to X Corps V.E.S. Billet having shelled from 12 p.m – 3 a.m. All animals removed to neighbouring fields.	
" "	12/8		Admitted two animals. M.V.S. moved to (Sheerny?) R 15 b. 6.7 on Boescheps Berthen Road.	

Army Form C. 2118.

WAR DIARY
or
INTELLIGENCE SUMMARY. 40th Mobile Veterinary Section Vol XXV
(Erase heading not required.)

Instructions regarding War Diaries and Intelligence Summaries are contained in F. S. Regs., Part II. and the Staff Manual respectively. Title pages will be prepared in manuscript.

Place	Date	Hour	Summary of Events and Information	Remarks and references to Appendices
Sheet 27 R15 b 7	13/9/18		Admitted three animals including one float case. DADVS visited Section	
	14/9/18		Admitted one animal.	
	15/9/18		D.A.D.V.S visited Section.	
	16/9/18		Eight animals admitted.	
	17/9/18		One stray animal admitted. Thirteen animals evacuated to Corps M.V.E.S.	
	18/9/18		Six animals admitted including four animals suffering from Dermatitis (Mustard Gas) from M.G. Bat.	
	19/9/18		Fourteen animals admitted. ADVS Corps visited Section.	
	20/9/18		Seven animals admitted. Twenty six animals evacuated to X Corps V.E.S.	
	21/9/18		Three animals admitted.	
	22/9/18		Five animals admitted.	
	23/9/18		Three animals admitted. Inspected lines with DADVS in British area to select suitable site for Clipping Depot.	
	24/9/18		Evacuated ten animals to X Corps V.E.S.	
	25/9/18		Admitted two animals.	

Army Form C. 2118.

WAR DIARY
or
INTELLIGENCE SUMMARY

(Erase heading not required.)

HQ Mobile Veterinary Section Vol XXXV

Place	Date	Hour	Summary of Events and Information	Remarks and references to Appendices
Shs-f-7 R15-b-f-7	26/8/18		Admitted three animals.	
	27/8/18		Admitted seven animals. D.A.D.V.S visited Section	
	28/8/18		Three animals admitted. Thirteen animals evacuated to X Corps V.E.S.	
	29/9/18		Admitted five animals. One animal cast and returned to duty.	
	30/9/18		One animal admitted. Seven animals evacuated to X Corps V.E.S.	

H W Mortimer
Capt AVC
OC 40th Mobile Vety Section

1/10/18

40th Mobile Vetery. Section.

War Diary.

Vol. XXXVI.

October 1918.

WAR DIARY
INTELLIGENCE SUMMARY
(Erase heading not required.) 40th Mobile Veterinary Section / C.XXXVI

Army Form C. 2118.

37
30

Place	Date	Hour	Summary of Events and Information	Remarks and references to Appendices
Sheet 27 R.15.c.6.7	1/8		96.99 animals admitted: Orders received to move M.V.S. forward to H.Q. 11th Div.	
" "	2/8		Two animals admitted: five animals evacuated to X Corps V.E.S.: M.V.S. moved to Camp at 1 Sh.57-28 m.17.63.3.	
Sheet 28 M.17b.3.3	3/8		D.A.D.V.S. visited Section: Admitted six animals.	
	4/8		Admitted seven animals including two Flat-Cases.	
	5/8		Four sick animals admitted. Evacuated twenty-one animals to X Corps V.E.S.	
	6/8		Three sick animals admitted: one animal suffering from left carpus destroyed.	
	7/8		Two animals evacuated to X Corps V.E.S. Admitted four animals. United Kennel Asst. to find another Cant. No Cant. was available.	
	8/8		Six animals including two Flat-Cases admitted. One suffering from septicaemia.	
	9/8		Ten animals admitted.	
	10/8		D.A.D.V.S. visited Section. Admitted seven animals	
	11/8		Five animals admitted: one animal (Rider) destroyed suffering from Debility	

WAR DIARY
or
INTELLIGENCE SUMMARY.

(Erase heading not required.) HQ - Mobile Veterinary Section 1 CXXXVI

Army Form C. 2118.

Remarks and references to Appendices
I - XXXVI

Place	Date	Hour	Summary of Events and Information	Remarks
Sheet 2F M.17.c.3.3	11/10/18		and village. Twenty four animals evacuated to 6X Coy V.S.S. The Staff Surg. method of conducting brocehett the Vid of Rops Canvas in the Tail used presently case evinced for a trial as invalid.	
	12/10/18		Report on Sick stray, mated forwarded to D.A.D.V.S. The 2nd animals admitted including two Staff-Cases attached on Command. posion to Capt Andrews A.V.C. during my temporary absence on leave to United Kingdom	
	13/10/18		H.H. Maluna C.O. rtd the 13/10/16 of 40 M.V.S.	
	14/10/18		Took over command of Section during Lieut. The Luiris absence on leave to U.K. admitted seven sick animals.	
	15/10/18		Seven sick animals admitted to A.V. hospital Section evacuated animals to X hospital.	

Army Form C. 2118.

WAR DIARY
or
INTELLIGENCE SUMMARY. 40th Mobile Vety Section
(Erase heading not required.)

Instructions regarding War Diaries and Intelligence Summaries are contained in F. S. Regs., Part II. and the Staff Manual respectively. Title pages will be prepared in manuscript.

Place	Date	Hour	Summary of Events and Information	Remarks and references to Appendices
Sheet 28 M17B 3.3	16/1/18		Admitted four sick animals. Evacuated thirteen sick animals to I Corps D.V.S. underlying eight. Cast cases. One sick animal destroyed. Fifty-five one sick animal admitted to N.V.I Corps.	
	17/1/18		One sick animal admitted. One sick animal evacuated to I Corps D.V.S.	
	18/1/18		Section proceeded to Boeschepe rendez-vous instructions from D.D.V.S. Two sick animals admitted. Three sick animals became destroyed of kear pound myocarditis.	
Houthem	20/1/18		Section moved to Boeschepe making one half at Mons G Farm sick animals admitted. One sick animal admitted.	
Boeschepe	21/1/18		Section moved to Lebleke making one half at Mons G Farm sick animals admitted. Two sick animals admitted. One sick animal sold to butcher for the sum of 200 francs.	
Lebleke	22/1/18			

WAR DIARY
or
INTELLIGENCE SUMMARY.

Army Form C. 2118.

Place	Date	Hour	Summary of Events and Information	Remarks and references to Appendices
AELBEKE	23/8		Handed over section to D.A.D.V.S.	
	24/10/18		Admitted 8 sick animals, including 1 strac-case. Aethenkem grazan	
	25/10/18		Admitted 2 sick animals & 1 stray animal. 35 animals evacuated to X Corps. V.E.S.	
	26-10-18.		Admitted four sick animals.	
	27-10-18.		Admitted three sick animals	
	28-10-18.		Admitted seven sick animals. One mule discharged - Tetanus.	
	29-10-18.		Admitted five sick animals, including one stud-case, five sick animals evacuated to X Corps V.E.S.	
	30-10-18.		Admitted five sick animals. One horse discharged womb gun-shot-neck. E.M. sick animals evacuated to Corps V.S.S.	
	31-10-18.		Admitted five sick animals. A.D.V.S. X Corps visited section.	

J. A. Moseley
Major

17.

Army Form C. 2118.

WAR DIARY
or
INTELLIGENCE SUMMARY.
(Erase heading not required.)

40th Mobile Vety Section
XXXVII
VII
VII 3 8

Place	Date	Hour	Summary of Events and Information	Remarks and references to Appendices
HELBEKE	1/8		Admitted two animals.	
	2/8		Admitted two animals.	
	3/8		Admitted seven animals; Evacuated eight to X Corps V.E.S. Suspected Section.	
	4/8			
	5/8		Admitted one; Handed over command of Section to Capt. METIVIER (A.V.C.) on return from leave. Absence	
	6/8		Took over charge of Mobile Vety Section from Major J.A. Bosley (DADVS); admitted six animals including one Sh.j.	
	7/8		Admitted six animals; Evacuated twelve animals to X Corps V.E.S.	
	8/8		Admitted three animals	
	9/8		D.A.D.V.S. visited section. Instructions received to be prepared to move forward on the 10th. Admitted four animals.	
OELBEKE	10/8		Admitted three animals. Evacuated fourteen animals to X Corps V.E.S. Section moved off at 3 p.m. from Albeks to Escape Files, en route to destruction of Bridge over the Scarpe River and Mini Bridge	
Potts			on the POTTS - Escape after road halted for the night at POTTS.	

Army Form C. 2118.

WAR DIARY
or
INTELLIGENCE SUMMARY.
(Erase heading not required.)

HQ # Mobile Vety Section Vol XXVII

Instructions regarding War Diaries and Intelligence Summaries are contained in F. S. Regs., Part II. and the Staff Manual respectively. Title pages will be prepared in manuscript.

Place	Date	Hour	Summary of Events and Information	Remarks and references to Appendices
Ecaussines	11/8		Section moved from Potter to Ecaussines. D.A.D.V.S notified section	
	12/8		Admitted one animal; Stray animal admitted to 6th Clause	
	12/8		109 Brigade Transport officer 90th Brigade (Infantry)	
	13/8		Admitted four animals	
	14/8		Admitted three animals	
	15/8		Admitted four animals	
	16/8		Admitted one animal. Evacuated thirteen animals to X Corps V.E.S: Section moved at 11 a.m. destination BELLEGHEM	
BELLEGHEM	17/8		Admitted six animals. 2/Lt/Cpl Wright this am at Horse Ambulance sent to Ecaussines to collect 21 animals (14 horses 7 mules) belonging to 16 M.V.S (29 Division): 18 M.V.S having to move forward.	
	18/8		Admitted two. One L.D. (Rdng 7 yr) belonging to 96 A.F.A Brigade destroyed (fracture Tibia) and to Butcher. 300 transferred to Field Transferred seventy six animals of 16 M.V.S. to X Corps V.E.S: Sick animals of 40 M.V.S also evacuated to X Corps V.E.S.	

(B6915) Wt. W14422/M1160 35,000 12/16 D, D. & L. Forms/C./2118/14.

Army Form C. 2118.

WAR DIARY
or
INTELLIGENCE SUMMARY.
(Erase heading not required.)

Instructions regarding War Diaries and Intelligence Summaries are contained in F. S. Regs., Part II. and the Staff Manual respectively. Title pages will be prepared in manuscript.

40th Mobile Vety Section V.C. XXXIII

Place	Date	Hour	Summary of Events and Information	Remarks and references to Appendices
BELLEGHEM	19/8		Admitted three animals.	
	20/8		Admitted five animals.	
	21/8		Admitted ten animals.	
	22/8		Admitted one animal. D.A.D.V.S. marked Rabbin	
	23/8		Admitted two animals: one flat-cane – Rider belonging to Capt. Cowan (9th Infantry Brigade). Evacuated fifteen to I Corps V.E.S.	
	24/8		Admitted seven animals.	
	25/8		Admitted four animals.	
	26/8		Admitted three animals. Evacuated thirteen animals to X Corps V.E.S.	
	27/8		Admitted eighteen animals.	
	28/8		Admitted six animals. Evacuated seven animals to X Corps V.E.S.	
	29/8		Admitted nineteen animals.	
	30/8		Admitted seven animals.	

H.S.M. G. Cpl A.V.C. R. Johns V-t/s
O.C. 40 Mobile V.S.

War Diary
— of —
40th Mob. Vety. Sec.
for Month of
November 1918.

Volume XXXVII

War Diary.
40th M.V.S.
December 1918.
Vol. XXXVIII.

Army Form C. 2118.

WAR DIARY
or
INTELLIGENCE SUMMARY.
(Erase heading not required.)

Unit: 45th Mobile Veterinary Section / VI XXXVIII

Place	Date	Hour	Summary of Events and Information	Remarks and references to Appendices
BELLEGHEM	1-12-18		Evacuated twenty-six animals to No 7 V.E.S (XIX Corps). Admitted one.	
Croix au Bois	2-12-18		Unit moved with Divisional Artillery to Croix au Bois	
Eotlinghem	3-12-18		Unit moved to Eotlinghem	
Renescure	4-12-18		Unit moved to Renescure	
	5-12-18		Admitted ten animals	
	6-12-18		Admitted nine animals	
	7-12-18		Admitted four animals. Evacuated nineteen animals (St Omer.)	
	8-12-18		6 No 23 Vety Hospital	
	9-12-18		Admitted five animals	
	10-12-18		Admitted twenty-one animals	
			Five animals admitted including one stray. Evacuated thirty animals to 23 Vety Hospital	
	11-12-18		One animal admitted	
	12-12-18		Admitted four animals, evacuated five to 23 Vety Hospital	
	13-12-18		Admitted eight animals	
	14-12-18		Six animals admitted. Evacuated twelve animals to No 23 Vety Hospital	

Army Form C. 2118.

WAR DIARY
or
INTELLIGENCE SUMMARY.
(Erase heading not required.)

Army Form C. 2118.

Instructions regarding War Diaries and Intelligence Summaries are contained in F. S. Regs., Part II. and the Staff Manual respectively. Title pages will be prepared in manuscript.

HQ Mobile Vety Section Vol XXXVIII

Place	Date	Hour	Summary of Events and Information	Remarks and references to Appendices
(Reserve) Remount	15-12-18		Admitted one animal.	
	16-12-18		Admitted one animal evacuated his arrivals to 23 Vety Hospital	
	17-12-18		Admitted six arrivals	
	18-12-18		Evacuated nine arrivals to No 23 Vety Hospital	
	19-12-18		Returns and Office Work.	
	20-12-18		Admitted two arrivals	
	21-12-18		D.A.D.V.S. visited M.V.S. on his return from leave.	
	22-12-18		Admitted two arrivals	
	23-12-18		Examined admitted	
	24-12-18		Four animals admitted. Eighteen animals evacuated to 23 Vety Hospital.	
	25-12-18		Xmas Day. D.A.D.V.S. visited Unit.	
	26-12-18		Admitted two arrivals.	
	27-12-18		Admitted one arrival	
	28-12-18		Office Work.	
	29-12-18		One arrival admitted	

Army Form C. 2118.

WAR DIARY
or
INTELLIGENCE SUMMARY.
(Erase heading not required.) 40th Mobile Vety Section Vol XXXVIII

Place	Date	Hour	Summary of Events and Information	Remarks and references to Appendices
Rencous	30-12-18		Fourteen animals admitted	
	31-12-18		Admitted eight animals and evacuated	
			Arrived to to no 23 Vety Hospital	
			H.P. Mostinus Capt - R.A.V.C	
			OC 40 M.V.S	
			4/1/19.	

40th M.V.S.

War Diary
for
January 1919.

Vol. XXXXIX.

S. Kirchner
Capt. R.A.V.C.
a/O.C. 40 M.V.S.

Army Form C. 2118.

WAR DIARY
or
INTELLIGENCE SUMMARY. HQ Mobile Vet Section Vol XXIX
(Erase heading not required.)

WO 40

Place	Date	Hour	Summary of Events and Information	Remarks and references to Appendices
Renescure	1/1/19		Admitted six animals;	
"	2/1/19		Admitted six animals Sent two Stray mules collected for Two M.S. Ans.	
"	3/1/19		Admitted two animals; Fourteen animals evacuated by Road to 23 Vety Hospital. Tuberculin by mots Ambulance (2.3 Vety Hospital	
"	4/1/19		Admitted six animals;	
"	5/1/19		Admitted one animal;	
"	6/1/19		Six animals admitted.	
"	7/1/19		Evacuated eleven animals by road to No 23 Vety Hospital Instructions received to move M.V.S. to Aire on the 10th.	
"	8/1/19		Visited Aire and arranged billets	
"	9/1/19		Advanced party march to new billets at Aire. admitted Six Brood Mares.	
Aire	10/1/19		Moved to Aire; Fifteen Brood Mares received Transfer to 23 Vety Hospital one sick animal admitted.	
"	11/1/19		Nine Brood Mares admitted. Two sick animals admitted	

Army Form C. 2118.

WAR DIARY
or
INTELLIGENCE SUMMARY.

(Erase heading not required.)

40th Mobile Vety Section Vol XXXI

Instructions regarding War Diaries and Intelligence Summaries are contained in F. S. Regs., Part II. and the Staff Manual respectively. Title pages will be prepared in manuscript.

Place	Date	Hour	Summary of Events and Information	Remarks and references to Appendices
Aire	11/9		Twenty-three Brood Mares transferred to No 23 Vety Hospital. Six animals evacuated to 23 Vety Hospital	
" "	12/9		Two Brood Mares received	
" "	13/9		Four sick animals admitted	
" "	14/9		Four sick animals admitted	
" "	15/9		Two stray animals admitted	
" "	16/9		Four animals admitted. Evacuated six (6) animals including one Hort- Case to 23 Vety Hospital. Two Brood Mares transferred to 23 Vety Hospital on to Dans Clg.	
" "	17/9		Admitted one animal. Evacuated six animals to 23 Vety Hospital	
" "	18/9		Office Work. Vety Board classified N°C horse at Section	
" "	19/9		Admitted one animal	
" "	20/9		Admitted three animals	
" "	21/9		Admitted two animals	
" "	22/9		Handed over command of 40 M.V.S. to Capt Little R.A.V.C. on proceeding to Divisional HQ to obtain D.A.D.V.S. Mr Major Bowley. Sick: [illegible signature]	

A6915 Wt. W14422/M1160 26,000 12/16 D.D. & L. Forms/C.2118/14.

Army Form C. 2118.

WAR DIARY
or
INTELLIGENCE SUMMARY.
(Erase heading not required.)

Instructions regarding War Diaries and Intelligence Summaries are contained in F.S. Regs., Part II. and the Staff Manual respectively. Title pages will be prepared in manuscript.

40th Mobile Vety Section

Place	Date	Hour	Summary of Events and Information	Remarks and references to Appendices
Gpe	23		Set remounts evacuated two animals admitted	
Ave	23/8		A.D.V.S. XII Corps ratified instructions one to	
"			take over section Capt Fetherington to	
"			proceed to Poperinghe. Two animals	
"			admitted	
"	24		Inspected Dis Lines for abattoir/ration	
"	25		Admitted one sick animal	
"	26		Admitted one sick animal	
"	27		30 Div Train animals medical inspection	
"	28		Completed two sick animals evacuated	
"			three sick animals	
"	29		Admitted one sick animal	
"	30		Evacuated sick animals	
"			Two stray animals collected from	
"	31		farmer at Elbpughieren. One section D	
"			proceeded to Staging Camp Bayenghem	

A. Andrews
Capt

A6945. Wt. W14427/M160 35,000 12/16 D.D. & L. Forms/C/2118/14.

Vol 41

War Diary.
40ᵀᴴ M.V.S.
February 1919.
Vol. XL.

Army Form C. 2118.

Vol XL

WAR DIARY
or
INTELLIGENCE SUMMARY.
(Erase heading not required.)

Place	Date	Hour	Summary of Events and Information	Remarks and references to Appendices
Cine Apl	1		Office work and usual routine	
"	2		Office work and general routine. Reinforcement D Sqdn arrived to come to Retron	
"	3		Admitted one sick animal & sent over 2 horse & section 3 Cy. nos. Received instruction for A.D.V.S XIV Corps to move to Steenwoorde	
"	3		Nos 5Th & 7th Stabs over from 7/6S	
"	4		Admitted two D cases	
"	5		Admitted two D cases & moved to Steenwoorde	
"	6		Took over from Capt. Wright - pellets, etc 8 7/6S & motor ambulance. Handed over 8 D horses from trench to till to 3/6S. Took over 18 sick animals from 7/6S. Admitted four sick animals	
"	7		Admitted two D animals & one sick animal	

A6945 Wt. W14422/M1160 35,000 12/16 D. D. & L. Forms/C./2118/14.

WAR DIARY
or
INTELLIGENCE SUMMARY.

(Erase heading not required.)

Army Form C. 2118.

Place	Date	Hour	Summary of Events and Information	Remarks and references to Appendices
Steenvoorde Feb	8		Admitted one Dog as sick animal.	
"	9		Officers work of general routine.	
	10		O.C A.V.S XIX Corps visited Station. Admitted two sick animals. A distinguishable mule paralysis.	
	11		Admitted one mare & one Donkey one C 2 animal. Evacuated 9 sick animals to 23 Vety Hospital 6 C to sick to 22 O.S & 6 animals C 2 to Stationary Camp Lingens. Office work & General return to DADVS 39th Divis unit & section	
	12		Instruction received from O i/c XIX to ratio Personnel attending horse sale at Cassell 1.30 o'clock received instruction to proceed to Cassell to see Col. XIX Corps to take four men to bring 8 to 23	
	13		Handed over M.U.S. to Capt [illegible]	
	14		Any instruction received from ADVS XIX Corps quoted.	

WAR DIARY
or
INTELLIGENCE SUMMARY

Army Form C. 2118.

(Erase heading not required.) 40TH MOBILE VETERINARY SECTION

Place	Date	Hour	Summary of Events and Information	Remarks and references to Appendices
Steenvoorde	15th		One sick animal admitted	
"	16th		Admitted two sick animals	
"	17th		One sick animal admitted. Section horse transferred for sale to Officer i/c 19th Corps Sale	
"	18th		Seven sick animals evacuated to 23rd Vety Hosp. One animal admitted	
"	19th		Four Z animals despatched to Staging Camp Rexpoede	
"	19th		Fourteen animals admitted	
"	20th		Seven sick animals admitted. Two dogs admitted for destruction (Auth.) 19 Corps	
"	21st		Admitted one sick animal. Evacuated twenty two animals to 8th V.E.S.	
"			Two dogs despatched to 15th V.E.S. Meuzeen	
"	22nd		Sixteen animals admitted	
"	23rd		Three sick animals admitted	
"	24th		Two animals admitted. Twenty two animals transferred to 8th V.E.S. Lille	
"	25th		6 sick animals admitted	
"	26th		Seven sick & forty four Z animals admitted	
"	27th		Seven sick animals admitted. Fifty eight animals transferred to 23rd Vety Hosp. St Omer. Six men transferred for Tembery duty with 23rd Vety Hosp. Auth. A2V.S. 19 Corps	

Army Form C. 2118.

WAR DIARY
or
INTELLIGENCE SUMMARY. 40th Mobile Veterinary Section
(Erase heading not required.)

Place	Date	Hour	Summary of Events and Information	Remarks and references to Appendices
Steenwerde	Nov 28th		Four sick animals admitted. Evacuated eight animals to 23rd V.etty Hosp.	
"				

Signed,
Lt. Col. R.A.V.C.

WAR DIARY.

40th MOBILE VETY. SECTION.

for

MONTH OF MARCH 1919.

VOL. XLI.

[stamp: 40TH MOBILE SECTION 1 APR 1919 A.V.]

Sinclair Captain
R.A.V.C.
O.C. 40th M.V.S.

Army Form C. 2118.

WAR DIARY
or
INTELLIGENCE SUMMARY.

(Erase heading not required.) 40th MOBILE VETERINARY SECTION

Vol. XLI

Instructions regarding War Diaries and Intelligence Summaries are contained in F. S. Regs., Part II. and the Staff Manual respectively. Title pages will be prepared in manuscript.

Place	Date	Hour	Summary of Events and Information	Remarks and references to Appendices
	MARCH			
Steenvoorde	1st		2 sick animals admitted.	
"	2nd		Admitted nine sick animals. Seven riding horses belonging to western transferred to Horse-Staging Camp, Eigne, also one other rider. Six over evacuated to 23rd Vety. Hosp.	
"	3rd		Capt. S. Little RAVC. takes over command of Unit. One sick horse admitted.	
			C.Blest Lt. Col. R.A.V.C.	
"	4th		Admitted four sick animals. Evacuated twelve animals to 23rd Vety. Hosp.	
"	5th		Admitted two sick animals. Evacuated two sick animals to 23rd Veterinary Hospital.	
"	6th		Admitted seven sick animals. Evacuated eight animals to 23rd Vety Hosp. Section was moved to billets in Steenvoorde.	
"	7th		Admitted one sick animal. Pte. H.M.Brown 4474 sent to concentration Camp.	
"	8th		Admitted seven sick animals. ADVS xix Corps visited the section evacuated two animals	
"	9th		Evacuated six animals to 23rd Vets Hospital	
"	10th		Admitted two sick animals	

WAR DIARY or INTELLIGENCE SUMMARY

Army Form C. 2118.

Vol. XLI

40th Mobile Veterinary Section

Place	Date	Hour	Summary of Events and Information	Remarks and references to Appendices
Steenwerck	March 11th	1919	Admitted five sick animals. Evacuated two animals to 23rd Vety. Hospital. ADVS XIX Corps visited Section	
"	12th		Admitted one sick animal. Evacuated five animals to 23rd Vety. Hospital	
"	13th		Admitted one sick animal. Evacuated two animals to 23rd Vety. Hospital	
"	14th		Office work & general routine	
"	15th		Admitted two sick animals. ADVS XIX Corps visited section	
"	16th		Collected one stray animal from civilian at Trotzlehem	
"	17th		Admitted five sick animals	
"	18th		Evacuated seven animals to 23rd Vety. Hospital, & on stray animal to XIX Corps Collecting Corp. Anzer	
"	18th		ADVS visited section	
"	19th		ADVS XIX Corps visited section. Admitted two sick animals	
"	20th		Collected two sick animals & evacuated to 23rd Vety. Hospital. Admitted a sick animal	
"	21		Evacuated two animals to 23rd Vety. Hospital. Admitted five sick animals. ADVS XIX Corps visited section	
"	22"		Admitted seven animals sick. Despatched GS Wagon complete to No.1 Cy. 30 Div. Train RASC units	
"	22nd		Authority of ADVS XIX Corps. Evacuated nine sick animals to 23rd Vety. Hospital	
"	23rd		Collected sick mule (flat water) from 30 DAC. RFA. Evacuated eight animals to 23rd Vety. Hospital	
"	24th		Admitted thirteen sick animals	

Army Form C. 2118.

WAR DIARY
or
INTELLIGENCE SUMMARY. 40th Mobile Veterinary Section

Vol. XLI.

(Erase heading not required.)

Instructions regarding War Diaries and Intelligence Summaries are contained in F. S. Regs., Part II. and the Staff Manual respectively. Title pages will be prepared in manuscript.

Place	Date	Hour	Summary of Events and Information	Remarks and references to Appendices
Steenwoode	April 25		Collected one sick animal from Armed Stages Corps Esquelbecq by ambulance evacuates position sick animals to 23rd Veterinary Hospital at Omer.	
"	26		Collected four men temporarily attached 23rd Vety Hospital by authority of ADVS 19th Corps.	
"	27		Admitted two sick animals. ADVS XIX Corps visited section.	
"	28		Office work & general routine. ADVS XIX Corps visited section.	
"	29		Office work & general routine.	
"	30		Admitted three sick animals.	
"	31		Admitted three sick animals. Arranged sale for butchery for two horses for sum of 800 francs.	

J. Stephen Capt. RAVC
OC 40 M.V.S.

[Stamp: 40th MOBILE SECTION 1 APR A.V.C.]

War Diary

40ᵗʰ M.V.A.

Vol. XLII.

April 1919.

WAR DIARY
or
INTELLIGENCE SUMMARY.
(Erase heading not required.)

Army Form C. 2118.

Volume XLII
40th Mobile Veterinary Section

Place	Date	Hour	Summary of Events and Information	Remarks and references to Appendices
Steenwoorde	April 1st		Dispatched two horses for Battery. ADVS XIX Corps visited the section. Allotted two sick animals for Ayre by motor ambulance. Admitted one sick animal.	
"	2nd		ADVS XIX Corps visited section. Sergt Jeffers RAVC reported for duty from 35th Div.	
"	3rd		Office work + general routine. Returned two RASC animals to 1 Coy 30 Div Train by	
"	4th		authority of ADVS XIX Corps. Dispatched 7 & Warrer. Pte Trant to Concentration Camp Hazebrouck. Evacuated four animals (Botchu cases) to 15th V.E.S. Proveren.	
"	5th		Office work + general routine.	
"	6th		Admitted one sick animal.	
"	7th		Admitted one sick animal. ADVS XIX Corps visited section. Sergt Jeffers, Pte Rutherford	
"	8th		R.A.V.C. dispatched to Concentration Camp Hazebrouck.	
"	9th		Admitted two sick animals. Cpl Henderson, A/Lc Cpl Wright sent to Concentration Camp. Evacuated eight sick animals to No 4 Vety Hospital Calais by rail. Admitted four sick animals.	
"	10th		Office work + general routine.	
"	11th		Obtained one horse Bernalier + sold it for Battery at St Omer for fr 660.	Initials
"	12th		Office work + general routine.	
"	13th		Admitted one sick animal.	

Army Form C. 2118.

WAR DIARY
or
INTELLIGENCE SUMMARY.
(Erase heading not required.)

Army Form C. 2118.

Volume XLII
40th Mobile Veterinary Section

Place	Date	Hour	Summary of Events and Information	Remarks and references to Appendices
Steenvoorde	14th		Total sick animals for Litchy 575h - 660 hs.	
"	15		Admitted eleven sick animals.	
"	16		Still one animal for Litchy. 680 hs	
"	17		Admitted ten sick animals. ADVS XIX Corps visited section	
"	18		Evacuated twenty one animals to No.4 Veterinary Hospital Calais	
"	19		Admitted one sick animal & all two sick animals for Litchy. 562 5hm - 517 5hs	
"	20		Admitted six sick animals	
"	21		Admitted ten sick animals	
"	22		Admitted one sick animal & sold three animals for Litchy. Tos 1330. Handed over command of Section to Lt Col. & Velo ADVS XIX Corps having received orders to proceed to England for duty. Paid out field cashier. Shewn the sum of Four thousand two hundred & eighty francs for sale of ten horses & one mule for Litchy.	
	23		Captain Little proceeded to Boulogne - Also Suprest of R.A.V.C. 2153 evacuated 9 sick animals to 4 Base Veterinary Hospital - Calais	
	24		Admitted 1 sick animal.	

WAR DIARY
INTELLIGENCE SUMMARY.
(Erase heading not required.)

Army Form C. 2118.

Vol. XLII.

40th M.V.S.

Place	Date	Hour	Summary of Events and Information	Remarks and references to Appendices
St Omer	April 25		One cycle horse conveyed by motor ambulance sold to Butcher St Omer for 714 Francs.	
	26		Received instruction to move by road to Neufchatel (Pas de Calais) as cadre for attachment to 30th Divisional Train — Instructions given as to Route numbers of proceeding to Senior N.C.O. Transport to start on the 27th.	
			[signed] Lt. Colonel. O.C. 40th M.V.S.	
Dannes	27		Horse Transport proceeded to Arques in route for Neufchatel.	
	28		Section reduced to Cadre strength moved to Dannes (near Boulogne) by Motor Ambulance + joined No 4 Company 30th Divisional Train.	
	29		Motor Horse Ambulance despatched to XIXth Corps HQrs Coast to report — Captain Taylor R.A.V.C. — Transport of Unit arrived.	
	30		General Routine	

[signed] O.C. 40 M.V.S.

Army Form C. 2118.

OFFICER-IN-CHARGE RECORDS
No.
28 OCT 1919
ROYAL ARMY VETY. CORPS.

WAR DIARY
or
INTELLIGENCE SUMMARY.
(Erase heading not required.)

Instructions regarding War Diaries and Intelligence Summaries are contained in F. S. Regs., Part II. and the Staff Manual respectively. Title pages will be prepared in manuscript.

Place	Date	Hour	Summary of Events and Information	Remarks and references to Appendices
Dunkerque	6th August 1919	40"	40 M.V.S. Wagons + Stores + Equipment embarked at Dunkerque for shipment to CHILWELL.	

Jas Gillett Lieut
No 138991 O.C. M.V.S.
40
RAVC

100 015/226/2

30TH DIVISION
DIVL TROOPS

30TH DIVL TRAIN ASC
1915-MAY 1919

Sent

186 — Coys ASC
189

Army Form C. 2118

WAR DIARY
or
INTELLIGENCE SUMMARY
(Erase heading not required.)

Instructions regarding War Diaries and Intelligence Summaries are contained in F. S. Regs., Part II. and the Staff Manual respectively. Title Pages will be prepared in manuscript.

Place	Date	Hour	Summary of Events and Information	Remarks and references to Appendices
HAVRE	4 Sept	9 PM	Arrived from SOUTHAMPTON and disembarked at the Quay. Superintended disembarkation of horses & vehicles of Headquarters. Coy & moved with Coy to Rest Camp No 5. Reported to recvg camp orders. Brick instructed that all blankets were to be handed in. Went to BASE HQrs and told there had been instructed at ALDERSHOT to bring blankets & 13 blanket wagons in all went. BASE HQrs allowed LOQ & later instructed me to return blankets. Some much of Division had travelled without them. Recvd instructions to entrain at 7 am 5 Sept. No casualties to horses or men except loss of one or two prison nose straps.	
In Train	5 Sept	6 PM	Entrained 15 times this morning with two days rations with Signal Coy RE. Orders en route to ULTRAM at AMIENS	
FLESSELS	6 Sept	10 PM	Detrained about 1 am at FLESSELS 5 Sept. At AMIENS experienced some difficulty & clearing station in fairly affected owing to little departure & all lights out. One Company that made entraining after dawn started & refused to keep horses on ropes. Kept to Sig. Coy wagons with signal Coy & FLESSELS — Headquarters Coy & Hq of A & B Coys at AMIENS. On marching the forward troops were refused to FLESSELS & Headquarters Coy to Ox Ox AMIENS. as ordered. Joined up with them by 6 Cross roads where road diverged two miles beyond FLESSELS. One wrong marching was not regarded after and followed them by General Coys after moving ruling by Squadron wrong road file two & four. Coy would and entered FLESSELS at 3.30 am 1st Sept. Rations at Divisional HQs to see them trimmed. Reported again from men at 8 am & visited HQ Coy at VAUX Tents. Brick very satisfactory.	
"	7 Sep	11 PM	Went with SSO to Rontheuil at CANAPLES. Visited No 4 Coy at KENACOU RT discussing supply arrangements with Divisional HQ & was approved. Then Start No 3 Coy who of 20 units to VIENACOURT. Instead of to COISY owing to wheeled Text to stay at VAUX. Brick with & met their marchings into St VAST. So sent them to HQ 9r by for the arrival at daybreak to prepare Rations	
"	8 Sep	9 PM	Inspected No 3 Coy at VAUX & No 2 Coy at MOLLIENS au BEAU found horses & vehicles in good condition	

1875 Wt. W593/826 1,000,000 4/15 I.R.C. & A. A.D.S.S./Forms/C. 2118.

Army Form C. 2118

WAR DIARY
or
INTELLIGENCE SUMMARY

(Erase heading not required.)

Instructions regarding War Diaries and Intelligence Summaries are contained in F.S. Regs., Part II. and the Staff Manual respectively. Title Pages will be prepared in manuscript.

Place	Date	Hour	Summary of Events and Information	Remarks and references to Appendices
FLESSELLES	9 Sept	9 A.M.	Discussed arrangements for producing units moving. 51st attached to other divisions with S.S.O. also with Dis H.Q. on horses arrangements	
	10 Sept	8 A.M.	Went with S.S.O. — Received the heavy difficulty in drawing rations arranged attention of Syftem with him. The Syftem was being filled by our convoy in afternoon. His Syftem to your rations in more at supplying tonight. Supply column wagons to draws from Railhead and at Railhead then unloaded all supply and dumped at pit at T Supply column Syftem distant about 1½ miles at Renteau, full over supply led later enabled first destriebute but made at the Zery holder. Forward by movements of troops and delivered also three Vemoist a tent baller Visited no 3 & 4 Coy during day. I was most of worked well— wagons for Railhead through refill worked hard to match up to 7 T supply all spare wagons to CAMAPLES to assist Supply at omy to companies. moved convoy there with the Inspected H.Q. Coy on return from chemmed gave men Lecture on aeroplane men were clean & smart in appearance lectr to no 2 Coy.	
	11 Sept			
	12 Sept			
	13 Sept		Instructed us — Dis H.Q. that they wished me to arrange checks of companies attached to various divisions with S.S.O. No difficulty carried by much. The supplies to 15 refer divisions and staff Vehicles if we are instructed to produce a day a so be able to reduce to right and reduced the number £13 & will in Divisional train ques at Mains. — Supply was very ready They 50³ have to sift divisional trains concerned. S.S.O. informed that the would not interview was with S.S.O.N.S. Arm arranged	

Army Form C. 2118.

WAR DIARY
or
INTELLIGENCE SUMMARY

(Erase heading not required.)

Instructions regarding War Diaries and Intelligence Summaries are contained in F.S. Regs., Part II. and the Staff Manual respectively. Title Pages will be prepared in manuscript.

Place	Date	Hour	Summary of Events and Information	Remarks and references to Appendices
FLESSELLES	14 Sept	9 P.M.	S.S.O. went to St Ouen & arranged about supplies & refunded action taken to divisional & 9th ordnance ration mps.	
	15 Sept	"	Stored equipment up with field cashier 10th day corps. as cases open, visited railhead.	
	16 Sept	"	Sent S.O. to Bois du TAILLES refilling point to 5 Divs. Wrote issues to staff. Wrote officers to units of the division army to supplies arriving with S.S.O. & div. point chief in the division to France for dumps & arranged by 10th staff. Visited all companies & instructed them as regards dumps.	
	17 Sept	"	Area success. Nos 3 Coy Div. move in a few days.	
GUILLAMCOURT	18 "		Moved by motor march at 7 am the morning from FLESSELLES & supply train to R.O.'s accompanied Nos 1, 2 & 4 Coys to CAYEUX & arranged them to move. Divisible nine Ratels will be detachable a few days for their French troops move.	
	19 "		Inspected refilling points selected by S.S.O. the four refilling points are to FOURILLOY, CORBIE, BONNAY & SAILLY LAURETTE — arranged with S.S. convoys of supplies Staff. arr — as all supplies R.Q. Trucks to CANAPLES to 3rd field supply Dept — to draw supplies & ordering accoutrements & Lorghum Lanternate to intermediate supplies also lorry to draw extra supply adopt delivered to Bele the guns	
	20		Visited Composition at CAYEUX & made billeting arrangements at WEINECOURT for the prisoners at divr H.Q.'s reported them to enquiry wagon was the promised rod that unite were to supplies in the second was completed wagon reserves to date.	

1875 Wt. W593/826 1,000,000 4/15 J.B.C. & A. A.D.S.S./Forms/C. 2118.

Army Form C. 2118.

WAR DIARY
or
INTELLIGENCE SUMMARY

(Erase heading not required.)

Instructions regarding War Diaries and Intelligence Summaries are contained in F.S. Regs., Part II. and the Staff Manual respectively. Title Pages will be prepared in manuscript.

Place	Date	Hour	Summary of Events and Information	Remarks and references to Appendices
WEINKOURT	21 Sept.	9 p.m.	Interviewed A.M.G.O. Division. Stated that only a few mule Cart Stretcher bearer troops. General Corps were to issue, having to unload baggage wagons to find early & enable move. Arranged to at least get supplies & men of Wagons truck also all Supplies & Blanket wagons. Instructed O. i/c to submit reports. Moved back there also to any 5 mile for troops & with H.Q.s that I would meet there and try and 5 mile for any gun instructed lorries to go when returned by mules from breakfast wagons for horse condition. visited all Buttle — had interviews with S.S.C. & div. and O.C.	
	22	"		
	23	"	Arranged with Headquarters that 1st Div transport must to meet in charge of an officer, that as several lorries were relating the Supply Wagons to sell in then emergency transport to the trenches. What must fetch. It	
	24th	"	Received orders that that tonight 18 Blanket wagons (S.S.) to Dullouis to Indian Cavalry Corps. Despatched there under officer at 7 p.m.	
	25th	"	Interview with Div ... Went thoroughly into all supply arrangements with S.S.O. regarding lorry unit to draw at supply points the brave together	
	26th	"	Conference at Div. H.Q. regarding supplies returned to R.S.C. & Brigades. M.S. reason to write Supply wagons to try change the method Signed would then Jam attempts were Mutiar troops to supply could not be making up the Battle	

WAR DIARY
or
INTELLIGENCE SUMMARY
(Erase heading not required.)

Army Form C. 2118.

Instructions regarding War Diaries and Intelligence Summaries are contained in F. S. Regs., Part II. and the Staff Manual respectively. Title Pages will be prepared in manuscript.

Place	Date	Hour	Summary of Events and Information	Remarks and references to Appendices
WEANACOURT	26th Sept	9	at the most distant points in less than 3 hours. explained also that I could do no other transport work if I had no baggage wagons. arranged to leave certain units their baggage wagons filled with technical equipment that could not be unloaded at present. Suggested storage of baggage as probability was units would not take it with them in advance.	
	27th Sept	"	Reported to Hd Qrs that some wagons were still outstanding from Divisional Troops also gave them full list of condition of horses & complaints against units who had not paid men or who had allowed horses to be worked when unfit & under fed them. Proceeded to St VAST to inspect damage done to wood by Divn Ammunition Coln also visited owner at AMIENS. Whose claim was too high he refused to reduce same. So sent it to Hd Qrs for transmission to claims committee.	
	28th Sept	"	Dispatched remaining eight Limbered wagons to Reserve advanced Depot at 8 am. Interviewed acting Provost Marshall re three brothels in the village arranged for French authorities to take action. Saw S.S.O. regarding S.O.s not visiting their coys often enough. discussed the feeding of 200 labour men who had arrived & not been indented for. Inspected horses of all Companies	
	29th Sept	"	Went to Divn Head Qrs & then to refilling point. visited all coys billets & inspected horses. owing to heavy rain & roads very muddy harness was not in satisfactory state impressed on OC Coys the necessity of harness being kept clean & serviceable	
	30th	"	Visited Divl Hd Qrs & Hd Qrs of Divn Cavly with reference to Coal Transport arranged to leave 2 wagons to be moved by 1st Line Tpt: ordinary Routine work.	[signature] Lt Col Cdr 2 Div Train

WAR DIARY
or
INTELLIGENCE SUMMARY

Army Form C. 2118

(Erase heading not required.)

Instructions regarding War Diaries and Intelligence Summaries are contained in F.S. Regs., Part II. and the Staff Manual respectively. Title Pages will be prepared in manuscript.

Place	Date	Hour	Summary of Events and Information	Remarks and references to Appendices
WELINCOURT	1st Oct	10th	Paid claims for damages to crops grown at CORBIE. FEESSETS and SAINT SERVOTIN.	
	2nd		Went to Divisional Headqrs. & to S.S.O. reported difficulty in obtaining coal. Was permitted to buy 5 tons important quantity train to Brigade arranged at hd Qrs. 14th Bn. Found two wagons without reins & staying bringing it into hd Qrs. for these from R.E.-Butt's. Visited refilling point 16. Drew coal at 3 S.O Hr & brought wagons in as ready for transport & more Refilling in and supply could not be reached before morning of following ult. to supply — lorry supply so for still not received any more for distribution. Usefully primed by wagon with delay on excellent supply of Rye Pate.	
	3rd Oct	9 A.M.	Interview with S.S.O. regarding coal. He managed to give two books of 27 B. drums coal at ½ — Steam. I am anxious to cast wood & trech pioneer butts at first. Arranged transport to cast wood. Such parade party arranged with 2nd Bn. Cutting started about 10 km from hy per day to have Bn. party at HARBONNIERES at wy to start 10 km per day. Hr d Hd Qr Bk. 22 3 bn the end of the 3rd of November truckels at Dist Hd Qrs. Hook of 22 3 bn. Detour works arranged with Dist Hd Qr that above could be arranged & running	
	4th		Went received 3 m.l. for 2 others for orders.	
	5th Oct		Rode to Bn at HARBONNIERES. Interview with S.S.O. arranged transport to draw wood. Sent two trap boot start out details regarding supply of coal through to be brought to M. after 9 P.M. Satisfactory arrangements made two Pontoons to two Brittoon made in billeting after Chance	
Cont.	7th Oct		Went to Field Cashier XII Corps. cash to draw money for Chnus Class BOR Tranche.	
			Went to S.S.O. 11th Q. Petroleum Mutual DA & A.D.S.S. Forms/C.2118. Spent with 2 Brewery Trans settling Prises without General	

Army Form C. 2118

WAR DIARY
or
INTELLIGENCE SUMMARY

(Erase heading not required.)

Instructions regarding War Diaries and Intelligence Summaries are contained in F. S. Regs., Part II. and the Staff Manual respectively. Title Pages will be prepared in manuscript.

Place	Date	Hour	Summary of Events and Information	Remarks and references to Appendices
VIGNACOURT	Oct 7.	9/15	Received information from Divn HQ & S.S.O. Capt HANNAY asking me to try to ensure that the two rod- [illegible] recruits his promise to [illegible] strength it was recommended in Amiens till he finish difficulties [illegible] in [illegible] with units [illegible] made to call phoretics arrived by Divn HQ 9/3. The lorry pushed them again. Still return goes on 24th July.	
"	8	"	Borrowed mineral supply guidebooks with S.S.O. & cut down HQ 9/3. Wd't revised all lorries & saw to allotments of new lorries on wagons. Won [illegible] a wagon to carry [illegible] lorry informations.	
"	9	"	Went in Car to BRAY & VIGNACOURT & May [illegible] in [illegible] from [illegible] filled settling at BRAY & Paris mayor of VIGNACOURT to settle well [illegible]. Capt KNAPMAN arranging [illegible] attended conference at Divn HQ 9/3 arranging re-supply of lorries & more F.E. roads.	
"	10	"	Visited Divn HQ 9/3 Worked out scale of fuel [illegible] with [illegible] who accidently discharged his rifle (No[?]9/036679 Dr Collins) when in sentry. Reported action taken to Divn HQ 9/3 [illegible] [illegible] to Salvation [illegible] to Conference of [illegible] arranged extra parade & [illegible] Divn HQ 9/3. That [illegible] lorries were stuck in [illegible] [illegible] with S.S.O. that [illegible] of [illegible] worked low but [illegible] [illegible] to carry [illegible] to [illegible] [illegible] [illegible] [illegible].	
"	11	"	Visited Divn HQ 9/3 [illegible] [illegible] [illegible] [illegible] Gutzebux[illegible] & MARCELCAVE to [illegible] [illegible] to Divn HQ 9/3.	

1875 Wt. W593/826 1,000,000 4/15 J.B.C. & A. A.D.S.S./Forms/C. 2118.

WAR DIARY or INTELLIGENCE SUMMARY

Army Form C. 2118

Place	Date	Hour	Summary of Events and Information	Remarks and references to Appendices
WEDNESDAY	13 Oct 15	9 A.	Interviews at Brig H.Qrs. I wish SSO on the line that SSO of 27 Div is disposed the charge of Bde from the Division in exchange with Bde of 27 Div who exchange Div as S. Bn. with supply & Reg. Officer, to forward of about 14 days. Went to H.Q. 6th Inf. Bde & re inspected the 1st & 2nd Bn. of 7th & 13th Inf. Bde. Afternoon 1st Beds. Regt. 3. Bedfordshire & 2nd Hampshire Regt. having moved forward the subsequently.	
	11 od	"	Inspected 189 (No.4) Coy. on Recy. H.Qrs. & 2 attached to 27 Div. was told that for a fortnight the Wiltr. mess H.Qrs. & Capt Chelms in Gd. to LAUNCOURT unnecessary supply grouping with SSO of Ned Ides LIDDEL Comdg. 27 Div. Tram. Div. stated he understood that any from the horse to Lier was permanent & told me quadrupeds of His Officer of by coming to the tram Inspected first time transport of Bde. Regt. as very rough then at 7 H. Officer was a good Knowledge of the work Captn. LIDDEL Comdg. Dep Coy. (Inc of 422 Divn Tram) reported arrived & started that the & a civilian head team transferred from another Coy to 27 Div. as the Coy twenty Returned to the tram Who that the Sgt. Major was a decent man Enquiries. Reported to Brig. H.Q. 9 Visit of 89 by were coming every tram permanently that 7 Strongly Suspected to the Coy. Officer being changed that I had not kept the bigger Officer where sending my log. The feet of the 2nd Cl. Sergt. further that the Bn were very worn wet painted expectations to Bde, & other Interviews with A.D.V.S. of 27 Div. writing in his Tran. Officers & with a R.T.O.S. with reference to fuelled fuel & top of the Reg. Very good accomodation meadow posted for Bde. Ho Cho. Regt. Every tram fair SSO of Div there various plans for Defences of Brewn. also see ADMS of Div. First conference. Pro-posed GOC Bde for field Ambulance. Inspected 68th	
	14 od	"		

WAR DIARY or INTELLIGENCE SUMMARY

Army Form C. 2118

(Erase heading not required.)

Instructions regarding War Diaries and Intelligence Summaries are contained in F.S. Regs., Part II. and the Staff Manual respectively. Title Pages will be prepared in manuscript.

Place	Date	Hour	Summary of Events and Information	Remarks and references to Appendices
WIENCOURT	15 Oct	9 A.M.	Attended conference at Divl. H.Qrs. Subject: Final relative positions of Army Corps. The 4 Corps is to hold up supply line, also frontier. Deaths & news expected all to be at G.C. point. Heard that next of Roman Battle Group Armed Woman gunned that the Depot was not enough. Previous with 100 RIDLER Battery arranged in time to see return at rallying point. Went to MARELCAVE to investigate claim for stolen papers, removed pipe for ammunition also very much regret that Major Spooner of the Cheshire & R clear hampers via case of unprimed shell. Were to Rogers station. Interview with S.S.O regarding Provl. brought or not unprimed. Instructed them that S.O.3 Provl. inspr. O.C. units of any shortage or shortage in action Provl. only of Provl. is 2nd Provl.	
	16 Oct		Interviews at S.S.O H.Q 9.30 a.m. S.S.O.S Office went with Inspector to transport &c. In 4 Coy arrangements for the Inspection [of] Brigade Transport. Inspection 66th Field Ambulance & 1/5th Tpt of Cheshire Regt in afternoon. Interview at S.D.S H Qs & impacted publy of Transport & ammn &c. of 9th Kent Scene & 4th K.O.R. Fusiliers 1/4th Suffolk Regt. 12 teams &c.	
	17 Oct			
	18 Oct		Col Long A.D.S went round stable. Mr Interview with Inl. S.C. regarding information & transport for R.E Stones, Inspection of Team by Inl S C in afternoon. Infantry 66 Field Ambulance & visited 1/5 Field Ambulance regarding repairs reported	
	19 Oct		Returning routine work	
	20 Oct		Visited the Divni with minor movement of stores & transport of division, made arrangements with S.T.O for supplies & ammunition. Brought up rations. Attached Officers of 6/5 of 5 Water Proven separately	

1875 Wt. W93/826 1,000,000 4/15 J.B.C.& A. A.D.S.S./Forms/C.2118.

Army Form C. 2118

WAR DIARY
or
INTELLIGENCE SUMMARY
(Erase heading not required.)

Instructions regarding War Diaries and Intelligence Summaries are contained in F.S. Regs., Part II. and the Staff Manual respectively. Title Pages will be prepared in manuscript.

Place	Date	Hour	Summary of Events and Information	Remarks and references to Appendices
VEINCOURT	22 Oct	9 A	Interview with Div. HQrs & with S.S.O. regarding changing supply route. Instructed Lt. Laurence to take No 3 Lay in place of Lt. Fisher who is to go to SERNY with Div. Hears — To AMIENS & to Hippodrome thence Racecourse. Received from Tierney & Thorne to VILLERS BRETONNEAUX tomorrow. Received 380 Light Draft horses & exchanged same with all Tierney draft horses in hand of Division. Capt. Hammay S.S.O. left for PARIS	
VILLERS BRETONNEUX 23rd			Interview at Div. HQrs regarding arrangements for evacuating the Div. Forage Stall in abeyance. Moved to VILLERS BRETONNEAUX & camped in wood. Received additional 12 horses to go to Divisional Lt. FISHER took No 3 which S.S.O. Capt. Darcy Hudson returned at Div Head Qrs to arrange for Capt Manvers(?) (Div 9 + 5)	
"	24 "	"	Appointed Lt. PARKER A.D.S. Camp in Place of CAPT HUDSON. Still at Div HQ. arranged details of Transport & Supplies for Issues tomorrow.	
"	24 "	"	Interview at Div. HQrs was instructed they 2nd Army & France, they wished to accompany the Division. It is very Bad. Who has to wait weeks arrived with Supply Wagon to move them. Manners & Borgnis Commanders arranged Transport for tools were ago from Capt HUDSON	
"	25 "	"	Arranged transport for 65 Bde M.T. vehicles. 1 15 motors to D.A.C. Transportation Capt. HUDSON to take Me Supply Wheels from TH-TINDELL (?) REEN the Horse has been detailed to go with Div. to Supply Vehicles with O.C. re feeding &c.	

WAR DIARY or INTELLIGENCE SUMMARY

Army Form C. 2118

(Erase heading not required.)

Instructions regarding War Diaries and Intelligence Summaries are contained in F.S. Regs., Part II. and the Staff Manual respectively. Title Pages will be prepared in manuscript.

Place	Date	Hour	Summary of Events and Information	Remarks and references to Appendices
VILLERS BRETONNEUX	26 to Oct	9 p.m.	Interviews at H.Q. re Supplies etc. D.D.S. & DT. Army arranged that cars by Divisional H.Q. arranged that all Supply – R.O.H. to 8o except at Tirdell Green who is all to that Coy Motor reserve now also that they're yester Supp Trains to 2 Hoffman to Koutran 50 as the transport officer that supplied by ADJST being to intend Vet-Section necessary impd. ADVS has checked that the Train will relieve all sick animals & units.	
"	27	"	Interview at DATHQ re building horse stow in case owing to the when weather. Went to Depot Intelk's got loaded equipment supplies arranged with French authorities for two trucks to entrainment to sick horse Sup to the Train. Interview with Lt-Denn of Supply Coy re reference to feeding of Arty & units soft machine for some days on Supply Officers may make net every time Birkhead Nos 3 & 4 (8gr) or Villers BRETONNEUX re Supply details known.	
"	28	"		
"	29	"	Sepdy details left and of the officer also reminder of Divnl HQ – arranged visiting for Jos's ho	
"	30	"	to Toutule – (RETURN Left Br P Clearing Station on Investigated arrangement moved with Dir. Coy in Buttle Vehicles on – & let to H.Q. re worse of food to with references of rationing horses also to suppose Supply Off. Gds. Div arranging Irwing	
"	31		Interview in arty HQ – also with Lt-Denn re purchase of vegetable stores —	

1895 Wt. W593/826 1,000,000 4/15 J.R.C. & A. A.D.S.S./Forms/C. 2118.

Bo h Sz: Iran
vol I

121/7656

Nov 15
mi 16

Confidential

WAR DIARY
of
Lt-Col C.M. Anville

from 1st Nov to 30th Nov 15

Volume 3

Comdg 3rd Pk District Tournai
Feb 22 Dist Tournai

WAR DIARY
or
INTELLIGENCE SUMMARY

(Erase heading not required.)

Army Form C. 2118

Instructions regarding War Diaries and Intelligence Summaries are contained in F.S. Regs., Part II. and the Staff Manual respectively. Title Pages will be prepared in manuscript.

Place	Date	Hour	Summary of Events and Information	Remarks and references to Appendices
VILLERS BRETONNEUX	1 Nov. 15	8 P.M.	Moved No 3 Coy into Billets obtaining ordinary work	
	2"	"	98th 99th & 100th Bdes R.F.A. entrained. Obtained Tpt officers to accompany each Bde to collect G.S. Wagons at LONGPRÉ. Selected officer for horse returning from duty Revn. Rebn. with T.O.C. 14th Horse Trsp. in mixed Trains.	
	3rd	"	Recd from Arty & Engineer Sent agent with same to HAVRE. Arty Hd Qrs & 9th/IX Lon & BORDER Horse entrained. Sent XII Corps strength of Train Recd orders from XII Corp that Train would be attached to 18th Divn from 5th. Tnspt to be Received to DOURS Sent Capt Miller to DAOURS to arrange billets. He made return quite & reported same to 18th Divn. Wired S.S.O. 18th Divn. Feeling strength	
	4th	10 P.M.	Received instructions from 18th Divn not to move to DAOURS unless further orders. To Record Officers at night to Record issue of following day. Sent Lt Kemble to clear heavy stuff/tins from 27th Divn.	
DAOURS	5th	"	Proceeded with Train to DAOURS & Billeton men.	
	6th	"	" 18th Divisional Hd Qrs & reported. Wired O/C 3rd reserve of work with to AA DADH.Q. Recd orders in this afternoon to proceed to AILLY LE HAUT CLOCHER to join 30th Division.	
AILLY LE HAUT CLOCHER	7th	10 P.M.	Marches with Train. Here I reported No 1 Coy in Run Running Coys & Camped outside. Reported at Divisional H.Q 9.3 Interview at 9.30 Hd Qrs with S.S.O. arranged of following Orders & sent Lyt to then Brigade Areas No.1 there No 2 BELLANCOURT. No 3 Coy NEUVILLE. No 4 Coy LA HAIE. Four Transport Supplies from 30th Train to replace 1 Capt & 3 Subs	
	9th		Went to see ADSOT at BEAUQUESNE to see if 13 Typ Cart would be exchanged	G.L.

Army Form C. 2118

WAR DIARY
or
INTELLIGENCE SUMMARY
(Erase heading not required.)

Instructions regarding War Diaries and Intelligence Summaries are contained in F.S. Regs., Part II. and the Staff Manual respectively. Title Pages will be prepared in manuscript.

Place	Date	Hour	Summary of Events and Information	Remarks and references to Appendices
AILLY LE HAUT CLOCHER	10th	10 AM	Interview with B.G.C. 35th Div. Arranged Transport meeting unit's arriving. Discussed supply question with S.S.O.	
	11th	"	Moved HQ. Getting trunk lines to Army Hd. Qrs. to conduct own interviews with div. trains to work S.O. Supply Col. But situation seem to be unable [&] feeding of troops a worry on Trunk	
	12th	9 PM	Interview with D.S.C. & Supply & Transport question. Went to Paris. Stayed with S.S.O.	
	13th	"	Interview with Divl Hd Qrs regarding units Benham Wagons & representatives with Supply Wagons. Re attitude to Train to Tabackers 27th Indian Taylor & Saunders whiskey there arrived others Record for S.S.C. & Three cyphers to work to Indian Desist Train. Went to Knul Front.	
	14th	9 PM	Interview at Divl Hd Qrs & with S.O. Supply Col. & Capt Ferrier left to join LAHORE Div. Train. Major Sargeon & Capt D. Hack to join Meerut Div Train. Capt. Wyatt returned. Decides to move by division into PLESSIEL AREA. Interviewed three trains of all Companies.	
	15th	"		
	16th	"	Found Supply trains in PLESSIEL area. I had into days supply with Div into truck to Gordon. Got 2nd army for horse gun Supply 10th in Supply Wagons delivered at Transport for morning's delivery 19th. On consumption. 19th.	

Army Form C. 2118

WAR DIARY
or
INTELLIGENCE SUMMARY
(Erase heading not required.)

Instructions regarding War Diaries and Intelligence Summaries are contained in F. S. Regs., Part II. and the Staff Manual respectively. Title Pages will be prepared in manuscript.

Place	Date	Hour	Summary of Events and Information	Remarks and references to Appendices
ALLY-LES-HAUT-CLOCHER (?am)	17th	9 PM	Sent I.R.O.S. to new area to bring worn clothes & vegetables. Details dispersed to new refilling point. No 3 & 4 Cos marched to new area. HQ G — By 9. No 2 to leave Brunn. Interview with Adjt. HQ G/S	
FLESSELS	18	"	Moved with No 1 & No 2 Cys into new area. Settled in. 1 lorry in a.m. reported to Divd HQ G/s. T/S M/T Vehicles of 26th Divn 1st line.	
	19.	"	Went round refilling points. Interview with Divd M/T G/s	
	20	"	Inspected No 3 & 4 Cys.	
	21	"	" Arranged with OC No 1 re loading of Vehicles of 26th Divn at FLESSELS Stn. Interview at Divd HQ G/s. Inspected M/T line transport of the B.g & B.De.	
	22	"	Inspected M/T Line Transport of the 91st Bde. Interview OC No 3 by adjutant to H. Interview by Divd of G/s re Brigr J Divn into new area.	
	23			
	24	"	Went with SSO HQ new area & inspected roads & forward refilling points. Interview with OC 36th Divd Train re places to hand to Divd purchases.	

WAR DIARY
or
INTELLIGENCE SUMMARY

Army Form C. 2118

Place	Date	Hour	Summary of Events and Information	Remarks and references to Appendices
FLESSELS	25 Jan	9 P.M.	Interview at Divl. H.Qrs. to arrange supply of petrol for Division when moving on 28th to get Rolls moving into Flesselles on 27th, also arranged details of petrol wheels with Div. Divnr.	
"	26.	"	Conference at Divl. H.Qrs. to ascertain names of officers recommended for Rewards.	
"	27	"	Arranged details of move of Corps not made known to infantry until Div'l Staff.	
FIENVILLERS	28	"	Moved to FIENVILLERS. Arranged Billeting. Went to BERNEUIL to report to Imperial Holder. S.S.O. regarding to Divl H.Q. 9th LE MEILLARD. Conference with S.S.O. regarding supply of gasoline, & supplies for travellers arriving on 30th. to the Div. of munts. attached to 4th Divn.	
"	29	"	Interview at Divl. H.Qrs. who instructed that a car to go out to Army School 3rd Army to see Weavers simply & briefly overruled our Genl. arranged daily convoy of 15 wagons for morrow carrying for travellers. Inspected No 2 by BERNAVILLE — No 1 by. BERNEUIL & informed on of change to force arrived of Army or no. DOULENS entered for morrow by abouts.	
	30th		Visited all refilling points & Rail Heads. Return at 8-30 H.Qr.	

30ᵗᵉ Division
vol: 2

12/7809

30ᵗᵉ Division

Dec 15

<u>Confidential</u>

WAR DIARY

of

Lt Col C. M. Ainslie
30th Div¹ Train

From 1 Dec 1915   To 31st Dec 1915

VOLUME I

Army Form C. 2118

WAR DIARY
or
INTELLIGENCE SUMMARY

(Erase heading not required.)

Instructions regarding War Diaries and Intelligence Summaries are contained in F. S. Regs., Part II. and the Staff Manual respectively. Title Pages will be prepared in manuscript.

MAP AMIENS SHEET 12.

Place	Date	Hour	Summary of Events and Information	Remarks and references to Appendices
FIENVILLERS	1 Dec	9 PM	Interview at – Divl HQ 9th Report orders for to–(Tacty. Capt) Mellish to proceed to GHQ for duty with Supply Col. 7th Indian Transfer over us by 57th Divn to Tiff for Builhead or no 1 Coy sent out. Night with empty lorries to arrive refugees. Received transport. Interview re carrying out Divl HQ 6 Regards move 7, 9th, Bde to trenches & 91 from trenches to all units. Know 2 Wheelers per unit. This included 13 Maltese wagon extra per Bde total of 36. Supposedly to furnish will always Woodcarts. Etc. Attended conference at Etap & improvements in the area.	
	2nd		Interview as Divl HQ 9th Recd battle of moves are detailed transport Arty still arriving & needs very heavy. Had brought how increased passages. Intercommunication between lorry & train HQ quo very difficult. Owing to distance. Bad roads. Convoys that took by 7 HQ of Cavalry Divn a motor bicycle attached. This would save many delays. Despatched from no Coy, 10 SS wagons to report to 48 & 4th Divns to Etang to Blangerval & unit relieving 57th area went to report passes.	
	3rd			
	4th		Lt Beaumand reported his arrival from 28th Reserve Park. Interview at Divl HQ 6th Sent 25, SS wagons to the 37th Divn at Oudenville arranged supply & Tpt details for arty moving to trenches. Capt Burgess Tpt completion lesson. Interview with OC no 1 Coy regarding horses of wagons and arty horses to bearers	
LE MEILLARD	5th		to LE MEILLARD. No move made. SS O. cap. Beccher Offa S. Vet Offa accompanied.	

Army Form C. 2118

WAR DIARY
or
INTELLIGENCE SUMMARY
(Erase heading not required.)

Instructions regarding War Diaries and Intelligence Summaries are contained in F.S. Regs., Part II. and the Staff Manual respectively. Title Pages will be prepared in manuscript.

Place	Date	Hour	Summary of Events and Information	Remarks and references to Appendices
LE MEILLARD	6th	9m	Afternoon at Divl HQ & 2/Lt HOTTON leaves tonight for leave via Boulogne	Trace AMIENS SHEET 12
"	7th		14th Inf. delivery returns late.	
	8th		Went with SSO to Rue Hippocrat. Discussed refilling points	
	9th		Went to No 1 Coy to investigate Divl HQ moves. Return at 10.0 via Bray	
			" 3 Coy. On running log to german artillery trains. Draft write manoeuvres last No 1 Coy. — 2 unit of Foster required for research for B.H.T. Sebast- HAURE	
	10		Visited No 1.3 & 4 Coys. Conference machinery maps. Shows arranged with Divl HQ & 2 Tiart from W/S rooms. Divds shows supplies in Infantry transport to handle to all weapons in work for CRE in Infantry Scheme. Arrangement for replacing dumps	
	11		Letters ar Divl HQ Gr. De Commanding Interior & fellow for Thursday. Machines in villages to Divtm Steams & supply trucks. S.S.O. to arrange movements if necessary.	
	12. 13.		Was with SSO to inspect machines Thursday. Went to No 1.3 & 4 Coys for leave 189th Inf Bde. Took lorry Hd Qr also horses accompanied with S.S.O.	
	14.		Went with DAQG. to go over new area & select refilling points between	
	15-		Interview at Divl HQ. Brig. Gen. Capt. Thompson reported from Engrs.	

Army Form C. 2118

WAR DIARY
or
INTELLIGENCE SUMMARY
(Erase heading not required.)

Instructions regarding War Diaries and Intelligence Summaries are contained in F.S. Regs., Part II. and the Staff Manual respectively. Title Pages will be prepared in manuscript.

Place	Date	Hour	Summary of Events and Information	Remarks and references to Appendices
LE MEILLARD	16th	9 p.m.	Sent 3 trained NCOs to Base. Recvd 3 reinforcement in their places. Detailed 6 Wagons from No 4 Coy to assist No 1 Coy in move of HQrs to Brucamps. Arrived at Divnl HQrs.	MAP AMIENS SHEET 12
	17th		Conference with A.D.S.T. Officer. 3 NCOs or Privates 3rd Army. Received proforma of stores to drawn in great case from stores in issue. Shortage of Lard, Barley & Woods St. Inspected No 4 Coy in afternoon.	
	18th		Interview with District HQ Gen D.S.S.O. re Supply question in general. Went to No 1 Coy.	
	19		Went to supply points with S.S.O. February routine work.	
	20		Went with S.S.O. to supply points, indents of Divnl HQrs.	
	21		Handed over duties to Capt Kemp upon return or leave. Detailed HQrs for 21st Bde joining this division. Intervw at Divnl HQ Gen.	
	30th		Arranged Type for march of Divn to new area. Reported return from leave to Divnl Gen. Train Inspection by I.G.C.	
	31st		Interview Divnl HQ Gen. Conference with O.C. Coys re future Transport of Divn. also with Supply Officer regarding Supplies during move.	

EM Crawde H.Cl.
Capt & 33rd Div Train

30th Sir L. Pam
Vol: 3

Confidential

War Diary
of
Lt. Col. C.M. Amistie.
Cmdg 30th Divl Train.
from 1 Jan 16 to 31 Jan 16.

Volume I

Army Form C. 2118

WAR DIARY
or
INTELLIGENCE SUMMARY
(Erase heading not required.)

Instructions regarding War Diaries and Intelligence Summaries are contained in F.S. Regs., Part II. and the Staff Manual respectively. Title Pages will be prepared in manuscript.

Place	Date 1916	Hour	Summary of Events and Information	Remarks and references to Appendices
LE MEILLARD	1 Jan	9 a	Interview with DSO and D.A.Q. Lectured to Train of Officers on Types of Supply Work and Organization.	
"	2		Detailed more lorries from XIII Corps for move of Division ordinary work.	
"	3	pm	Went to DADST with AQ and BGRAS re change of Railhead in new area. Received wire from 5th Army Train that these taken over but Vacancy filled at present. Cancelled move of No 253 Coy into huts ordered. But sent 30 + 6 Coy to other Entire Brigades 3 Officers Staff 3 Transport Wagon to remain with these.	
	4		Wired all units to return Baggage + Supply Wagons, Ambulances and Saw DADST who will look up question of Baths.	
	5		Ordinary routine work made final arrangements of wagons for major have been 14 lorries + 36 5/5 wagons from XIII Corps of traffic moved.	
	6		Went to No 1 Coy re transport arrangements. Return at DSS 7 pm. No 2 + 3 Coys to move to new area in 5th.	
	7		Went to ETINEHAM to see BQO SDD. Returned to HQ 5 pm 8 m.	
PONT NOYELLES	8		Went to ETINEHAM to check Test re detailed HQ and 1 and 2 DADTS. Returned to PONT NOYELLES No 253 Coy had arrived there.	
"	9		Routine work PONT NOYELLES. Influenza SO 1 Offr at DADTS.	

Army Form C. 2118

WAR DIARY
or
INTELLIGENCE SUMMARY

(Erase heading not required.)

Instructions regarding War Diaries and Intelligence Summaries are contained in F. S. Regs., Part II. and the Staff Manual respectively. Title Pages will be prepared in manuscript.

Place	Date	Hour	Summary of Events and Information	Remarks and references to Appendices
PONT NOYELLES	10th	9 a.m.	Went to ETINEHEM to arrange for billets. Checked with previous K.O.H.G. Routine work. Interview with H.Q. G.S.	
ETINEHEM	11	"		
	12	"	Moved to ETINEHEM. Arranged for work inspected Ruffling Sqn. Elevators.	
	13	"	Routine work. Arranged Tpt. for R.E. & Det. 1st Pers Carr reported.	
	14	"	Routine work. Worked out Scheme for Transport & Forge for Range at FOISSY (canal) all forage from 22nd Div. Stores from Pionnes. Hire instead of rail head.	
	15		Went to find Ground with S.S.O. to save improved routes for men & mules. Roads not ment — always very bad state. Drew up scheme for movement of the horses & Rations. Saw to transport for tpt to proceed to —	
	16			
	17		Went with D.A.Q.M.G. to see LOCKS on Canal to find 1 practical to launch pontoons. Drew up Scheme to enclude horse transport for Supply Col in the event of Tpt —	
	18		Interview with Div. M.O. Completed Scheme.	
	19		Routine work. Went round refilling points.	
	20			
	21		Inspected new refilling points with S.S.O. Forage to Rail head evacuated Horses from Village. Wood. If any tpt. required Horses at tpt to get up keeping numbers of tpt as Horses are not up to day well as otherwise arranged for S.S.O. to go to 2nd Divnl trans & Supply & Horses they they help to rain in Brithon	

1875 Wt. W593/826 1,000,000 4/15 J.B.C. & A. A.D.S.S./Forms/C. 2118

Army Form C. 2118

WAR DIARY
or
INTELLIGENCE SUMMARY
(Erase heading not required.)

Instructions regarding War Diaries and Intelligence Summaries are contained in F.S. Regs., Part II. and the Staff Manual respectively. Title Pages will be prepared in manuscript.

Place	Date 1916	Hour	Summary of Events and Information	Remarks and references to Appendices
ETINEHEM	23 Jan	9 pm	Went to Refilling Points & arranged with OC D.A.C. Teams of lorries to Rv through FRENCH AREA	
	24		Went with DAQMG to inspect BRAY railway station. The Party visited FROISSY (EAUVE RIVER SOMME) YORK & BRAY. I may be used for forage from Abbeye to serve the roads. Inspected the Ly.	
	25		Ordinary routine work. Went forward. Staffs 4, No 2, 3 & 4 bns. Interviewed W. Div & OC Qm.	
	26		Went to FROISSY Ferry Reports. Shelled. Others arrived. Storage Forage dump to CAPPILY fort. 2g - Interviews to Divisions & at 9 pm FROISSY again shelled. Infantry at CAPPILY & DC 28/29 moving transport & rather & detailed waggons. Interview at Divns for O's ordinary routine work. Arranged supplies for REA going from 5 to 9 am.	
	27			
	28			
	29		Returned. All transport no. 11 pulled out. Orange in ETINEHEM. Held ready to start forward. Made Officer arranged for 6 supplies for next meal. Awaiting the German attack.	
	30		Replaced broken vehicles. Noticed 9.5 F Battery with tractors & drawn repeatedly through the gas.	
	31		Ordinary routine work. Went to Refilling Points. Made arrangements to transport divine only after Much fire infantry Company to Werter. Being shelled all horses & teams to be ready to clear at 5 mins notice.	

JR Connell Lt Col
ADS 30 to Dec 31

30th Div.
Train
Vol. 4

Confidential
_____

War Diary

of

Lt Col C. N. Ainslie
Comdg 30th Div Train

From 1st Feb 1916   To 29 Feb 1916
(Volume IV)

Army Form C. 2118

WAR DIARY
or
INTELLIGENCE SUMMARY

(Erase heading not required.)

Instructions regarding War Diaries and Intelligence Summaries are contained in F. S. Regs., Part II. and the Staff Manual respectively. Title Pages will be prepared in manuscript.

Place	Date	Hour	Summary of Events and Information	Remarks and references to Appendices
ETINEHEM	1 Feb	9 P.h	Interview ad. Brent Fd. 9th all Trey T othes how coming by railtruck. Went to FROISSY with SSO to see arrangts. dep: 3 Troops for SAILLY Rh. they all distings. to Vanise VIGNETT f. waters.	
	2 Feb		Went with SSO to inspect vegetable station at BRAY. BRAY was shelled + shre many times to the minute. Interview 2p. no 9th G.S.	
	3 Feb		Arranged with Div Rd. gr. to alter hour of refilling to the morning. Interview Wagon Sergt. Them wd. after chufs.	
	4 Feb		Inspected S.S.D, by gr at MORLANCOURT. ETINEHEM slightly shelled in afternoon. Evening Interview wd. Div. Fd. gr.	
	5 Feb		Interview bi-div Fd. gr. Refilling pour today wd. 10 am working of afternoon arranged to leave our wagons after refill. until dark for vehicles going to BRAY & onward. Bray & onward shelled.	
	6 Feb		12 S.S. Wagons reserve cavalry attacked. Div. by gr RE work. Instances wanted pour Div gr. re. attachment of co.k tosp. Div. Sectry. S.S.o. Sow Corps. + arranged tout VIII Corps suffer. to get petrol speed.	
	7		Sdinner. Brentier. Work. Went to Ruckhead. Work EFS.	
	8		Inspected no 1 Coy. & allotted Lorries that had arrived at Ruckhead.	
	9		Interview Brent Fd. 9.5. regarding Scheme of transpt. self supplying by camel & horse. Cont. Re Wagons 2 Coys to the attachment to CE	
	10		No 1 Coy moved to SAILLY LAURETTE. $50 Wagons 9 9th Rds early to be attached to No 1 Coy for work for C.R.E. Went with Div 9 x. y	
			SSO to ECLUSE to plan refilling point. Wrote to SAILLY LAURETTE to see arrangements.	
	11			

WAR DIARY or INTELLIGENCE SUMMARY

Army Form C. 2118

Place	Date	Hour	Summary of Events and Information	Remarks and references to Appendices
ETINEHEM	12th		Interview of Div HQ arranged new suppling arrangement white PERRY CORBIE ROAD closed. Interviewed or J. Interviewed Baths regarding running of Bph for two units which two some. SSO D.51 Sp. SD. interviewed my SSO regarding that this nothing open this above.	
	13th		Interview at Div HQ. I went to interview with SSO gave directions for works for wagon from new supplying point through French lines. Inspected No 1 Bn at SAILLY LAURETTE.	
	14			
	15		Went with SSO to new area to see supplying points + interviewed OC 51 Bn. I saw his limber + OC 53 came here to see. Infants the interview Div HQ + OC gave instructing as to Supply of the arrangements for more	
	16			
	17		Interview Div HQ + OC I gave details of system I have rejected + arranged for No 4 Bn to remain where they were. Fresh meat to SAIUY LAURETTE Dep IVI Br	
	18		More counter orders in regard Sup: Interview at Div HQ.	
	19		Interview at RA HQ OC + arranged Supply: The details of move APM. Visited ECLUSE LOCH with CRE + CO and I SP & made necessary arrangements + minimum: all supplies leaving Road + Road to Line by Barge	
	20			
	21		Went to RAILHEAD with SSO I inspected pos 20 + 420.	
	22		Went to new supplying point with SSO + some refilling	
	23		Interview w SSO Spl Offr arranged arrangements regarding arrangements for supplies made	

Army Form C. 2118

WAR DIARY
or
INTELLIGENCE SUMMARY

(Erase heading not required.)

Instructions regarding War Diaries and Intelligence Summaries are contained in F.S. Regs., Part II. and the Staff Manual respectively. Title Pages will be prepared in manuscript.

Place	Date Feb-	Hour	Summary of Events and Information	Remarks and references to Appendices
EINDHEM	24		[illegible handwritten entry]	
	25		[illegible handwritten entry]	
	26		[illegible handwritten entry]	
	27		[illegible handwritten entry]	
	28		[illegible handwritten entry]	
	29		[illegible handwritten entry]	

Confidential

War Diary of Lt Col. C M Anstie A.S.C.
30th Div Train

From 1st March

To 31st March.

Vol 6

Army Form C. 2118

WAR DIARY
or
INTELLIGENCE SUMMARY
(Erase heading not required.)

Instructions regarding War Diaries and Intelligence Summaries are contained in F.S. Regs., Part II. and the Staff Manual respectively. Title Pages will be prepared in manuscript.

Place	Date	Hour	Summary of Events and Information	Remarks and references to Appendices
ETINEHEM	March 1st	9 p.m.	Interview at D.D.M.G. Went to refilling point at BUSSE ÉCLUSE. Superintended that arrangements discussed in the morning's CRE Inquiry provided for unhorsed transport.	
	2nd		Sent to Conference to Confer with G.S.O.3rd. Secured writer out and spare men, horses, & wagons. Mr. G.C. [illegible] that they be [illegible] to patrols without [illegible] these to be [illegible] by train & different to their H.B.C. vehicles.	
	3		Went to ÉCLUSE to see refilling. Made arrangements for relief of 13th Div. Arming.	
	4th			
	5		Interview at D.D.M.G. ref [illegible] works. Inspected [illegible] horses in [illegible].	
	6th		Went to ÉCLUSE & [illegible] by the [illegible] brought forward & the [illegible] to join them from the [illegible].	
	7			
	8		Patrolled the Div. area [illegible] performance arrangements for move of Div.	
	9		Went to No.1 [illegible] [illegible] delivery of [illegible] of Div. [illegible] area.	
	10		[illegible] arranged with D.S.M.F. for [illegible] move. Two interviews [illegible] with G.S.O.	
	11		Interview [illegible] at [illegible] [illegible].	
	12			
	13		Went to [illegible] area & saw O.C. 18th Div. [illegible].	
	14		Worked out [illegible] move with [illegible] D.Q. to G.D. [illegible] [illegible].	
	15		Went to [illegible] with [illegible]. Inspected [illegible] & work, & CO of 8 [illegible].	

WAR DIARY or INTELLIGENCE SUMMARY

Army Form C. 2118

Place	Date	Hour	Summary of Events and Information	Remarks and references to Appendices
ETINEHEM	16 Feb 9/8		Went with Daroch to new area to see if 18 SDS est instructors would start. 18 SDS would take over hosp in the Essars. To see if Station in town ready.	
	17		19.15 still complete uproar. Mov. 3 Coy moved to SAILLY LAURETTE. No 2 Coy to BEHENCOURT. No 1 Coy to CORBIE. Interview at SHORE 8:30 pm.	
	18		Cleared Railhead at CORBIE to new area. Fish + ment passes from S.S.O. Buffets at CORBIE + 15 places which arrived at Railhead. Inspection + distribution of Forage and distribution.	
	19		Went to Railhead to get forage sent out by fish to A HUSSEY BEHENCOURT + wagon to Infantry farms at LA NEUVILLE. Returned at 9.10 pm.	
MONTIGNY	20		Moved to MONTIGNY with Team. 9/8 3/8 9 SDS H⁰ 9/5 H⁰ trains etc.	
	21		On leave. Interview at S.S. H⁰ 9/5 returning returns work.	
	22		Inspected No 2 Coy at BEHENCOURT	
	23		" " " " S.S.O + Capt Knox + Wynne. Leave. Interview Dis 9/8 9/5. A.D.O.S. Returning. S.S.O. discussing Supply Wynate at present. 9/8 H⁰ 9/5 Etrun to DAOURS opening No 1 Coy to CORBIE.	
DAOURS	24		Moved with 88 H⁰ 9/5 to DAOURS. Interview with Major BEADON +S.O. pm Sailly LAURETTE.	
	25		Visited No 1 Coy at CORBIE + No 3 Coy at SAILLY LAURETTE.	
	26		Interview at Dis H⁰ 9/5 SDS to move to new area on 28th. Made necessary supply arrangements. 9/8 SDS 15 returns good made in YBRAY area.	

WAR DIARY
or
INTELLIGENCE SUMMARY

(Erase heading not required.)

Army Form C. 2118

Place	Date	Hour	Summary of Events and Information	Remarks and references to Appendices
DAOURS	27.	9½.	Went to Railhead CORBIE to No 1 Coy. Completed arrangements to move — OC No 2 Coy Report No T/4 14362 Dr HOSTLER L killed by accident through horse stepping into arm of Company.	
AILLY Sur SOMME	28.		Moved to AILLY Sur SOMME. & No 1 Coy to LONGPRÉ. No 2 Coy to SAILLY LAURETTE	
	29		Moved No 3 Coy to VAUX. Visited new refilling points.	
	30		Moved No 4 Coy to VAUX & No 3 Coy to LONGPRÉ. Went with DADOS to GOC & OC to to 13 Corps re Motorable regarding Tpt Railhead to LONGPRÉ There being no Motor there suitable & that CORBIE as Railhead. Visited No 1 & 4 Coys.	
	31		Visited HQrs RFA re retention of baggage wagons between Div Tpt &c.	

30th Div Train 1916

Confidential

—— War Diary of ——

Lt Col C S H Ainslie. DSO
Commanding. 30th Divl Train

From April 1st 1916
To.   April 30th 1916

WAR DIARY or INTELLIGENCE SUMMARY

Army Form C. 2118

Place	Date	Hour	Summary of Events and Information	Remarks and references to Appendices
AILLY SUR SOMME	1 APL	9 m.	Returned Div HQ. Ordinary routine work. Interview ADMS. re withdrawal of Standard Trench furniture & S. Weapons.	
	2		Inspected No 1 Coy at LONCPRE	
	3		Inspected No 3 " "	
	4		Inspected No 2 " at SAILLY LAURETTE	
	5		Inspected No 4 " at VAUX — all Coys in good working order	
	6		Interview at Div HQ. Re move of Field hosp. R.E. & exchange of 21st & 9th Fd Ambs	
	7		Interview Div HQ. Dr Finished No 4 Coy re move of B.E. at VAUX. Ordinary routine work.	
	8		Interview Div HQ. Dr Finished No 2 Coy. LONCPRE	
	9		Dealt with prisoners No 1 Coy — LONCPRE. Went to Paris Plage	
	10		Went round refilling Points — I selected sites for refilling Points-yesterday	
	11		Handed over to Major Kenahman command of Field Ambce my period of temp. Record without to return No/Field Ambce & 3 gas s-	
	12		Interview Div Md Gr.	

Ts.D. Greenall M. Col.

Comdg 30 F. S. D.

Tr

Army Form C. 2118.

WAR DIARY
or
INTELLIGENCE SUMMARY.
(Erase heading not required.)

Instructions regarding War Diaries and Intelligence Summaries are contained in F.S. Regs., Part II. and the Staff Manual respectively. Title pages will be prepared in manuscript.

Place	Date	Hour	Summary of Events and Information	Remarks and references to Appendices
AILLY-SUR-SOMME	APRIL 13th		Lt. Col. AINSLIE proceeded to ENGLAND on leave. MAJOR L. KNAPMAN assumed command of 20 "G" Sub. Train. Interview with D.H.Q. Interview received re disposal of surplus animals.	
"	14th		25 Wagons + mules. Interview with D.H.Q. Instructions received to uproad to Train says, that all wheelers are to be represented by April 25. —	
"	15th		Interview with D.H.Q. General Routine work. Proceeded to 2 Co at SOLT LAVRETTE + also Detachment of Coy to st Same Village — Horses + harness in good condition.	
"	16th		Interview with I.H.Q. Gradie R.E. re extra wagons for Trades Carting. Routine work.	
"	17th		Interview with I.H.Q. Routine Routine work.	
"	18th		Lt. Col. AINSLIE returned from leave (Gerning to below Keading all officers from ENGLAND) to resume of command of 20 Sub. TRAIN. MAJOR L. KNAPMAN returned to No 1 Company.	

Army Form C. 2118

WAR DIARY
or
INTELLIGENCE SUMMARY
(Erase heading not required.)

Instructions regarding War Diaries and Intelligence Summaries are contained in F. S. Regs., Part II. and the Staff Manual respectively. Title Pages will be prepared in manuscript.

Place	Date	Hour	Summary of Events and Information	Remarks and references to Appendices
AILLY SUR SOMME	18.		Returned from leave & reported at DDS HQ 6pm. Interview DDS HQ 9pm told who should go for transport — Major KHAPMAN	
	19		Visited No 4 Coy at VAUX.	
	20		No 1 " LONGPRÉ	
	21			
	22		Recd word todo to march to ETTINEHEM area — visited our supply Depot arranged return. Div HQ pm	
	23		Ordinary routine work	
	24		Interview Div Sup Sgt 6am. Move of Coys to new area performed hors tanys	
	25		A.D.V.S. & I inspected unshaven AT VAUX & LONG-PRÉ. Delivery wagons work. Sent Div HQ for supply wagons — I wish to inspect 1st time Try Hrs	
	26		Interview D.D.S Hqs 6pm ordinary routine work.	
	27		Known No 4 Coy Ordinary routine work	
	28		Or supplies 18th ???. Came over for information re The new reserve. Interview Sub HQ 9pm	
	29		Visited No 1 & 3 Coys LONGPRÉ	
	30		Went to ECLUSE & returned on horseback. Sent 4 coyt of all Corp. Interview div Sup HQ 9pm on return	

CONFIDENTIAL

War Diary of Lieut Col; C.M.Ainslie.

Commdg 39th Divisional Train

FROM   May 1st 1916

TO   May 31st 1916

Army Form C. 2118

WAR DIARY
or
INTELLIGENCE SUMMARY
(Erase heading not required.)

Instructions regarding War Diaries and Intelligence Summaries are contained in F.S. Regs., Part II. and the Staff Manual respectively. Title Pages will be prepared in manuscript.

Place	Date	Hour	Summary of Events and Information	Remarks and references to Appendices
AILLY SUR SOMME	1 May		Intervie Ass Adj gre No 2 Coy moved from SAILLY LAURETTE to ECLUSE Camp.	
	16		No 3 Coy from LONGPRE to CORBIE	
	2nd		No 3 Coy moved from CORBIE to ECLUSE Camp & No 4 Coy from VAUX to CORBIE	
			Made final arrangements for ASC moves.	
	3rd		No 4 Coy moved from CORBIE to ECLUSE. Instructed No 1 Coy to send advance party from LONGPRE to ECLUSE to recover Intercom Ass Coy	
ECLUSE MERICOURT	4th		Ordinary routine work	
	5th		Moved to ETINEHEM. + Visited camp at ECLUSE	
			Interview Ass Adj gre ordinary routine work	
	6			
	7		Moved to ECLUSE + visited all companies arranged transport details for supply + wagons for RE work	
	8th		Interview Ass Adj gre ordinary routine	
	9th		" " " " " " arrangement - wire DJ H&gs	
			" method of man handling returns	
	10		Showed Ass Adj gre Various methods of carrying water & on DR on stretchers to on two boys slung over shoulders. Latter most favored. Capacity 40 rations.	
	11		Intervie Ass Adj gre re haring ambulance to purchase hospital	
	12		AMIENS by Wagt. Ass Adj/DJ start for LONGPRE Pl Damage done by Turks	

Army Form C. 2118

WAR DIARY
or
INTELLIGENCE SUMMARY
(Erase heading not required.)

Instructions regarding War Diaries and Intelligence Summaries are contained in F. S. Regs, Part II. and the Staff Manual respectively. Title Pages will be prepared in manuscript.

Place	Date	Hour	Summary of Events and Information	Remarks and references to Appendices
ECLUSE MERICOURT	May 12th	9h.	Ordered to front. Major was unavoidable. Major to hand over to Major Kirkby. Men trucks & Staff.	
	13th	"	Proceeded on leave & handed over to MAJOR KNAPMAN.	
	14th	"	Visited H.Qrs.	
	15th	"	Visited H.Qrs. – Made arrangements for removal of reserve dumps & elected depot for present dumps to mile from camp. Received instructions re reorganisation of Div Artillery + general + Bef adc Ammn Colums. Action taken to recall four G.S. Wagons from B.A.C. now surplus to Estab'n. new depot allotted for Bread & Meal dump for Lorries.	
	16th	"	Visited H.Qrs. – Exchanged four Mark IV wagons from Inf' Brigade. In Mark II. The four Mark III wagons were then received new at R.F.A. as complete turn outs for evacuation.	
	17th		G.S. returned from B.A.C.	

With the Bee S.S.
Old System of 4 B.A.C.
              1 D.A.C.
Total B.A.C. + D.A.C.

	Baggage S.S.	Supply S.C.	Drivers	Horses
	4	4	8	16
	4	5	9	18
	—	—	17	34
			10 – 20	
	3	3	13	26
		4		8

New System D.A.C. For 13 a/t Cafs.
                    Extra Forge.

J.S. Surplus to Estab'n →

Army Form C. 2118

WAR DIARY
or
INTELLIGENCE SUMMARY
(Erase heading not required.)

Place	Date	Hour	Summary of Events and Information	Remarks and references to Appendices
ECLUSE MERICOURT SUR SOMME	MAY 17th		Visited Hd Qrs. — nominated Capt Mayne. 7 w & B to supervise all walkways in refer. to G.R.O. No 1476. The C.R.A paraded a number of Rellies & R.A. Horses. Many of these were exchanged with units who have R. & H.S. they needed to Change for remount reasons; Issued orders for return of Leans handed (mens) & appointed Survey Board to inspect "same report."	
	18th		Visited Hd Qrs. — Visited C.R.E. re extra Majors — Made arrangements for this Wake Carts to work on road between Bray & Pont 80 Carts to remain at Bray. Drivers & horses to return to Camp daily. Made arrangements with S.S.O re 1st wire of Green Lorries, also trucks issued to Div Train.	
	19th		Visited Hd Qrs. — 8 extra G.S. Wagons sent to Bray for C.R.E. Majors. 8 extra G.S. Wagons sent to Bray. Drivers full day work report to remain. Horses & Drivers to return to Camp. Drivers full day work report daily at R.E. Park. BRAY. 7 a.m. night work at 7 p.m.	
	20th		Visited Hd Qrs. Visited BRAY re Wake Cart work & attached four horses & four A.S.C Drivers to 202 fs R.E. Bray for this work — Routine work —	
	21st		Visited Hd.Qrs. Instructions received re Move of 53 B DE of 18 Div will take over from 51 fr R Bde. Commencing night 23/24 Arranged to meet Lt Col. Gross. O.C. 18 Div Train 11 AM 22nd ////. 4 N.C.O's Sent to attend a Course of Div Anti-Gas Officers	

1875 Wt. W593/826 1,000,000 4/15 J.B.C. & A. A.D.S.S./Forms/C. 2118.

Army Form C. 2118

WAR DIARY
or
INTELLIGENCE SUMMARY
(Erase heading not required.)

Instructions regarding War Diaries and Intelligence Summaries are contained in F.S. Regs., Part II. and the Staff Manual respectively. Title Pages will be prepared in manuscript.

Place	Date	Hour	Summary of Events and Information	Remarks and references to Appendices
ECLUSE MERICOURT SUR SOMME	May 22		Remittee End. to FIELD AMB. H.D. horse (to No 2. G. Train) another Cllrsfrom HQ Drs No 2 44569 dated 18th inst. Visited SALLY LAURETTE to meet Lieut. Col. Snow O.C. 18th DIV TRAIN & made arrangements with him in Ref. to move of 33 Bde of the 18th Div.	
	23rd		+ 89 Bde. to "Div Hd Qrs" Routine work. Reported to Div HdQrs. Visited HdQrs. Arranged with Staff Capt. 1 Div Artillery that any Field Amb. Drs available to J.S. troopers in the Train would be at his disposal for Carting logs from ECLUSELOCK to right flight of left flight group. R.F.A.	
	24th		Lt W. Annis returned from leave to V.K. & G.S. when command of Train.	
	25"		Interview Div Mr. OT + with RAMP OT re purview of Forage wagon to R.A. re RA when same is a very bad state. Inspected Lines + horses forage etc + c/o.	
	26		Interview Div Mr. O.T. Visited Rail head.	
	27		Inspected Reserve ratios at SAILLY LAURETTE	
	28		Inspected Reserve rations to MARICOURT + BILLON NORTH to detail rate for 6 days	
	29		Arrangement accordingly	
	30		reconnaissance marching & supplying escort when at SAILLY LAURETTE	
	31		supported in the Field for Annual detail of Mules of RAMC or supply to the French	

1875 Wt. W593/526 1,000,000 4/15 J.B.C. & A. A.D.S.S./Forms/C. 2118.

C O N F I D E N T I A L

WAR   DIARY

of

Lieut. Col. C.M.Ainslie.A.S.C.,
Commdg 30th Divl. Train

FROM..........JUNE 1ST.
TO............JUNE 30TH

WAR DIARY
or
INTELLIGENCE SUMMARY
(Erase heading not required.)

Army Form C. 2118

Place	Date	Hour	Summary of Events and Information	Remarks and references to Appendices
ECLUSE MERICOURT	June 1st	9/12	Went to SAILLY LAURETTE to receive Ration Store & Accumd Transport of certain stores detailed transport for more of 9th Rifle Brigade. With DAA & QMG	
	2nd		Arranged to draw from 9th Res Pk H 30,000 reserve rations, the storage which first time almost 10,000 per day. Got horse what in turn were wounded & wagon taken by chaplain	
	3rd		New 15,000 reserve ration & transported to MARICOURT returning with horse	
	4th			
	5th		Drew remaining 15,000 reserve rations. Inspection Div HQ & QT Mr & C inspection	
	6th		Went to AMIENS & 8th [?] for then sent over for 30 [?] field ambulance & 3 S wagons	
	7th		Div AT & QT approved of handover of DADOS & handover arranged. Enquiry for more of 9th Rifle & the cause of	
	8th		21st Rifle to keep leave made and supply arrangements. Interview Div DQ & QT & travel supply arrangements — Res Rats	
	9th		indicating ration work	
	10th		Capt Moss struck off strength. Capt Parry to report for 33 days to	
	11th		interview Div AT QT arranged details of reserve (4 days) Rations 62 street	
	12th		interior — Div MARICOURT in theory of 2 Infantry Brigades Ration Pr. sailed globally for inland 20 ration in RES Packs	

Army Form C. 2118

WAR DIARY
or
INTELLIGENCE SUMMARY
(Erase heading not required.)

Instructions regarding War Diaries and Intelligence Summaries are contained in F.S. Regs., Part II. and the Staff Manual respectively. Title Pages will be prepared in manuscript.

Place	Date	Hour	Summary of Events and Information	Remarks and references to Appendices
ECLUSE	June 13th	9pm	Interview 2nd Art O. arranged lorry for ammunition & grenades to ASSIST R.A. arranged lorry to complete reserve ration at MARICOURT.	
MARICOURT sur SOMME	14		Ordinary routine work	
	15		Made final arrangements regarding wine & rations. Mess June — Three days wine to be stored at MARICOURT to fulfil nights by M. Fox. Supp. wines being made to receive, all rations packed. Preliminary at refilling point. Interview 2nd Art O. & wire or 9th Div Train. Div move not this am.	
	16		Conference of O.C.'s regarding wine & rations after embarkation full details expected to follow & forms orders issued.	
	17		Interview Div H.Q. An extra lorry reserve grub, for forward issue. Div armed arranged. Convoy 1 30 wagons to close ammunition.	
	18		Interview 2nd Art O. Re ordinary matters will lorry for ammunition to MARICOURT. From 26 S.S. wagons with grenades etc to MARICOURT.	
	19			
	20			
	21		Capt. H.M. HINDE reported for duty from Base. Interview 2nd Art O. lorry. Ammunition to MARICOURT & ordinary supply petrol.	
	22		Interview Div H.Q. O. to lorry H.Q. for lorry. Ammunition supply & ration to MARICOURT.	
	23		Interview 2nd Art O. Petrol to MARICOURT 92 Coves. Reserve Ration & ammunition convoy. (T Stores)	

Army Form C. 2118

WAR DIARY
or
INTELLIGENCE SUMMARY
(Erase heading not required.)

Instructions regarding War Diaries and Intelligence Summaries are contained in F.S. Regs., Part II. and the Staff Manual respectively. Title Pages will be prepared in manuscript.

Place	Date	Hour	Summary of Events and Information	Remarks and references to Appendices
ECLUSE MERICOURT sur SOMME	24		(U Day) Interview this a'n'n re arranged convoy to carry food from BRONFAY FARM & ammunit'n to U.W.Rs. Arranged to hire dump men & Rations on 2 Days.	
	25		(V Day) Arranged supply petrol him to keep him also trucks & motorcycles arranged supplies to 95th Rgts moving into the area	
	26		(W Day) Interview this a'n'n & p'n	
	27		(X Day) " " " Sent 5" water truck to MARICOURT dm with water for petrol him, water supply having failed. Moved into dump Rest-	
	28		(Y Day) Detached 5 S.S.Wagons for C.R.E. to take Trestles material to Trenches & 6 S.S. for C.E. XIII Corps. One attached to BRONFAY.	
	29		(A Day) 1 20 S.S.Wagon taking water to BRONFAY. Interview this a'n'n & p'n received instructions regarding petrol, coal & Trains. Sent lorries & water supplies up to BRONFAY & arranged accommodation	
	30		(B Day) Interview this a'n'n & p'n. Trains to move to SAILLY LAURETTE next w'd.	

J.R. Chandler M/A
Capt & 30? DAC Train

CONFIDENTIAL

War Diary

of

Lieut Col C.M.Ainslie. A.S.C.
Commanding 30th Div Train

From   July 1st 1916

To   July 31st 1916

Army Form C. 2118

WAR DIARY
or
INTELLIGENCE SUMMARY
(Erase heading not required.)

Instructions regarding War Diaries and Intelligence Summaries are contained in F. S. Regs., Part II. and the Staff Manual respectively. Title Pages will be prepared in manuscript.

Place	Date	Hour	Summary of Events and Information	Remarks and references to Appendices
ECLUSE.	1 July	9 pm	Interview Div HQ: made arrangements re move of Train to SAILLY LAURETTE. Arranged for Barges to take place of haul of Depot.	ALBERT Confidential Sheet - 57 D 3 62 D 3
	2 "		Hdqrs SAILLY LAURETTE. Selected and ground for Train Hrs. arranged with 9th Div Train to take over reserve ration at MARICOURT.	
	3 "		Interview Div HQ. I reported that All troops had fresh meat & bread daily who permit of ration. Except 21st Bde who have one day tinned by their own request.	
SAILLY LAURETTE	4		Moved Train to SAILLY LAURETTE. Interviewed Barges. French shortage in milk on starch taken over. Other supplies of bread Train which they have now made up. Other supplies corn stopped too Barges cannot get away to home. Have Barges at Gt. Train in demand.	
	5		Interview Div HQ: 9 - DADQMG - DADSST inspected supply arrangt.	
	6		Inspected all arrange sent wagons to BRONFAY FARM to collect salvage.	
	7		Interview Div HQ. Ordinary routine work.	
	8		Arranged convoy nights to CRE to take stone from had from Rail Hd Train Trenches.	
	9		Inspected Camps. Visited new prepared Railhead near BRONFAY FARM Interview Div HQ 9 - attached to wagons I see from Pair & RE for road work - usually two ASC officers. Interview Div HQ 9 - Ordinary routine work.	
	10			
	11			

WAR DIARY or INTELLIGENCE SUMMARY

Army Form C. 2118

(Erase heading not required.)

Place	Date	Hour	Summary of Events and Information	Remarks and references to Appendices
SAILLY LAURETTE	July 12		Interview S.S.O. H.Q. Made arrangements for Supplies & Transport for move of 9th & 21st Rifles.	
	13		10 S. Sd gm attached RE. delivered also S.S.S Wagons attached. 13 Lorries made arrangement for move of 29th Rifle & Trench mortar.	
	14		Div H.Q. moved to CORBIE. arranged T.M.S Supplies for R.E. Cyclists collected horse drawn Remounts for various units in the Div.	
	15		Arranged Transport to move 9 95th & 21st Bdes to back area.	
	16		Supplies all units at various lgs. Interview S.S. H.Q.	
	17		Arranged for a forward refilling point for 5 days ration on BRAY-ALBERT Road. As no lt lays to supply there.	
	18		Interview S.S. H.Q. arranged T.M.S Supplies for the 313th mining Tnch to this area. Jnr day prepared to proceed to forward area.	
	19		Air Tenders refilled here for last two trains taken. Interview S.S. H.Q.	
	20		Interview with O.C. 1st h Bde Train regarding taking over units to be when they come there. Arranged T.M.S Supply for S.A.A. & Signal Sect. morning forward to day.	
	21		Rec'd Order to march Wn. Troops to 2 DSS. Sm. & move to BERNANCOURT.	
BERNANCOURT	22		Moved Troops to BERNANCOURT. & drew from Northward also arranged for 2 DSS.	
	23		Interview X. S. Tpl. 6th Arranged transport from Remmt to BRAY ALBERT Road.	

Army Form C. 2118

WAR DIARY
or
INTELLIGENCE SUMMARY
(Erase heading not required.)

Instructions regarding War Diaries and Intelligence Summaries are contained in F.S. Regs., Part II. and the Staff Manual respectively. Title Pages will be prepared in manuscript.

Place	Date 1916	Hour	Summary of Events and Information	Remarks and references to Appendices
BRAY ALBERT Rd	24 July		Moved Train & refilling point to BRAY ALBERT Rd. Attached 10 S.S. wagons fr R.E. work daily, also 2 fr each Bde fr Stores fr maintenance	
	25		Men Div H.Q. & ordnance water work. Exchanged W.D. horses to D.S. for worn out horses	
	26		Inspected all horses in Train ordinary routine work.	
	27		Interior Div H.Q.	
	28		" "	
	29		Visited Railhead. Purchased wood fr S.S. wagons, Feedboxes &c	
	30		Interior Div H.Q. Issued Petrol lamps to Bdes fr Water Supply. Sent out transport wagons to all Infy Bdes for move fr Line.	
	31		Interior Div H.Q. Made Supply arrangements for move fr Line fr Infy Bdes as far as possible accurately further details unknown.	

Lt Colonel A.T.F
Comdg 20th Div Train

Green Vol 10

WAR DIARY

OF

LIEUT COL C M AINSLIE A.S.C.
COMMDG 30TH. DIV: TRAIN.

FROM AUGUST 1ST
TO AUGUST 31ST } 1916

WAR DIARY
or
INTELLIGENCE SUMMARY
(Erase heading not required.)

Army Form C. 2118

Place	Date	Hour	Summary of Events and Information	Remarks and references to Appendices
BRAY ALBERT ROAD	1916 Aug 1		Moved from to POULAINVILLE. Interview with D.D.M.G.S. & mules & Troops Billeted Town Bays & Depot. Orders for 110 lorry to proceed to 24 HOURS on 2nd & from 110 Q.M.D. remove lorry to HALLENCOURT	
POULAINVILLE	2		Instructed all units having Transport there this Herewith who they hereafter of Div Hd Qrs Q=D	
HALLENCOURT	3		Visited supply Bush. & saw supplies dumped. Billeting app. & repairing Div Hd Qrs selected temporary supply point in new area. & fixed up military horses at stations of Entrainment	
St. FLORIS	4		Made full arrangements for Div Selected Rwy head for Point Detraining for Div HD Qrs lorry point general & Retaining Stations & met Divs	
	5		Morning workable with next lorry on arrival & inspected all lines on the new lines.	
	6		Visited 39th Div Train & went round to see how standing to Billet the Div to take over.	
	7		Interview Div Hd Qrs made supply arrangements for move of Div to new area. Sent S.S.O. to new area to select supply point.	
	8		Interview Div Hd Qrs Made transport arrangements for Troops. Saw S.S.O. 39th Div & arranged to feed units supplied by motor lorries	

WAR DIARY
or
INTELLIGENCE SUMMARY

(Erase heading not required.)

Army Form C. 2118

Place	Date	Hour	Summary of Events and Information	Remarks and references to Appendices
St Pol	9th		Visited refilling points in area. Made final supply arrangements.	
	10		Instructed that No 3 Coy could not be billeted in BETHUNE. Visited LOCON & arranged billets for Train. Tps & R.E. Coy & adjt. 39th Div Train & Sn'r Supt of Pk. Retsd of work for Corps & RE.	
	11		Interview S.D. Dir 9th. Ordinary routine work.	
LOCON	12		Moved Train Hqrs 9th to LOCON & visited Camps & Hqrs.	
	13.		Interview S.D. Dir 9th. Arranged detail for Horse Tpt to draw Purchases in place of lorries. Drew by lorry yesterday & today 3 miles in place of lorries. Drew by lorry yesterday & today & turned Nos 1 to wanted all Fuel Pnst tn Railway on Supply Cot on adv dump. Turn in reserve. OC no 2 See 6 E. Reserve Park wharves. Detailed two wagons in whty for 39th Inf Bde. C.E. Supplementd first day's clearing at Railhead (BETHUNE) by Horse Tpt. Turned all fgrmg for both wharves at Railhead.	
	14		Interview S.D. Dir 9th & Q. Ordinary Routine work. Inspected all by-passes the "Train". ADVS Various Inspected all horses in Train.	
	15			
	16			
	17			
	18		Interview S.D. Dir Q's. Ordinary routine work.	
	19		Revd instructions for No 2 Sec 6 Res Park to move on 20th & 31st Div wharves	

Army Form C. 2118

WAR DIARY
or
INTELLIGENCE SUMMARY
(Erase heading not required.)

Instructions regarding War Diaries and Intelligence Summaries are contained in F.S. Regs, Part II. and the Staff Manual respectively. Title Pages will be prepared in manuscript.

Place	Date	Hour	Summary of Events and Information	Remarks and references to Appendices
LOCON	Aug 20	9h	No 2 Sec & No 1 Sec Resn moved out — to No 1 Sec 1st army lines (H) Coy inspected in & replace same. Went round refilling point. Visit S.S.O. Interview S.S. Tpt O. received instructions to fill up stocks of supplies on Barges at — No 4 Field Supply Depot.	
	21		Went round refilling points. No 2 S.S. Barges to empty up that our loads were full — being taken out of traffic lanes.	
	22		Interview S.S. Tpt O.	
	23		Instructed that corps would inspect refilling points & I Tpt Lines of No 4 Coy to all Teen Vehicles.	
	24		Interview Div Tpt O. Ordinary routine work	
	25		Issued instructions re drawing supplies from Barges on the 31st S.S.O. in accordance with Corps orders for turnover of stock. Conference at — Corps re supply standards.	
	26		Interview Div Tpt O. with Dagos wound refilling points. Saw R.E. reference refusals to at Refilling points.	
	27		Inspection of Teen Vehicles by I.O.M. I.M.T. Army.	
	28		Went round Teen Standings with Dagos.	
	29		Visited Field Ambulances & inspected their WK Do M S.	
	30		Made final arrangements re warnipty Barges tomorrow.	
	31	8.00	Handed over Command of Train to Major KNAPMAN during my leave.	

Th. Quayle Lt Col
Comdg S.S. Tn. Div Train

CONFIDENTIAL

WAR DIARY

OF

LIEUT. COL. C.M. AINSLIE   A.S.C.

COMMANDING 30TH DIVISIONAL TRAIN

FROM:-   SEPTEMBER 1st 1916
TO:-   SEPTEMBER 30TH 1916

Army Form C. 2118

WAR DIARY
or
INTELLIGENCE SUMMARY
(Erase heading not required.)

Instructions regarding War Diaries and Intelligence Summaries are contained in F.S. Regs, Part II and the Staff Manual respectively. Title Pages will be prepared in manuscript.

Place	Date	Hour	Summary of Events and Information	Remarks and references to Appendices
LOCON	1916 Sept. 1		Interview D.H.2. Visited No 2 + 3 Coys of Train re Winter accommodation	
	" 2		Interview NCO's of men. Interview D.H.2. Made necessary arrangements for Pole Bargees Wagons to move 90th Bde to FESTUBERT. Section of Line at 21st Bde move to Reserve Area. Visited No 1 + 4 Coys of Train re Winter accommodation of NCOs + men	
	" 3		Interview D.H.L. Arranged with D.A.D.O.S. re local purchase of timber for repair of Wagons. Interview with C.R.A. re returns of supplies Train Baggage Wagons &c for W.E. Part III No 813, dated S.D.2. 22 July. The re-organization took effect from 3rd Sept.	
	" 4		Interview D.H.2 + Thundersley Train boys re-arrangements for Winter accommodation.	
	" 5		do — do — Routine work	
	" 6		do — do — Inspected horses at No 1 Coy lines.	
	" 7		do — do — Made necessary arrangements for move of 21st Infantry Brigade from GIVENCHY section 7 to 8 inst.	
	" 8		Brigade who relieve 89 Infantry Brigade in GIVENCHY section 7 + 8 inst Interview D.H.2 Routine work	
	"		Took over Command of Train from Major Knaggs	

1875 Wt. W593/826 1,000,000 4/15 J.B.C. & A. A.D.S.S./Forms/C. 2118.

Army Form C. 2118

WAR DIARY
or
INTELLIGENCE SUMMARY
(Erase heading not required.)

Instructions regarding War Diaries and Intelligence Summaries are contained in F.S. Regs., Part II. and the Staff Manual respectively. Title Pages will be prepared in manuscript.

Place	Date	Hour	Summary of Events and Information	Remarks and references to Appendices
LOCON	9		Interview Genl Hd Qrs. Visited supplying units & worked in Progress of building Shedding etc.	
	10		Inspected No 4 & 5 Cos. Genl HQ. & Employee Supply & Shipping. Wecam to ABBEVILLE	
	11		Interview Div Hd Qrs Berghuer No 167. Interviewed D.S Hd Qrs were convened to Forces. So Inspect supply & Train HQ 62	
	12		Inspected No 2 Co. & Visited Railhead	
	13		Interview Div Hd Qrs Moved from Hd Qrs. Buzh to Nd Killed my to New Hd Qrs. Image Farm. Cancelled	
	14		Interview Div Hd Qrs Made Supply & Train arrangement for move of A D of E Staff on 15th. Train has arrived.	
	15		Interview Div Hd Qrs. Made Supply & Train arrangements for move of Div (his div) to new area.	
	16		Went to Railhead & supplied Park. Spent of 31st Div & Train to arranged to thought over make supp Railhead to also handed over to Have lines of Billets	
BETHUNE	17		Marched from Hd Qrs to BETHUNE. T Train lys ready to entrain	
DOULLENS	18		Marched Train Hd Qrs to DOULLENS. Selected Supply Point billets Coys. & Pars H.Q. Div Supply Col.	
	19		Hd. Qrs Coys at Staff as arrived. made Supply & Transport to marched to W.CNACOURT Horses No 21st Train-	

1875 Wt. W593/826 1,000,000 4/15 J.B.C. & A. A.D.S.S./Forms/C. 2118.

WAR DIARY
or
INTELLIGENCE SUMMARY
(Erase heading not required.)

Army Form C. 2118

Place	Date	Hour	Summary of Events and Information	Remarks and references to Appendices
DOULLENS	20 Sept	9h	Made arrangements for the move of the Bde. to KENACOURT area. Sent on HQ Supply Col. & Lorries.	
VIGNACOURT	21 "		Moved from DOULLENS to VIGNACOURT. No 2 Coy to OHINCOURT, No 3 Coy to HERSERE. Nos 4 Coy to WARGINE S. Moved to NW heavy supply cot with Bde. Suffering lots experienced in arrival. Teams to clear railhead tomorrow. As all transport & supply wagons heavy put reserved in area.	
			7h 15 men Went to Rlye. Loaded for 2nd Supply Col. attaining 15 Lorries & arranged similar trip.	
	22		Visited Nos 2, 3 & 4 Coys. Schemes for Sept 6th.	
	23		Went to railway Station & Railhead. Owing to Railway Lorries to No 1 Coy Coy. There were insufficient trucks to clear supplies by Railway wagons off Rlye Coy. for Bdes.	
	24		Arranged to clear supplies for Bdes. Rlys demanded (?) by Lorries. Visited No 1 Coy.	
	25		Cleared Lorries (Remnants) for 3rd Div from Railhead. Returned Air Hd 9th Man. Supply 9 Tpt wagons for move of Bnde.	
	26		At 5.6. JERNAN COURT. Inspected No 2 Coy. Made arrangements for more of Supply Park.	
	27		Made arrangements for supplies to 9th Div & Supplies to ALLONVILLE necessary for Tpt? Transfer of ammo by road with a move to move the whole of line from tomorrow as no train was available for the train.	

WAR DIARY
or
INTELLIGENCE SUMMARY

(Erase heading not required.)

Army Form C. 2118

Place	Date	Hour	Summary of Events and Information	Remarks and references to Appendices
VIGNACOURT	28/4/16		Ordinary routine work. Interviews with O.C.	
"	29"		Inspected No 4 Coy. ordinary work with H.Q.	
"	30		Inspected No 3 Coy. Interviews with H.Q. O.C.	

J.H. Curnock Lt Col
Comdg 3rd Pioneer Bn

SECRET.

D.A.G.,
    3rd Echelon.

    I beg to forward herewith please, original copy of War Diary for the period, June 1 - 30th.

In the Field   Lieut Col.
July 1st 1916.   Commdg 30th Divisional Train.

Vol 12

Confidential

WAR   DIARY

of

Lieut; Colonal C.M. Ainslie A.S.C.,
Commanding 30th Div. Train

FROM;-   October 1st 1916

TO;-   October 31st 1916

Army Form C. 2118

WAR DIARY
or
INTELLIGENCE SUMMARY
(Erase heading not required.)

Place	Date	Hour	Summary of Events and Information	Remarks and references to Appendices
VIGNACOURT	1 Oct 1916		Interview DDS re: GS:-	
	2		" " Arranged supplies & Petrol for move of Bdes to new area. A 2nd Horse to be made to relay. - Supply wagons wagon to move forward. Battn. & Mony on 4th Trip by Train.	
	3		Supply & Baggage wagons reported to all units & Divn ancillary supplies	
	4		Moved to REREMONT. No 2 Coy to DERNANCOURT. No 3 Coy to BOIRE No 4 Coy to REREMONT. Went round Lines with Lt.Col. Ref & XX	
REREMONT	5		Inspected No 2 & 3 Coy Lines. T Supply W.R.	
	6		Issued supplies for 2, 3 & 4 Coys that sent supply wagons to them units. Nos 3 & 4 Coy Divnre to furnish new system after refilling. For them Coys arranged new refilling points in forward area. Cleared supplies for DY Supply Railhead by Horse Trp.	
	7		Interview DS Hq gs Ordnance indents work. No 3 & 4 Coy Railhead Bde.	
	8		Inspected no 1 Coy in forward area	
	9		No 3 & 4 Coy agreed drew area. BRAY-ALBERT Road.	
	10		No 2 Coy refilled to BRAY-ALBERT Rd. Made supply & Op. arrangemt	
E.11 Central	11		Moved & set up Qrs to E.11. Central, unheated Cars.	ALBERT confirmed Sheet

Army Form C. 2118

WAR DIARY
or
INTELLIGENCE SUMMARY
(Erase heading not required.)

Instructions regarding War Diaries and Intelligence Summaries are contained in F.S. Regs., Part II. and the Staff Manual respectively. Title Pages will be prepared in manuscript.

Place	Date	Hour	Summary of Events and Information	Remarks and references to Appendices
E 11 Central	1916 Oct 11		Provided twenty S.S. wagons for R.E. work. Moved Brigadier to advanced printers. Supplied 4 S.S. tendered Asphalt tarmac in front store & two S.S. Do attached to each Bde Gp 6-	ALBERT Combined Sheet
	12			
	13		Railhead changed to EDGE HILL. Interview DD Sup G.S. Moved 2,3,& 4. Coy to E 11 Central. Supplied twenty S.S. wgns M.T. R.E. work	
	14		Railhead changed to ALBERT. Closed down Supplies to Refilling Point, & Reverts to units. Moved No.1 Coy to E.11 Central. Interview 41st Div. re petrol. Issued 1000 water troughs to Reserve &c. ordinary routine work.	
	15		Received instructions that Railhead would change to OLD FRICOURT on 19th & selected sites Pr by G Brunne	
	16			
	17		Flew reconnts for Sidings from Railhead & distributed to units	
	18		Moved ADS to FRICOURT & rec'd instructions late evening that Railhead in FRICOURT would not move. Moved Coy back to E.11 Central. Interview DDS Sup Gr 6-	
	19			
	20		Interview Sir Wm G- Ordinary routine work	

Place	Date	Hour	Summary of Events and Information	Remarks and references to Appendices
F/M Central	21		Made arrangement to move to Vicinity of RIBEMONT then less No 1 Coy to move by Rdos.	
RIBEMONT	22		Moved today to RIBEMONT made arrangements for ...	
	23			
	24		Visited new area to forward infantry Roads - ? DW of ADS & Supply & ? ? compounds	
	25		COsC moved Rgl Head With Bdes to VICKERS BOCAGE & TALMAS & adjusted the M... Sure TPs on road & ? Bdy to ...	
LUCHEUX	26		T&SH commanced absorption ... to new posn. & moved Tm Hq to ... . Inspected new Tpp in new area	
	27		Interview with OC 46th Gas Rms...	
	28		Visited Tns Cap & Infty Bde ...	
	29		Made double issue supplies moved supply details ... Ind	
	30		Move No 2 & 4 L.Gs to LABRET No 3 L.G. to GOMBERMETS moved Tn for L.G. to BAVINCOURT	LENS 11
BAVINCOURT	31		to clear railhead by dusk. ?	

CONFIDENTIAL

WAR DIARY

OF

Lieut Col C.M.Ainslie A.S.C.
Commanding 30th Divisional Train.

From.... November 1st 1916.

To......November 30th 1916.

Army Form C. 2118

WAR DIARY
or
INTELLIGENCE SUMMARY
(Erase heading not required.)

Instructions regarding War Diaries and Intelligence Summaries are contained in F.S. Regs., Part II. and the Staff Manual respectively. Title Pages will be prepared in manuscript.

Place	Date	Hour	Summary of Events and Information	Remarks and references to Appendices
BAVINCOURT	Nov 1st		Interview DDS & AD QMG moved horses & DDS troops reported to M — was under orders for issue. Detailed wagons of Res Park section for drawing supplies for Railhead for these situated troops. Detailed baggage wagons for clearing Railhead for Btns.	
	2nd		Inspected No 2, 3, & 4 Coys and arranged with C.R.E. for provision of matured ties here standings. Detailed wagons for that with Issue for Canteen	
	3rd		No 2 Sec 27th Res Park to issue daily 27 wagons for clearing Railhead for DDS troops & 465 DDS attached 36th DDS in manner to 10:35 wagons for R.E. Work. Civ. Lorries now being available to assist	
	4th		Interview ADDS & DDS 3rd army. S.S.O. Visited VII Corps regarding terms for making hay that has been purchased. As they rather refused to 6 lbs per horse in Pack.	
	5th		Drew up scheme for horse TM scheme for horses on leave & those after hard frost. Went round Lys Sec refugee typed Drivers attached to them for 14 days instructions in programme of work & submitted same to G.O.C. Interview DDS 4S(?) QMG ordinary written work.	
	6th		Sent 2nd Lt Filter & Cox to report to 3rd army HQ QMG DDS T office for units with army Headquarters forwarded. Jews AE re	
	7th		Two 3 Tops Drive Horse Standings. Went with ground work DC No 3 Coy to select site for same	
	8th			
	9th		Interview DDS about ordinary written work arranged with VII Corps to arrange certainty for the Corps. See Dilutts to see owners of Watches in area	

Army Form C. 2118

WAR DIARY
or
INTELLIGENCE SUMMARY
(Erase heading not required.)

Instructions regarding War Diaries and Intelligence Summaries are contained in F. S. Regs., Part II. and the Staff Manual respectively. Title Pages will be prepared in manuscript.

Place	Date	Hour	Summary of Events and Information	Remarks and references to Appendices
BAVINCOURT	10th		Interview D.A.D.O.S. re supply of coal to Divnl Baths, Laundries, Sooth Kitchens &c &c. Wrote reliance the attendance to the Officer. Drafted letter re subject.	
	11th		Ordinary routine work. Interview with Staff Capt 46th Divn re transport.	
	12		Pet 415 H.S. & Bath forming division. Ordinary routine work.	
	13		Inspected progress of horse standings at 403 Coy. Ordinary work. Pot — Bay employed only slow progress owing to scarcity of material.	
	14		Inspected Nos 2/3 & 4 Coys. Train inspected by 2nd D.D.S. of 3rd army. Ordinary routine work.	
	15			
	16			
	17		Started scheme of woodcutting for VII Corps. Early & 170 German Prisoners employed in felling trees & both Field Army in cutting & stacking. Encountered Pty of T.M. officers attached to Head Quartering. Both	
	18		Inspected Nos 4 Coy. Supply of Ration arrived for Ch. Foreher Turner Late Staff Ord — Divisional Morgan for 2.9th Bde for more Interview G.O.C. Div re instruction of Staff Sgt Officers	
	19			
	20		Inspected No 3 Coy & refilling points.	
	21		Visited No 1 Coy who moved up with Baty to LUCHEUX	
	22		Attended Rivithead & Saphinkid Clearr.	
	23		Interview D.A. D.Q. &c. & M.C.R.E. re wood cutting.	

1875 Wt. W593/826 1,000,000 4/15 J.B.C. & A. A.D.S.S./Forms/C. 2118.

Army Form C. 2118

WAR DIARY
or
INTELLIGENCE SUMMARY
(Erase heading not required.)

Instructions regarding War Diaries and Intelligence Summaries are contained in F. S. Regs., Part II. and the Staff Manual respectively. Title Pages will be prepared in manuscript.

Place	Date 1916	Hour	Summary of Events and Information	Remarks and references to Appendices
BAVINCOURT	24 Nov		Went with S.S.O. round various units. Where workshop is in progress & estimated tonnage available. Exchanged 4.8 Reserve Park Wagons with 48 D.A.C. Wagons & 30th D.A.D. Wheel reported for work in this area	
	25		Interview D.D.S. T&T Pks arranged transport retard for A.E. Workshop 30th D.A.C.	
	26		Interview D.D.S. T&T Pks gas relieving workshop work.	
	27		Interview D.D.S. T&T Pks & 5 O.C. B Echelon D.A.C. regarding Transport relieved.	
			relieving workshop work.	
	28		Interview D.D.S. T&T Pks made arrangements for Tyres & Supplies for 3rd D.A.D. Lorry-unit this area.	
	29		Interview No 1 Coy 46th D.S. Train re Exchange War steam lorries. Inspected same. Relieving various units	
	30			

[signature]
Major J/C 3rd D.J. Train

CONFIDENTIAL

WAR DIARY
OF

Lieut Col G.M.Ainslie D.S.O.
Commanding 30th
Divisional Train

From ;- December 1st 1916
To   ;- December 31st 1916

WAR DIARY
or
INTELLIGENCE SUMMARY
(Erase heading not required.)

Army Form C. 2118

Instructions regarding War Diaries and Intelligence Summaries are contained in F. S. Regs., Part II. and the Staff Manual respectively. Title Pages will be prepared in manuscript.

Place	Date 1916	Hour	Summary of Events and Information	Remarks and references to Appendices
BAVINCOURT	Dec 1		Interview D.A.D.T. O.C. Delivery Rubbish W.D.A.C. Inspected No 3 Coy. made arrangements for new horse lines	
	2			
	3		No. 1 Coy moved to BAVINCOURT	
	4		Inspected woodcutting with S.D.O.	
	5		Went to Rouilbeau & superintended clearing	
	6		Inspected No 4 & 2 Coys.	
	7		Interview D.D.S.D. H.Q. O.C. 1st Army & Div. Officers attending a course	
	8		Inspected 1st - 5th June Tpt. & 17th Tpt. D.A.P 13 Tpt Pts — 5 Anchor Regt.	
	9		Ordinary routine work	
	10		Inf. Battn. cleaned supplies for Rubbish P.W. — 30 Tn. supply wagons received 460 loads of Ammunition for Army	
	11		Interview D.a. D.T.O.s & Surrey 15th D.A.C. wagons assisting to shortage of horses in army arranged loads to be supplied at unit - horse lines to keep wagons clear of Tpt. tomorrow.	
	12			
	13		Took over horses Transit et Rouilbeau & issued to Div. S.O.C. inspected "Tram" [illegible]	
	14		Interview D.a. D.T.O.s superintend clearing Rouilbeau	
	15		Ordinary routine work. Visited attached Inf. Tpt Officers along Tpt. Course. Inspected No. 3 Coy	

WAR DIARY
or
INTELLIGENCE SUMMARY

(Erase heading not required.)

Army Form C. 2118

Instructions regarding War Diaries and Intelligence Summaries are contained in F. S. Regs., Part II. and the Staff Manual respectively. Title Pages will be prepared in manuscript.

Place	Date 1916	Hour	Summary of Events and Information	Remarks and references to Appendices
BAVINCOURT/16 DEC	17"		Interview Ass. Dir. Pm Railway Routine Work.	
	18"		Ditto	
	19"		Personnel attached 7th Division after Return with lorries proceeded in Motor Trucks when moved off Tm.	
	20"		To Major Knapman — Ordinary Routine Work.	
	21"		Interview Dir" Hqrs.	
	22"		do. Inspected the Horse Lines & Three Generators of No 2 & 4 Corps of Train.	
	23"		Interview Dir" Hqrs.	
	24"		do. do. Interview with C.R.E. De improvements to Drivers Sleeping accommodation.	
	25"		do.	
	26"		Interview with Dir" Hqrs. Arrangements made to return 15 G.S. Wagons of the 27 R. Park attached for Railhead duty to the 3 Brigades Coys of the Train. Three were replaced by Servis Lorries, i.e. 2 to each Brigade of the Railhead duties.	
	27"		Interview with Dir" Hqrs. — Notice No 2 & 3 Bgy of Train	
	28"		Ordinary Routine work —	
	29"		do. do.	

1875 Wt. W593/826 1,000,000 4/15 I.B.C. & A. A.D.S.S./Forms/C. 2118.

WAR DIARY
or
INTELLIGENCE SUMMARY

(Erase heading not required.)

Army Form C. 2118

Place	Date	Hour	Summary of Events and Information	Remarks and references to Appendices
RAVINCOURT	30th 1915		Ordinary Routine work.	
	31st		do do do Resumed command of 33rd Train on return from leave.	

J.R. Crawley Lt Col
Comg 33rd Div Train

Vol/5

Confidential.

W A R   D I A R Y.

of

Lieut Col C.M.Ainslie D.S.O.
Commanding 30th Divisional Train.

From ;- January 1st 1917
To ;-   January 31st 1917.

WAR DIARY or INTELLIGENCE SUMMARY

Place	Date	Hour	Summary of Events and Information	Remarks and references to Appendices
BOUINCOURT	1 Jan 1917		Made Supply & Tpt arrangements for move of Divn Ress Arty to LUCHEUX area. Arranged with A.Q.G. XVII Div Train re Transport. Taking Div Horse Standings & Shelters	
	2"		Went round new lines & selected refilling point.	
	3		Interview Divn Tpt O. re Transport. New Train Wagons for Composite of Army Arty Bdes. earmarked as follows:— 7 S.S. wagons to 3 extra teams for 150 Fld (Arty). 1 G.S. & 3 Petrol lorries to 2nd line Tpt. ammunition W.O. & 2 S.S. wagons to bear horse Tpt. depôts on the breaking up of X.Y./150 H.Div). Battery	
	4⁴⁵		Received two S.S. wagons for D. (47) Batty attached to Heavy D.A.C. Army Arty Bdes.	
	5		No 3 Coy moved to HALLOY	
	6		No 2 Coy moved to COLLEMONT & No 4 Coy to BOSQUEMAISON S.S.O. 145 D.S. in armoury worked out. Cohe Duntn.	
NEUVILL ETTE	7		on Div Charge	
	8		Moved Train Hd Qrs to NEUVILLETTE. Inspected Standings etc of No 204 Coy.	

WAR DIARY or INTELLIGENCE SUMMARY

Army Form C. 2118

Place	Date	Hour	Summary of Events and Information	Remarks and references to Appendices
NEUVILLETTE	7		Inspected standings of No 3 Coy. Visited No 2 Coy + saw A.S.O. MARTIN	
			COURT re loading. 7 50 ton trucks.	
	10		Took over rest camp at BOSQUEMAISON. Interview DD re ice Safety Route to this area	
IVERGNY	11		Moved from 9nd Gp to IVERGNY. Orders to arrived of 62nd D.D. Visited No 2 Coy I Wood cutting in LUCHEUX FOREST. Arranged feeding + relative troops (Indians) attached for work.	
	12		Ordinary routine work.	
	13		Interview DD re No 9 works No 3 Coy.	
	14		Inspected No 4 Coy + refilling trenches.	
	15		No, Coy moved to IVERGNY.	
	16		" 4 " " " Adjt + Capt. Parks temps out day.	
	17		Interview DD HQ 9th re clearing Railhead + timber 2 hrs	
	18		Tpt. arrangements to do so from 2575 Inclusive.	
	19		To Bayen Post. No 3 Coy to BOSQUENMAISON. Fixed up party to work down in LUCHEUX + attempted withdrawal + cleared supplies by Issue S.S.	
	20		Inspected No 2 + 3 Coys. Arranged supply of water from	

Army Form C. 2118.

WAR DIARY
or
INTELLIGENCE SUMMARY.
(Erase heading not required.)

Place	Date	Hour	Summary of Events and Information	Remarks and references to Appendices
IVERGNY	21/Mar/17		Ordinary routine work	
"	22		Inspected No 1 Coy - went round refilling points	
"	23		Went to Headquarters in LUCHEUX forest - attended Methodical	
BOUQUE MAISON	24		Moved No 4 Coy & Train HQrs to BOUQUEMAISON. Accompanied	
"	25		S.A. O.i.c. of several issues etc. Delivered lecture on supplies & POL at Divisional School	
"	26		Ordinary Routine work	
"	27		Arranged details. City work & new area	
"	28		Inspected Train 8 & 9am. 7am trip to LE SOUICH	
LASOUICH	29		Interview 2nd 3rd 4th Coys Inspected refilling	
"	30		Attended Railhead. Inspected Nos 2 3 & 4 Coy	
"	31		Moved No 1 Coy to BAVINCOURT.	

Confidential

WAR   DIARY

of

Lieut.Col.C.M.Ainslie D.S.O.

Period.

From:-   @ 1rst.February 1917.

To:-   28th.February 1917.

Army Form C. 2118.

WAR DIARY
or
INTELLIGENCE SUMMARY.

(Erase heading not required.)

Instructions regarding War Diaries and Intelligence Summaries are contained in F. S. Regs., Part II. and the Staff Manual respectively. Title pages will be prepared in manuscript.

Place	Date	Hour	Summary of Events and Information	Remarks and references to Appendices
LE SOUICH	1917 Feb 1		Fixed up billing points at BAUINCOURT. Visited No 1 by	
	2		Followed VII Corps G.R.O. refilling points. Tried New appearance. Made supply to TPR arrangements for move of 3rd Division	
	3		Divisory position W.S.H.	
	4		attended Recitheid & went round hay dumps	
	5		Moved No 2 & 4 Coy to LABRET 3 W.S. Coy to BAUINCOURT also detachment of No 3 Coy to VALLEY for unloading	
LABRET	6		Moved Train Hqs Coy to LABRET	
	7		Interview Dn. DADS all Mot. RMS detailed for Corps from Armies arranged to clear Railhead with horse transport — 20 DAC Wagons to help.	
	8		Ordinary routine WrA	
	9		Interview Dn. MT. Ob. re distribution of loads etc.	
	10		Moved No 2 & 4 Coy to BAUINCOURT Div to LABRET Railhead	
	11		Inspected loading trucks of Train 23 in Coy.	
	12		For Two Coy to unload for reserve of 20,000 forage rations S.S. used stocks up to about heavy	
	13		Ordinary W/hrg up to SS used stocky up to about heavy to-day	

Army Form C. 2118.

WAR DIARY
or
INTELLIGENCE SUMMARY.
(Erase heading not required.)

Instructions regarding War Diaries and Intelligence Summaries are contained in F.S. Regs., Part II. and the Staff Manual respectively. Title pages will be prepared in manuscript.

Place	Date	Hour	Summary of Events and Information	Remarks and references to Appendices
LABRET	1917			
	14		Ordinary routine work	
	15		Inspected all coys returned to regiment	
	16		Interview Brig HQ ps regarding billets. Drove over to Thos Pt	
	17		Instructed Drove Thos coys to LABRET. Ordinary routine work	
	18		Moved No 1, 2, 3 of Coy to LABRET. Thos scheme to drive clearance, southward by Louse Pt including ordinance of Pts.	
	19		Moved No 3 b to LABRET. Inspected all horse lines again. Cleared southward of old PARA coy Pt. Purple workshops reported	
	20		Sent car (open) to supply coy workshops. Visited residence. Interview	
	21		Thos scheme received for their further clearance. Interview by those	
	22		Brig HQ ps. Ordinary routine work. Cleared rubbish by three	
	23		M — as usual.	
	24		Inspected No 2 + 3 coys. Thos scheme in force till further orders. Arranged	
	25		Change in a + D schemes brought clearing of roads.	
	26		Interview Brig HQ ps. Instructed No 1 + 4 coys saw Chieftain of Turco there for Residence.	
	27/28		Made arrangements to carry work for EE corps in BARLY. Interview Brig HQ ps. Ordinary routine work.	

Confidential.

WAR   DIARY

of

Officer Commanding 30th.Divl.Train.

Period.

From:-   1st.March 1917.

To:-   31st.March 1917.

Army Form C. 2118.

WAR DIARY
or
INTELLIGENCE SUMMARY.
(Erase heading not required.)

Instructions regarding War Diaries and Intelligence Summaries are contained in F. S. Regs., Part II. and the Staff Manual respectively. Title pages will be prepared in manuscript.

Place	Date	Hour	Summary of Events and Information	Remarks and references to Appendices
LA BRETÊ	MARCH 1st 1917		Inspected No 1 Coy Posts & lines.	
	2nd		Between sunset & 9 pm arranged to provide Lewis gun & 2 rifles. Patrolman for Enemy patrol for water for Twin.	
	3rd		Inspected rifles of unwounded reporting after 8 Pack animals instead of S. Wagons.	
	4th		Dummy relieve work	
	5th		Interview Div HQ Div	
	6th		Inspection HQ 2 & 3 Coys. Major Price reported as S.S.O. for 13th Res Batt.	
	7th		Attended withdrawal dress & stopping points.	
	8th		Made arrangements for purchase of wood near "BARLY" for workmen for VII Corps	
	9th		Discussion & inspection of Rifle by Expert Rep. 1st BEAUMETZ	
	10th		In delivery service of arms	
	11th		Ordinary Routine work. Major Kingham interned	
			New Hd QR & Tpt Wkrs. New Scheme again in operation to keep enemy occupied to clear Railhead by Major Page Capt F. all officers to Head of 12th Durham of Pioneers & Major Vaughan of	
	12th		heavy inf Essex	

WAR DIARY or INTELLIGENCE SUMMARY

Army Form C. 2118.

Place	Date	Hour	Summary of Events and Information	Remarks and references to Appendices
LABRET	MARCH 1917 13th	—	Interview with Div. Hd. Qrs. Routine office work.	
	14th	—	do do do do Noted Wood Cutting Party.	
	15th	"	Routine work. Visited D.T. & Brigad Dumps. Visited D.A.D.O.S. re Horses, Mules.	
	16th	"	Interview with Div. Hd. Qrs. Inspected 89 Horse Lines. Carried on 2. S. Maj. M.S.	
	17th	"	Routine office work. Visited Detachment of Train attached 303 B. Road Const.	
	18th	"	Interview with Div. Hd. Qrs. O.C. D.A.C.	
	19th	"	do Visited Refilling Points for Div. Troops. & BRIGADE Ons.	
	20th	"	do Div. Troops, Dump moved to BEAUMETZ	
	21	"	do 89 & 90 Bdes Refilling Dumps moved to BEAUMETZ	
	22nd	"	do Arranged for move of 21st Brigade	
	23rd	"	do 21st Brigade Refilling Dump moved to LABRET	
			arranged for move of 90th Brigade.	
	24th	"	do Arranged for move of 89th & 90 Bdes & Div Troops Refilling Dumps	
	25	"	do & Train Transport detachment to BELLACOURT.	
			do observation as to Supply & Transport arrangements to be made re	
			the issue of three days iron rations to 63rd Division.	
	26th	"	Interview with Div. Hq. Drs. Visited Supply Detachment BELLACOURT & Detachment on	
			+ Conference . " . " . Road moved to GOUY.	

Army Form C. 2118.

WAR DIARY
or
INTELLIGENCE SUMMARY.
(Erase heading not required.)

Instructions regarding War Diaries and Intelligence Summaries are contained in F. S. Regs., Part II. and the Staff Manual respectively. Title pages will be prepared in manuscript.

Place	Date	Hour	Summary of Events and Information	Remarks and references to Appendices
LABRET	MARCH 27		Interview with Div HQ's Visited Rest Head & Refilling Points Rail Head	
	28th		" CRA " " " " " " BEAUMETZ Detachment	
			do do do Brigade B's Supply transport Repaired from BEAUMETZ Detachment	
			do CRA + RE trying to procure Transport Lorries from Brigades for this purpose	
	29		Routine + Office work. Visited all refilling points. - Detachment to Rail head	
	30		Interviews with Div HQ's - 153 Brigade sent transport to work from Rail to Rail'y	
	31		dump. - Visited D.E. 153 Bgde rail'y up by it attached HQ of march	

R. Maguire
Major
Comdt 30 Div Train

CONFIDENTIAL

WAR   DIARY

Of

Lieut.Col.C.M.Ainslie. D.S.O.

Period.

From:-   1st.April 1917
To: 30th.April 1917.

WAR DIARY or INTELLIGENCE SUMMARY

Army Form C. 2118.

Place	Date	Hour	Summary of Events and Information	Remarks and references to Appendices
LABRET	1917 MARCH 31		Routinework. Visitd. Detachment + Refilling Points BELLACOURT + Routhead LABRET. Seven water carts taken from Routhd. with Harness + turned over to S.A.A. sec. Trspt.	3.30pm
— do —	APRIL 1		Visited HqQrs. + C.R.E. Made arrangements for 13th R.S. Diggers to form detachment at BELLACOURT for duty at BLAIRVILLE (night work) for R.E. Visited refilling points. Visited Railhead Trains in 1.15 pm.	
	2		Visited HqQrs. CRE + CRA. Arranged for transport of extra hay or straw (next morning) for 2 + 1 + 2 + 3 days supplies to R.A. — Visited Refilling Points — Numbers 2 + 1 Brigade to forward Area. 4 Bag. Waggon Cart — Advanced Refilling. Railhead Supply Waggon fly others and Pack moving in with approx 10 min apart P.O. with the Train to go — Supply wheel the horses of	
	3		Visited Hd Qrs — Supply wheel the horses of — Tested for 24 horses where he sicked the nid Detachment arranged Tact for 24 horses where he sicked. Via and Detachment arrangements made in event of I.T. Rations (u 2-1 - 1 Dumps, arrangements made to meet Q.M. in field to assist without delay. 2 + 2 + 2 + 3 days in field to meet without delay. No Supply Train arrival of this day.	
	4	V	Interview with HqQrs. — Train arrived out 4 am (yesterdays train) Visited detachment BELLACOURT. This morn at 6 am Withdrew Iron Rations for Tpt 1,2,13, arranged to make use of 1st Line Transport, supply, WC2 Refilling Points as no men of supplies owing 7-9am arrival of Train — Supplies moved at 2 pm forwards	
	5	W	Interview with Gen Hd Qs. Inspected all horses in detachment at BELLACOURT. Interview with C.R.A. arranged to refill Supply Extra forage Wagons of 150 + 158 Brigade. to recur	

Army Form C. 2118.

WAR DIARY
or
INTELLIGENCE SUMMARY.
(Erase heading not required.)

Instructions regarding War Diaries and Intelligence Summaries are contained in F.S. Regs., Part II. and the Staff Manual respectively. Title pages will be prepared in manuscript.

Place	Date	Hour	Summary of Events and Information	Remarks and references to Appendices
LABRET	6th		Visited Div H.Q. Morning & Evening. Arrangements made in re of Ambulances & supplies to 89 & 93 Brigade. Visited Refilling Point (at BELLACOURT. Arranged for R.E. stores & pickets.	
do	7th /12		Visited Sec. Hd. Qrs. Morning & Evening. R.E. pickets (14) to be returned to Coys. Arranged for O.E. Coys to have Supply Transport lessened to — BELLACOURT. Camp after delivery Supplies & Refilling from 2 — 1 day 13.3", 2 — 1 day 13.3". Interview with all O.E. O in Cs Re Transport. Also not to to 2 as to the movements of Supply & Baggage due to the reduction of following days S.	
BELLACOURT	8th		Visited Hd. Qrs. all Main Carts filled (?) Reliance placed by Horse Transport in Coal Mine. All Train Supply Transport Section's camped at BELLACOURT. Refilling Points — 13 Tank Armoury after cleaning suppliers at Refilling Point — Left at LABRET with Baggage Wagons. Town near BAVINCOURT, O.C. Co returning at LABRET. S.S.O. meeting at LABRET. (Yday.)	
do	9th		Visited BOISLEUX AU MONT to see proposed rest head in new area.	
do	10th		(2 day) Arranged to send out Advance for R.F.A Baggage Wagons & Supply Wagons. Visited Hd. Qrs with two wagons few Rations for the move forward to Wgn's line & of FICHEUX. Visited BOISLEUX-AU-MONT selected refilling points & Bn Camps. S.2 Central	

WAR DIARY
or
INTELLIGENCE SUMMARY.

(Erase heading not required.)

Army Form C. 2118.

Place	Date	Hour	Summary of Events and Information	Remarks and references to Appendices
BOISLEUX-AU-MONT	April 11th		Visited Div H.Q's morn & evening. Moved all O.C. Bry's with Bry/4r Sections from LARBRET to BOISLEUX-AU-MONT. S.B. & 89 A. III Corps expect a supply train in the two right Divisions attack BOISLEUX-AU-MONT on 11 or 12th. Arranged for supply transport return & supply details to move to S.B.T after move on 2 or 3 days. At 12th noon TRAIN holds S2 central.	
do.	12th		Visited H.Q. Div G. tanks - Moved Div Train back to LARBRET. 2:1 Brigade moved back to BIEVILLERS, 203.S wagon supplies twit to t his supply details. - By & supply wagons sent out to 2 yor 7.30 89 Brigade as move to BIEL area. POMMIER & BAILLEUVAL. 89 Brigade order supply wagons sent out to BLAIR VILLE, 89 Bde move on to return to rendezvous, Div Troops refilling joint moved to S2 central. R.F.A supply Queens Bucharest.	
LARBRET	13th		Visited Div Troops Brigades Bryds. refilling joints at LARBRET. 89 Brigade moved to back area Supply wagons did not return there overnight A.D.M.S & A.D.V.S. Rd to BA Brown detailed 30th Div R.A. 30 Div R.A. attd 33 Div. In moved areas Visited Div G to G2 at S2 central.	
do.	14th		Visited Div H.Q's. Arranged 5 horse am 7 moto cars at O.T. refilling point & twenty wagons from 3 Reynolds Cnp A.Q. Brigade Bottye wagons sent out to more 89"	
do.	15th		do. do. Selected sep.t for refilling point at COUIN for 90 Brigade	
do.	16		Visited H.Q H.S. Lieut Automatic Assumed Command Party to embarr AURIGNY today 3.45p.m to 11.p.m base Remount Depot BOULOGNE to collect 40 mules.	

Army Form C. 2118.

WAR DIARY
or
INTELLIGENCE SUMMARY.
(Erase heading not required.)

Place	Date	Hour	Summary of Events and Information	Remarks and references to Appendices
LABRET	April 17		Interior Div HQ. Inspected No 1 Coy.	
	18		Made supply & Pet arrangements for	
			" "	
	19		Work of Coys. B+C Sub Divs wired.	
			Inspected No 2, 3 & 4 Coy. Sent out baggage wagon	
			to units. Received charger to APRR's	
ACHICOURT	20		Interview D.W.M D= moved 3 & 4 Coys from WM B+C	
			ACHICOURT. Water rendered.	
	21		Moved no 2 Coy to ACHICOURT. Moved sections Coy 1	
			to main BEAUMETZ ARRAS road. Sent 2 Forks	
			of 160 other ranks to RSHWIDONE Gr Troops Gr Div.	
	22		No 2, 3 & 4 Coys moved from ACHICOURT to RSA. Inspected No 1 Coy Hdqr	
			with D.A. Q.M.G. Forwarded 400 Filter Tins for water to address 51 SIC	
			Front store.	
	23		Interview Div HQ. O/C "G" moved Supply Dump to RSA. Inspected WSAd to 1750.	
			Zone of No 2, 3 & 4 Coy	
	24		Attended rehearsal. Greeted by Capt	
	25		Interview Div HQ. O/C Delivery wheeled WSAd	
	26		No 3 Coy moved SERRCOURT. Made supply & Pet arrangements	
			for units of Div Made new area	

Army Form C. 2118.

WAR DIARY
or
INTELLIGENCE SUMMARY.
(Erase heading not required.)

Place	Date	Hour	Summary of Events and Information	Remarks and references to Appendices
Achicourt	27		Interview with the O.C. 8th Bde. Inspected Brew area. Fixed suppting Points	
	28		No 2 Coy moved to NUNEQ. Two Buffs & 8.9th moved to new area. Made arrangements for handing over Batteries units to 18th Bde	March.
	29		No 4 Coy moved to TACHINCOURT. Turned over 6mm mortar to ROELLECOURT. Visited supporting Points. Inspected No 2 3 & 4 Coy. Interview with 5th T.D.	LENS 11
	30		XIV Corps. attended weekend	

CONFIDENTIAL

WAR DIARY.

of

Lieut.Col.C.M.Ainslie D.S.O.

Comdg.30th.Divl.Train.

PERIOD.

From:- 1st May 1917.
To:- 31st.May 1917.

Army Form C. 2118.

WAR DIARY
or
INTELLIGENCE SUMMARY.
(Erase heading not required.)

Instructions regarding War Diaries and Intelligence Summaries are contained in F. S. Regs., Part II. and the Staff Manual respectively. Title pages will be prepared in manuscript.

Place	Date 1917	Hour	Summary of Events and Information	Remarks and references to Appendices
ROELLECOURT	May 1st		Inspected No 4 Coy.	
	2nd		Made supply & Tpt arrangements for move of Brigade to new area. Issued baggage & supply wagons to all units.	
DEUF	3		Moved train & Moro from to DEUF No 2 Coy to HAMOR FARM No 3 Coy to ERQUIERES No 4 Coy to SERAUCOURT. Inspected No 4 Coy. Interviewed Bn 4 Coy.	
	4		Travel two A.S. Wagons to Camp Canche XIX Corps for No 4 Coy in town. Inspected No 253 Coy. Interviewed Sen Tpt Or. Inspected No 4 Coy.	
	5		Visited Supply OC & northwest	
	6		Ordinary routine work went-worth three Lines of Sup	
	7		Arranged to move supplies to Rentheme for B9 & 21st 11th Div by Horse Tpt from HQ 1125 Coys.	
	8		Inspected No 3 Coy & attended southeast	
	9		" " No 4 Coy Interviewed 30th Suppls WT. Moved	
	10		supply Coms & of 21st Div to CROISETTE	

Army Form C. 2118.

WAR DIARY
or
INTELLIGENCE SUMMARY.
(Erase heading not required.)

Instructions regarding War Diaries and Intelligence Summaries are contained in F. S. Regs., Part II. and the Staff Manual respectively. Title pages will be prepared in manuscript.

Place	Date	Hour	Summary of Events and Information	Remarks and references to Appendices
OEUF	Aug 11th		Started Railhead by Horse Tpt for OG 2, 3 & 4, by rail to 5 & 6 in 7	Inspected
	12		Interview Div Tpt O=	
	13		Ordinary routine work	
	14		Much Supply & Tpt arrangements 5th Divn of OG 2, 3, 4 types	
VAL	15		Move then not go to WAIL	
	16		Inspected No 3 & 2 Coy Trains. East Wagons to 115 Lorries for troops	
	17		Interview Div Apt O= Inspected no 4 Coy Trains & Lorries	
	18		Made Supply & Tpt arrangements for move to new area. for Trust. Heavy March. Light Points OEUF NUNC Q CROISETTE R 20th Trust.	
	19		Interview HQ Apt O= Issued all Brigades with 2 days Supplies. Trust Baggage & Supply Wagon for am units. Rest. HQ & LD Stone for Frevent	
	20		Brigades Cavs moved towards new area	
PERNES	21		" " " moved to PERNES.	
NORRENT	22		" " " " NORRENT-FONTES	
FONTES	23		Interview Div Apt O= Issued regularly reports for 25th Tn	

Army Form C. 2118.

WAR DIARY
or
INTELLIGENCE SUMMARY.
(Erase heading not required.)

Instructions regarding War Diaries and Intelligence Summaries are contained in F.S. Regs., Part II. and the Staff Manual respectively. Title pages will be prepared in manuscript.

Place	Date	Hour	Summary of Events and Information	Remarks and references to Appendices
STEENBECQUE	24		Moved from Hd Qrs to STEENBECQUE. Joined up with Bn 28th Sept.	
CAESTRE	25		Moved from Hd Qrs to CAESTRE. Joined up with Pnrs 27th	
WATOU	26		" " " WATOU. S.S.O. had interview with DADS	
"	27		S.D.T. 2nd Army. Interview OC 224 Train in talking over two lines in respect. Interviewed Bde H.Q. Visited Railhead WAREN HOEK. Had much 224th Train to see supply posnt. No 2 by moved to G16c88.	23. BELGIAN Map
	28		Inspected No 2 Coy & No 3 Coy. No 4 Coy moved to G16c88. 2 No 1 Coy to WATU. Made supply arrangements for issue of 900 Rns to ST OMER area. Visited OC 24 Div Train & No 20th Coy.	
	29			
	30			
	31		Moved the HQ to G16c88. Interview 2nd HQ QS No 3 Coy moved to ST OMER area with 90th Bde.	

[signatures]

CONFIDENTIAL.

WAR. DIARY.

of

Lieut.Col.C.M.Ainslie D.S.O.
Comdg.30th.Divl.Train.

Period.

From:- 1st June 1917.
To:- 30th.June 1917.

Army Form C. 2118.

WAR DIARY
or
INTELLIGENCE SUMMARY.
(Erase heading not required.)

Place	Date	Hour	Summary of Events and Information	Remarks and references to Appendices
ROSEBOOM	June 1st		Interview Div H.Q. arranged to clear Rouckland by three Z/y from 3rd inst.	
	2nd		69 men s.w. employment (?) reported to replace Engineers taken over. Inspected No 1 Coy.	
	3		Cleared Rouckland (WIPPENHOEK.) by horse transport. delivery vehicles with	
	4		Inspected No 3 Coy in area 4 Divn - Engrs supply & Tppn as supports for more L 10th Bde to the army, attached & employed to Bomb Vers. for dump Interview with O.C. Inspected No 2 I + H/g the Posts spread on this (Ammny)	
	5			
	6th		No 3 Coy moved into this area. arranged for relief of unsupplied wagons from 9th Bde.	
	7		Inspected trees in waggon of No 3 Coy - arranged to have 2 Coy conv'd to hire 4 R.E. Field Coy.	
	8		Interview Div Hqd O.C. Ordnance Services with	
	9		Inspected all horses & employing counts	
	10		Lt. Taylor to S.J. re'd'd change of transport at Poperinghe Stove. Vice Lt. Foster.	
	11		attended of Rouckhead ordnance section dept arranged supplies to Div army botty Bdes to start	
	12		over wagon if Div hqrs to Estaire	

Army Form C. 2113.

WAR DIARY
or
INTELLIGENCE SUMMARY.
(Erase heading not required.)

Instructions regarding War Diaries and Intelligence
Summaries are contained in F. S. Regs., Part II.
and the Staff Manual respectively. Title pages
will be prepared in manuscript.

Place	Date	Hour	Summary of Events and Information	Remarks and references to Appendices
RUSEBOOM	June 13th 1915		Arranged to transfer reserve rations at 9/10 ES to 8th Bde R Charge /9 am - Morning Routine work.	
	14	5		
	15		Moved from to 922304 Redhead Changed	
	16		Lt Semertin relieved Lt Taylor at Bank Farm Field Sec. Iulesten. First two cars to P.T.B.Ds	See 129
	17		Two army field amb bbns (202-232) transferred for return to P.B.Ds Also 3rd Canadian Field any 1-42 many transf to b/p	
	18		Sent convoy of 18 wagons with two return to B.S (Bedford) Horses under Lt Kislingbury. Lt Kislingbury wounded & sergt & Base through. Nos 10 Casualty Casualty.	
	19		93rd Labour Bn attached for return one wagon returned for reloading. Detailed daily onwards to Wagon for Trenches by S Coy for 6 Lancer men.	
	20		Sent Buggy wagon for a section of Bearers 9/2 Bde to France	
	21		WATTEN Interval 50s 100s 9/2s arranged return for 90-8. Sec in half wire arranged to bring Eng Stores. Returned. Rerouted WATTEN area Tyrsted all horses. Sent to count all wagon & M.T. Etc.	
	22		Attached pending move - whilst went moved Vicinople 24th by attached to WATTEN to see Lt Cartie it & Suffolk there for 90E Bde. Proceeded to	
	23		WATTEN -	
	24		Return 225 M.O. Two men wounded & Canary nets.	
	25		Orders Ambulance W.M. -	

Army Form C. 2118.

WAR DIARY
or
INTELLIGENCE SUMMARY.
(Erase heading not required.)

Instructions regarding War Diaries and Intelligence
Summaries are contained in F. S. Regs., Part II.
and the Staff Manual respectively. Title pages
will be prepared in manuscript.

Place	Date	Hour	Summary of Events and Information	Remarks and references to Appendices
BUSEBOOM	26		Made Supply & Transport arrangements for move of 21st Bde to Zunnybeeren WATTEN — also to 95th Bde returning to the area.	
	27		Attended Railhead Interview. Did not go.	
	28		2nd + 15 marched to WATTEN. Advancing billeting worked.	
	29		2nd Scottish Rifles united vice 2nd Tenth [?] attached & changing	
	30		Advance when with attached Conference for H.Q. D.s. re Rail Transport Etc.	

Vol 21

Confidential

War.   Diary

of

Lieut.Col.C.M.Ainslie D.S.O.
Comdg. 30th.Divl.Train.

Period.

From:- 1st.July 1917.
To:- 31st.July 1917.

Army Form C. 2118.

WAR DIARY
or
INTELLIGENCE SUMMARY.
(Erase heading not required.)

Place	Date	Hour	Summary of Events and Information	Remarks and references to Appendices
BUSE BOOT	July 1st		Inspected all Field Works. Attended Reinforcement 2nd A&G Bde	
	2nd		Attended without details extra wagon to Transport Lines 1-12, 1st.	
			9 & for store to S. Forces 1st & 2nd Dumps detail.	
	3		Made supply to the arrangements for move of 2.9 & 9.0 Bde to	
			Back area. These moves settled & RE work.	
	4		Interview 2nd A&G 6th Division attended without	
	5		Interview O.C. 1st Div Trns re Transport No escape Richm Test	
			No 3 Coy moved to LA MONTAIRE Interview 2nd Mt 9th	
	6		" 2 " " to " Mt 9th & 6 WOLPHUS	
			" " " " POLINCOVE & Tren Mt 9 to 6 WATTEN	
	7		Interview 2nd Mt 9th 6 inspected no 4 Coy at WATTEN	
	8		No 3 Coy moved to WOLPHUS. Attended Conference re taking	
			RE stores up in Z Army, made supply arrangements for	
	9		X & Z days & for Z Army 1 Return p 1/526 to part	
			Turned in & Sup - with two days ran- 24,000 Rations	
			in addition to the quant in Supply Trains for use y	
			Thus T 10th days work	
			Ordinary without wank	
	10		Attended Readings in Pressnes over to see new scheme for	
WOLPHUS	11		supplying to ploy of new Cavalry from Cav Div -	

Army Form C. 2118.

WAR DIARY
or
INTELLIGENCE SUMMARY.
(Erase heading not required.)

Instructions regarding War Diaries and Intelligence Summaries are contained in F. S. Regs., Part II. and the Staff Manual respectively. Title pages will be prepared in manuscript.

Place	Date	Hour	Summary of Events and Information	Remarks and references to Appendices
WOLPHUS	July 12		Interview D.D.S. A.D. & D.S. Inspected No 2 Coy	
	13		Attended Rentheud Comtg. WATTEN	
	14		Major General Comtg. D.S. inspected Train.	
	15		Issued Surgery + Supply wagons to 9th Batt to issue	
	16		" " " " " " " " 24 " " "	
	17		" " " " " " " " 25 " " "	
	18		" " " " " " " " " " "	
STEENVORDE	19		Train A.D.S. moved. Drew Amn WIPENHOEK. STEENVORDE	
	20		Train A.D.S moved to STEENVORDE Interviewed D.D.S D.D & G.O.C.	
	21		Inspected Camp. Pho 2,3,5 & Coys. Attended Rentheud [RENINGHELST]	
	22		Inspected No 1 Coy at G 22.D.0.4. Interview with O.C. 18th Division re camps.	
			No 3 Coy moved to G 22.D.0.4. Detailed Cap. Parker I/C Tptr–ar–Bmot	
	23		Vice to return on 23rd	
			Sent 6 G.S. limbers to Bmot Stre under 2 Tpt-Fields 2 S & boys	
G 22.D.0.4	24		Moved to G 22.D.0.4	
	25		Moved Train for D.D & G 22.D.0.4. Sent 40 Barrels to Water to amounces Train to Pleas	
			Detailed S.S wagons + Water Carts for Rentforus Camp 2nd Corps to	
	26		CASUAL	
			Started one Water Cart for D.S Bmot Stre Orderly Nature WINH	

WAR DIARY
or
INTELLIGENCE SUMMARY.

(Erase heading not required.)

Army Form C. 2118.

Place	Date	Hour	Summary of Events and Information	Remarks and references to Appendices
G.22.D.0.4.	July 27		Attended Ruilhead & refilling	
	28		2nd Lt MALTBY reported for duty. 2nd Lt SCANLAN reported. Pte Rear Bombay Lt BELLAMY Sheet 28	
			Interior Economy. Sent out party preparing returns &c	
	29		Firewood. Two days when Sr Bn Sr Operation	
	30		Sent 20 horses & men to Bomb Stores & Pack Transport	
			SAA on 31st Instr. Instrns re types of S Bread testing Rum	
			for men in Trenches	
	31		Visited Bomb Store & attended Ruilhead & refilling	
			Casualties during past 3 months	
			Officers. 2 Wounded	
			NCO's & men 1 (Sgt) Killed 3 Wounded	
			Horses 2 Killed 8 "	
			Vehicles 1 G.S. Wagon D. 1 G.S. Limber destroyed	

Alexander ???
Comg 3rd Divn Train

WAR DIARY

CONFIDENTIAL

Lieut Col C.M.Ainslie D.S.O.
Commdg 30th Divl. Train.

FROM....... August 1st 1917

TO.........   "   31st 1917.

Army Form C. 2118.

WAR DIARY
or
INTELLIGENCE SUMMARY.
(Erase heading not required.)

Place	Date	Hour	Summary of Events and Information	Remarks and references to Appendices
G2DO4	Aug 1st 2nd		Attended Railhead. Interview D.S. A.D.S. made supply & typ arrangements for move of 21st & 90th Bdes to STEENVOORD area. attended refilling.	
	3		made supply & PH arrangements for move of D.S. Zoo Corps to new area. (STEENVOORDE area move cancelled.) GODWAERSVELDE No 3 by moved to ST. SYLVESTRE & No 4 by to EECKE, F.	
GODWAERS VELDE	4 5 6		Then A.D. Div. to No 2 by moved to GODWAERSVELDE Stabled Cars returned 21st Regence Coys Inspected Coys + Selected refilling Points D main Road from STRAZEEL - BAILLEUL Rd.	Sheet 27 Sheet 28
MERRIS	7		Div. Hd Qrs moved to MERRIS. No 2 by to X.22.A.3.3. No 3 by to STRAZEEL No 4 by to X.20.R.2.2. Interview R.S.O. Relichard.S.A. Points selected refilling points. 14.S.S. wagons reported to 37th Div. Sn Corps unit.	
	8		made supply & PH arrangements for move to St. Jan CAPPEL area. moved 2 & 3 Coys to X.11.C.6.9.	
	9		Attended railhead & of refilling Points in new area. moved No 4 by to X.11.C.6.9. Handed over command of Train to Major Knapman on proceeding on leave	
	10			

Army Form C. 2118.

WAR DIARY
or
INTELLIGENCE SUMMARY.
(Erase heading not required.)

Instructions regarding War Diaries and Intelligence Summaries are contained in F. S. Regs., Part II. and the Staff Manual respectively. Title pages will be prepared in manuscript.

Place	Date	Hour	Summary of Events and Information	Remarks and references to Appendices
ST JANS CAPEL	11/8/17		Train HQrs moved to St JANS CAPEL. Interview with Div HQrs re Sara-Rehers rations. No. 1 Co Train moved from 922.d.o.4. to BAILLEUL.	
	12/8/17		Inspected refilling points. Interview with Div HQ re allocation of Lorries for refilling & rations, convoys from Railhead to be used.	
			Same day Div. Artillery & No 1 Co Train transferred to 2nd Army GS.	
	13/8/14		Inspected 2, 3, 4 Coys Train.	
	14/8/14		Interview with Div Hdqrs. Hand rations drawn from Rations Column.	
	15/8/14		Detachment under Lieut Kettle in Ims convoy supplied 171th Coy RE, 77th Field Coy RE 171 South Lane.	
	16/8/14		Sent out Supply Boy/Wagon & Lieut Bellamy returned. Lieut Kettle. N.10. C.59. 0 & No 1 Cos	
			" Div Artillery returned London Farm	
			" relieved all two Coys.	
	17/8/14		2nd August. No 1 Co Train moved to MERRIS. Interview with Div HQrs re move of the 91st Bdes to LOCRE area. Div Artillery drew from HAEGEDOORNE. Railhead at 7.30 am. No. 3. relieved nlm at N. 10. C. 59.	
	18/8/14		Interview with Div Hqrs. detachment at N 10. C. 59 supplied to 2 relieved.	
			Coy & Lieutns. To Capt Thos. Nts.	
	19/8/14		Interview with Div HQrs. Detachment at N 10 C.59 withdrawn.	
	20/8/14		" " " " Interview 4 Aux. Trains re taking over lorries etc. 21st Bdes Boy Waynes Cart out to Strands for Coml. to New Area.	

WAR DIARY
or
INTELLIGENCE SUMMARY.

Army Form C. 2118.

Place	Date	Hour	Summary of Events and Information	Remarks and references to Appendices
to JAN 20/8/17 GAPEL	21		Interview with Oni Hodge re Orders to Move Area. 90th Bde Baggage Wagon Oned out to units informing to Move Area. S.S.O handed over to Capt Parker on Proceeding on leave.	
	22		Took over command from Major Knapman Interim	
	23		Moved No 4 Lry to M29 c93	
	24		Moved No 3 Lry to M29 c93 ,, ,, 2 ,, M29 c93 ,, No 1 Lry M34 c37 Horses in Wagon to 335 Road Construction Coy Inspecting dry Tents.	Train Bde on to BRANDUTKE Sent 20 HD interior Pn. no 33
	25		Interview An HQ for Ordinary Works	
	26		Attended Funeral. Interview 30th Suffolk Coy	
	27		Dispatched handy transfer Capt Parker for Chiew to request for PODLOSNE Interview Bn HQ	
	28		T/Capt TW Fairbairn reported to Clerkly Kenting for attached duty	
	4		Reviewed Wagon frained B9 & 90 Bdes for bridging works	
	29		Major Knapman instructed any pre or Train	
	30		Ordinary Rotation Work. Lr Wagon to S. Transport Works	
	31		It Peer left to Report ENGLAND on leaves Pn Infantry	

EH Marske Major
Comdg 20th "Div Train

C O N F I D E N T I A L

War   Diary

of

Lieut; Col; C.M.AINSLIE D.S.O.
Commanding 30th Divisional Train.

PERIOD

1st to 30th September 1918.

Army Form C. 2118.

WAR DIARY
or
INTELLIGENCE SUMMARY.
(Erase heading not required.)

Instructions regarding War Diaries and Intelligence Summaries are contained in F. S. Regs., Part II. and the Staff Manual respectively. Title pages will be prepared in manuscript.

Place	Date	Hour	Summary of Events and Information	Remarks and references to Appendices
DANOUTRE	1-9-17		Interview Brig. Gen 9th & 5 S Wagons to Bgd Ryle for review. Attended Rifle Mtg & Millerod	
	2			
	3		Ordinary routine work.	
	4		Inspected No 3, 2, 4 Coys.	
	5		Inspected No 1, 3, 2 Coys. Interview D.D.V.S.	
	6		Interview Bn Opp 9th Div. 7 D.A.D.V.S.	
	7		Horses of No 2 Coy shipped. No presentative for many returned 3 S.S. Wagons to 17 Additional Reserve Pk R.E. work.	
			IX Corp	
	8		Returned Capt BLYTHE for duty with 89th Bty in Supply Offr also there.	
	9		Capt BLYTHE transferred to new Interview Brig. Gen. Inspected 14 June Tpt on work. Returned 10 further S.S Wagons to IX Corp work.	
	10			
	11		49th Div A.S.C. attached for rations. Attended Presentation of Interview Brig. Gen O.C.	
	12		Ordinary routine work.	
	13		1st Canadian Res. Park Section of S.S Wagon attached for Corps work.	
	14		Interview Brig. Gen 9th & O.C. See Bio Coy M.	
	15		Adjt. Attended Funeral of my behalf of Pioneer transport interview Bn Railhead moving to BAILLEUL, Z.E.	

#353 Wt. W2544/1454 700,000 5/15 D.D. & L. Gp A.D.S.S. Forms/C. 2118.

Army Form C. 2118.

WAR DIARY
or
INTELLIGENCE SUMMARY.
(Erase heading not required.)

Instructions regarding War Diaries and Intelligence Summaries are contained in F. S. Regs., Part II. and the Staff Manual respectively. Title pages will be prepared in manuscript.

Place	Date	Hour	Summary of Events and Information	Remarks and references to Appendices
JANOUTRE	17/9/17		Interview R.S.O. BRULOOZE re clearing Railhead by horse Tpt.	
	18		Making detailed visit at Railhead.	
	19		Inspected No. 1 Coy. attended refilling. Interview OC 1st Canadian Reserved Park. Detailed 47 F. Sn. wagons to IX Corps. work Co.	
	20		Interview Sen. Sup. Offr. 9th attending Railhead. Cleared BRULOOZE Railhead by horse Tpt. refilled also at Railhead.	
	21		Interview Sen. Sup. Offr. Div. & c.	
	22		Attended Railhead. Inspected transport.	
	23		7 Lt. SWANSTON proceeded to ENGLAND for change to Infantry	
	24		Interview Div. Sup. Offr. re relief into war	
	25		Made arrangements to clear Railhead HAEGEDORNE	
	26		Interview with R.S.O.	
	27		Conference Div. HQ Q re Supplies &c with Staff Capt. Capt. REDMAN replied for stores. Inspected 1st Line Transport 89th Inf. Bde.	
	28		104 Bde R.F.A. attached for rations attended Railhead. Selected rifles hands in exchange of arms inspected 1st line Transport 21st Bde	
	29		attended Railhead. Inspected interchange of Ft. transport at Wk. Inspected 1st line Transport 90th Inf. Bde.	
	30		Die man Wounded during month. Interview OC Sup. Col.	

Th. Mauleh, H. Col.
Major SR DA [illeg.]

CONFIDENTIAL

War   Diary
     of

Lieut; Col C.M.Ainslie D.S.O.
From ;- October 1st 1917
To ;-   October 8th 1917.

     and of
Major L.Knapman A.S.C.
From ;- October 9th 1917
To ;-   October 31st 1917

Army Form C. 2118.

WAR DIARY
or
INTELLIGENCE SUMMARY.

(Erase heading not required.)

Instructions regarding War Diaries and Intelligence Summaries are contained in F. S. Regs., Part II. and the Staff Manual respectively. Title pages will be prepared in manuscript.

Place	Date	Hour	Summary of Events and Information	Remarks and references to Appendices
BANOUTRE	1917 Oct 1st		Interview with Hd Qrs attended Routhead	
	2nd		Inspected horses in 2, 3 & 4 Coy Lines	
	3rd		Committee remounts to Fd Amb & issued same	
	4th		S.S.O attended VIII Corps Conference. Pret P.M. & Hd Qr Os Committee Charges the the Railhead & issued remounts	
	5th		Inspected horses in No 1 Coy Lines Veterinary Routine Work	
	6th		2nd Lt Bellamy admitted hospital & evacuated	
	7th		Interview with Hd Qrs attended Routhead	
	8th		Handed over to Major KNAPMAN & proceeded on leave	
	9th		[signature]	

4353 Wt. W3544/1454 700,000 5/15 D. D. & L. A.D.S.S./Forms/C. 2118.

Army Form C. 2118.

WAR DIARY
or
INTELLIGENCE SUMMARY.
(Erase heading not required.)

Instructions regarding War Diaries and Intelligence Summaries are contained in F. S. Regs., Part II. and the Staff Manual respectively. Title pages will be prepared in manuscript.

Place	Date 1917	Hour	Summary of Events and Information	Remarks and references to Appendices
DRANOUTRE	6/October 8		Took over command from Lt. Col. CM. AINSLIE D.S.O. proceeding on one month's leave to ENGLAND. Handed over command not to Capt Col. PARKER. Capt. R.E. PORTER proceeds on two days leave to EMPLITO. Capt T.W. JACKSON came to A.D.r. Hqrs asking to assist nursing wife at Ostend. Left during down at recover. 2nd Lt. J.H. BARRY posted for H.Qrs (2) & all Byrnes Artillery Bdes.	
	9th		Visited Railhead Loading in Progress out BHM. Interview with 5th Hqrs A.C.P.E.	
	10th		Left Railhead at 11 am. Trade arrangements for all Between Boxes at Danoutre. Some issues to the Artillery tramways. Detrainments at Railhead. Visited 2nd Hqrs Bgd P.D.T. R.A.	
	11th		Left Railhead. Visited 2nd Troops Artillery Park & 2nd Hqrs.	
	12th		Interview with 2nd Hqrs (2) & CRE Ref to No 16 Lost 2 Submarine with Col Mackworth.	
	13th		One Horse Transport Engr from No 1 Bg reported to A.P.M. Poperinghe. Train Col Supplied Country Issue enough by Trau. Col.	
	14th		to see off Chayette on Payment were Capt J.H.B. & CRE on Capt T.W. JACKSON command Artis on Payment sees Capt J.H.B. & CRE on ten days leave to ENGLAND. Capt MITCHELL to BOULOGNE on tour for ten days leave to ENGLAND. ENGLAND on same.	

Army Form C. 2118.

WAR DIARY
or
INTELLIGENCE SUMMARY.
(Erase heading not required.)

Instructions regarding War Diaries and Intelligence Summaries are contained in F. S. Regs., Part II. and the Staff Manual respectively. Title pages will be prepared in manuscript.

Place	Date 1917	Hour	Summary of Events and Information	Remarks and references to Appendices
DANOUTRE	Oct 15	11.16	Interview with Div H.Q. Inspected Company Wagon Lines	
	16		" C.R.E. ref improvement of Lines	
	17		Visited Railhead & Div H.Q.	
			18th (Kings Liverpool) Batt. LIVERPOOL Bde and 17 Bn MANCHESTER Bn transferred 6	
			II ANZAC Corps Bayonne telegraphy re "Have sent"	
			"Sent them with fifteen horses. Vessel to E.T.O.E."	
	18		Inspected all Town transport or Platoons of Great H.Q. 2nd IN.H.3 & 5 returned from Base.	
			Visited Nº 6 Encamp Inspected Horse Lines	
	19		91st Brigade relieve 90th Bde as the nine Firms of Albany	
			Each Town altered accordingly	
			Interview with Div H.Q.	
	20		" Commenced " Several postern Frost Distillery	
	21		" " 2 Lt C.J. FROST reported for instruction re Forage	
			do Allowed Wanting a	
	22		do do Capt. C.L. PARKER with ENGLAND to report	
	23		do do To Nº 2 Infantry School BEDFORD	
			Vehicle Transport Lines & Railway Pont. Half Company	
	24		Allowed Rail Hd & Interview with C.R.E. re Camps	
			Overstepping of all Horses Clipped started	

Army Form C. 2118.

WAR DIARY
or
INTELLIGENCE SUMMARY.
(Erase heading not required.)

Instructions regarding War Diaries and Intelligence Summaries are contained in F. S. Regs., Part II and the Staff Manual respectively. Title pages will be prepared in manuscript.

Place	Date	Hour	Summary of Events and Information	Remarks and references to Appendices
DAINOUTRE	6.4.25		Offices at Rail H'a & visited ref Billy Beront	
	26		Interview with Out Posts. Capt. J.A. BARRY returned from 10 days leave.	
	27	do	Capt. T.W. Jackson assumed command of No 2 Coy.	
	28	do	Inspected New Billeting Ponds under construction.	
	29	do	Capt. H.M. HINDE proceeded on 10 days leave ONGESSINO	
	do	do	Capt. R? REDMAN assumed command of No 3 Coy.	
	do	do	Visited Rail H'a & Billeting Ponds	
	30	do	Inspected all by Posts & Redmans' Interview with CRE	
	do	do	re improvements to Camps	
	31	do	Capt. J.C. ME1305 reported for duty from Base Depot to W.I.Co.	
			Total Casualties for 04/25	
			O. Rank. Wounded 2	
			Horses Killed 1	
			do. Wounded 2	
			Mules destroyed Nil	

E.H. Egmore
Major R.E.
Commanding 3? [?] Train

1st December 1917.

CONFIDENTIAL.

WAR DIARY.

of

LIEUTENANT COLONEL C. M. AINSLIE D.S.O.

30th DIVISIONAL TRAIN.

PERIOD:- From 1st November 1917 to 30th November 1917.

WAR DIARY
or
INTELLIGENCE SUMMARY

Army Form C. 2118.

(Erase heading not required.)

Instructions regarding War Diaries and Intelligence Summaries are contained in F. S. Regs., Part II. and the Staff Manual respectively. Title pages will be prepared in manuscript.

Place	Date	Hour	Summary of Events and Information	Remarks and references to Appendices
DAINCOURT	Nov 1st		Interview with Sir H.Q. Inspected No 1 D. Lines. Arrangements made for Pack Transport Scheme. Formed Class of Instruction for Pack Loading Horses.	
"	2nd		Attended Roll Call of Vehicles at Refilling Points.	
"	3		" " " re Salvage of numbers on the event of an advance. 2nd Lieut E. Ware reported from Reserve Army.	
"	4		Routine Work —	
"	5		Inspected 1st Line Transport of 21st Brigade.	
"	6		Visited Railhead + Refilling Points.	
"	7		" " " Pack Transport. Supplied Supply Lorries.	
"	7½		Sir H.Q Drs. Arranged for the Supply + Baggage Wagons of 19th Kings + 18th Manchesters to report for move. Visited Rail Head + Refilling Points.	
"	9th		Sir H.Q. Inspected 89th Brigade 1st Line Transport. Supply + Baggage Wagons of 11th South Lancs (Pioneers) were seed out + reverts to Store.	
"	10th		Sir H.Q. Drs. Visited New Creek Brigade Refilling Points + Camps for the Horse Brigade Co. Handed over to Lieut Col AINSLIE DSO on his return from leave.	

Army Form C. 2118.

WAR DIARY
or
INTELLIGENCE SUMMARY.
(Erase heading not required.)

Instructions regarding War Diaries and Intelligence Summaries are contained in F.S. Regs., Part II. and the Staff Manual respectively. Title, pages will be prepared in manuscript.

Place	Date 1917	Hour	Summary of Events and Information	Remarks and references to Appendices
DRANOUTRE	Nov 11		Followed Div Hd Qrs. No 3 Coy moved to STRAZEELE with 90th Inf Bde	
	12		Fine weather. Cmdt. No 21 & 89th Inf Bdes. Inspected No 3 Coy horses & vehicles.	
	13		Interview DS Int Ors. Inspected horses No 1 Coy.	
	14		No 3 Coy moved to K.34c.53 Sheet 27. 14/9 Coy. RFA moved to METEREN. Train waggons attached to Batteries until completion of move. Arty attached to 5th Australian Div.	
	15		Railhead changed to WIPPENHOECK. No 4 Coy moved with 21st Inf Bde to STEENVOORDE. Interview with DDS.	
	16		No 2 Coy moved with Div Inf Bde to STEENVOORDE. Followed Div Hd Qrs to our new Rail Camp.	
STEENVOORDE	17		Div Hd Qrs moved to STEENVOORDE. Closed Railhead by 7H.1 – 9 delivered supplies less 3 empty Rations by 1st Zone. Interview R.S.O.	
	18		Div Hd Qrs. 6 – 7 letter Hd Qrs Railhead. Interview Divn Cmdg re more Oxen. Orders Osier Brush Supply to Type attended on finer morning.	
	19		Inspected No 38 Troops Ordnance Delivery Railhead MdW	
	20		Dry day. Inspected Supplies Brush – 7 broken Tins – bgs.	
	21		Interview with DS. 3g to Div. Two WESTOUTRE Inf Bdes also Lorries to withdrew entry from BRULOOZE Railhead.	

Army Form C. 2118.

WAR DIARY
or
INTELLIGENCE SUMMARY.
(Erase heading not required.)

Instructions regarding War Diaries and Intelligence Summaries are contained in F. S. Regs., Part II. and the Staff Manual respectively. Title pages will be prepared in manuscript.

Place	Date 1917	Hour	Summary of Events and Information	Remarks and references to Appendices
STEENVOORDE	22		Interview Div HQ re. made Supply & Tpt arrangements for Inf Bde moves	
	23		Moved No 1 Coy to M.5.c.29. Interview Asst Q 39 Div Train re billeting area.	
	24		Marched No 3 Coy to M11c3.8. Interview Div Aspt Q.I.	Sheet 28
	25		No 1 Coy church parade, on arty. Went round new area. Took over Coal dump.	
	26		No 4 Coy moved to new area. Visited No 3 & 4 Coy Tun.	
WESTOUTRE	27		Train Hd qrs moved to WESTOUTRE. No 2 Coy moved to new area. Railhead changed to DICKEBUSCH. Attended railhead & refilling.	
	28		Interview Div HQ re 2nd Army scheme. Motored Wytschaete XI Corps. Went round Refilling Points with Q. G. 39 -	
	29		Train inspected by Major General Commanding, attended Railhead	
	30th		Casualties by shell fire etc. Lt Naughton LT/C and 39 Div Train	

A5834. Wt.W4973 M687 750,000 8/16 D. D. & L. Ltd. Forms/C.2118/13.

CONFIDENTIAL.

WAR DIARY.

of

LIEUTENANT COLONEL C.M.AINSLIE D.S.O.

COMMANDING 30th DIVISIONAL TRAIN.

Period from 1st December 1917 to 31st December 1917.

WAR DIARY
or
INTELLIGENCE SUMMARY.

(Erase heading not required.)

Army Form C. 2118.

Place	Date 1917	Hour	Summary of Events and Information	Remarks and references to Appendices
NESTOOTRE	Dec. 1		S.S.O. Interview with S.D. of S.D.T. 2nd Army re new scheme of supplies and REPORTER reported to 2/11 Iny Bde as a Learner	Sheet 3g
	2		Inspected supply Dumps & Railhead with Major G.	
	3		Formal report of visit forward at H.36.C. for visits in the Line	
	4		Inspected all C.S.O. Lorries & Horses	
	5		Interview re new orgn of re new schemes	
	6		Ordinary routine work attended meeting	
	7/8		Interview	
			So far no attack has reported at D.T. link	
	9		Ordinary routine work	
	10		Attended meeting & rifle mtg at forward dumps	
	11		Inspected all new force Dumps	
			Interview Bds Hd Qrs re chances of unloading & clearing	
			Coal arriving in Broken wagons to limit unit generally	
	12		Ordinary routine work.	
	13		Interview Bde Hd Qrs Inspected supplies	
	14		Recd Reports from CRA & Dr Somme & arranged same	
	15		Attended Relieved & forward dumps	
	16		2nd Lt. Mc Manners reported for duty from Base. Have got the usual	Ref 5
	17		Ordinary Routine work	

Army Form C. 2118.

WAR DIARY
or
INTELLIGENCE SUMMARY.
(Erase heading not required.)

Instructions regarding War Diaries and Intelligence Summaries are contained in F. S. Regs., Part II. and the Staff Manual respectively. Title pages will be prepared in manuscript.

Place	Date	Hour	Summary of Events and Information	Remarks and references to Appendices
WESTOUTRE	18/17 1916		Lt Field proceeded to join R.F.C. Bunkhurst Popm 10/6/ Capt Meiggs reported to 2nd Scout Train-7th Divty respectively	
	19		2 No 2, 3 & 4 by	
	20		Afternoon Div HqtrsO? attended Railhead	
	21		Morning visited work	
	22		Interview Div HqtrsO? attended Refilln	
	23		Capt Hunter visited ? duty of MT several of detach	
	24		Morning visited work. Visited forward dumps & railhead	
	25		Interview Div HqtrsO?	
	26		Visited railhead forward dumps	
	27		attended Railhead & refill	
	28		Interview DS Hq O? U move to new area attended forward dumps	
	29		made supply & transport arrangements for move	
	30		February work schedule filed to Deputy Direct	
	31		i c Sup GODEMAESVELDT Rgt Hqrs. BELLE CROIX. LYNDE SERCUS attended railhead & refill [signature] 31st Div Train 36a	

A.5834 Wt. W.4973/M687 750,000 8/16 D. D. & L. Ltd. Forms/C.2118/13.

CONFIDENTIAL.

WAR DIARY.

OF

LIEUTENANT.COLONEL.C.M.AINSLIE D.S.O. COMMDG.

30th DIVISIONAL TRAIN.

Period   January 1st 1918 ------------31st January 1918.

Army Form C. 2118.

WAR DIARY
or
INTELLIGENCE SUMMARY.
(Erase heading not required.)

Instructions regarding War Diaries and Intelligence Summaries are contained in F.S. Regs., Part II. and the Staff Manual respectively. Title pages will be prepared in manuscript.

Place	Date 1918	Hour	Summary of Events and Information	Remarks and references to Appendices
WESTOUTRE	1 Jan.		Interview DS HQ D.S. Issued Supply & Night arrangements for 1st & 2nd FLORBIX	
	2 "		Arrangement supplying J. Pelican DS & DS No 2 & 3 "B" Supply columns routed refilling for HO's 905, 827, 898, 1st & 2nd Divisions Birmingham	
	3 "		No 1, 3, 5 & 6 Coy moved to BLANKINGHAM area. Refilled DS for AM & IV Corps & Cav Corps & 3rd & 6th Divisions Front Line	
	5		Refilled 297, 798 hours for move to Breebreur. Interview D.S. Ostern re arriving for Res. westhead at EBLINGHAM	
	6		Refilled at EBLINGHAM. Moved Supply arrangements for move to CORBIE area. No 2 & 5 moved to BLANKINGHAM area. Closed supplies for VILLIERS BRETONNEUX. 7th 905 1904 George	
BLARINGHAM	7		Moved to BLARINGHAM area	
CORBIE	8		moved from HQ 9th to CORBIE	
	9		Interview S. Supply Col re taking over to close East Tr.	
	10		Went round refilling points. trucks short. Supply arrangements for units arriving.	
	11		Interview DS & QMG re NESLE area. Detailed 100 Blanketwagon for units	
	12		No 1 Coy move to NESLE area. visited refilling points	
	13		No 2 & 3 & 4 coy moved to new area. NESLE & ROSIERES	

A5834 Wt W4973/M687. 750,000 8/16 D.D. & L.Ltd. Forms/C.2118/13.

Army Form C. 2118.

WAR DIARY
or
INTELLIGENCE SUMMARY.
(Erase heading not required.)

Instructions regarding War Diaries and Intelligence Summaries are contained in F.S. Regs., Part II. and the Staff Manual respectively. Title pages will be prepared in manuscript.

Place	Date	Hour	Summary of Events and Information	Remarks and references to Appendices
CORBIE	14		Attended Railhead & Supply Points	
NESLE	15		Made supply & Tpt arrangements for move to ERCHEU area. MOVED TO NESLE	
	16		Attended Railhead & Relieving Div Tpt O/s re details generally	
			Re to Three Scheme	
	17		Visited all Coys. Normal interior work ROYE	
			Interim Div Tpt O/s Coys. moved forward. No 1 & 5 APP. BETT.	
	18		Tpt for moved to ERCHEU. No 2 Coy to SOLENTE No 3 & BOVERCHY	
			Hm Tpt for moved to MIDILLE VILLETTE.	
			No 4 Coy to MIDILLE VILLETTE.	
ERCHEU	19		Attended FOREST Railhead re 21st Divn Supply. remainder of	
			Division drawing from NESLE. No 1, 3 & 4 by Railway inspected	2 & 3
	20		visited NESLE Railhead. No 2 Coy previously inspected	
	21		Inspected No 1 Coy.	
	22		Interview Div Tpt O. re move to forward area. CHAUNY.	
	23		Visited new men & tried repairing Tents	
	24		Inspected No 4 & 3 Coy.	
	25		Visited new area & saw supplies changed at Railway front	
	26		No 2 3 & 4 Coy moved to APPILLY Interim Div Tpt O/s	
	27			

Army Form C. 2118.

WAR DIARY
or
INTELLIGENCE SUMMARY.
(Erase heading not required.)

Instructions regarding War Diaries and Intelligence Summaries are contained in F. S. Regs., Part II. and the Staff Manual respectively. Title pages will be prepared in manuscript.

Place	Date	Hour	Summary of Events and Information	Remarks and references to Appendices
CHAUNY	28		Main HQ Qrs moved to CHAUNY. Visited Infantry Brks	
	29		Inspected No 2 3 & 4 Coys Divn S.T.MT.C.	SHEET —
	30		Interviewed Div HQ Qrs & attended infantry	ST QUENTIN
APPILLY	31		Main HQ Qrs moved to APPILLY. Attended overhead at 11AM. Casualties for the recorded issue to enemy shell fire	
			Officers Nil	
			Men Nil	The Church 11.24
			Horses Nil	Coy. HQrs DS. Team
			Wagons Nil	

35807. W16879/M1879 500,000 3/17 R.T. (1074) Forms/W3091/3

Army Form W.3091.

Cover for Documents.

Nature of Enclosures.

War Diary of
Lt Col E.K. Ainslie D.S.O.
Cmdg. 30th Divl Train

Period: Feby 1st to Feby 28th 1918.

Notes, or Letters written.

30 D Train
Vol 28

Confidential

Army Form C. 2118.

WAR DIARY
or
INTELLIGENCE SUMMARY.
(Erase heading not required.)

Place	Date 1918	Hour	Summary of Events and Information	Remarks and references to Appendices
APPILLY	Feb 1		Interview Div Hd Qrs. Inspected No 2, 3 & 4 Coys.	
	2		Attended Railhead & refilling	
	3		Inspected No 1 Coy. Ordnance Stores WKM	
	4		Interview with Q.M. Transport Supply & Transport arrangements for move.	
			Bdrs to ERCHEU area. No 4 Coy Horses & went – they go Annex. General Train transport refd. for & cleared by a/c.	
	5		Found Horses for Div Train Railhead HAM. Palestine Draft H.Q.	
	6		Attended refilling & Railhead	
	7		Interview Div Hd Qrs & S.S.O & SR in 2 Township Hd mounted	
ERCHEU	8		No 4 Coy moved to MOILLE-VILLETTE & then Hd Q.T.L. ERCHEU. Visited No 1 Coy.	
	9		No 2 Coy moved to BEAULIEU LES FONTAINES. Interview Hd Q.T.	
	10		No 3 Coy moved to BOVERCHY Attended Railhead & visited No 1 Coy. Sent 80 H.D. horses to work for Farmers & agriculture by 160 miles from R.F.A. 2nd Yr & Anderson	
	11		Work replaced in train Parc. Drawn Hd Q.T.	
	12		Visited refilling points &	
	13		Attended Railhead & inspected No 2 & 4 Coys.	
	14		Interview Div Hd Q.T. Ordnance MM.W. 3 Coys	

Army Form C. 2118.

WAR DIARY
or
INTELLIGENCE SUMMARY.
(Erase heading not required.)

Instructions regarding War Diaries and Intelligence Summaries are contained in F. S. Regs., Part II. and the Staff Manual respectively. Title pages will be prepared in manuscript.

Place	Date	Hour	Summary of Events and Information	Remarks and references to Appendices
ERCHEU	15.		Attached Railhead NESLE to HAM (8) 21st Infantry Division visited No 4 Coy. Obtained additional 25 men to assist in unloading scheme.	
	16		Interview Div. HQ re Railway Canteen work.	
	17		Interview with American Red Cross representative re visit of the French to procuring areas for Refugees. Visited Ham & Porquet —	
	18		made necessary arrangements. Interviewed Do. 1 Coy. Returned ER/W. Major REPORTER M.C. reported for duty to OC the Div. Train.	
	19		attended conference of infantry Brigades.	
	20		Made supply & transport arrangements re motor lorries. Interview Div. HQ re Air Interview No 2, 3 & 4 Coys.	
	21			
	22		Railhead changed to VILLERS (F CHRISTOPHE). Travelled to NESLE, then moved to VILLERS-S'CHRISTOPHE by L'ETHON & No 3 Coy. to AUBIGNY attended Railhead. Railway	
PITHON	23		From HQ Coy. moved to PITHON. Nos 2 & 4 EPPEVILLE.	
	24		Visited all units. Signed ... Lt Col R^{...}	attached Railhead work

Army Form C. 2118.

WAR DIARY
or
INTELLIGENCE SUMMARY.
(Erase heading not required.)

Place	Date	Hour	Summary of Events and Information	Remarks and references to Appendices
17th DN	25th A		S.S.O. attended Conf. of Supply at 5.1.91 Jun. 31st 6.12 re C.ps. S.S. Christoph- Villers systems work	
	26 "		Visited officer points made arrangements for test delivery of supplies by stages Rly to RWO Brigade groups.	
	27		Attended withdrawal interview div HQ 3=	
	28		Rect sight Rly Jun VILLERS S. CHRISTOPHE to ENTRELLERS working Jun. ground Garry by wagon + westerlies Rghly Point to mean units to div Rgt. Genery by 1st zone supply wagon memory for westerly HQ Train taken to extract Rack Train transfer to broad 45 minute for tos buf 1925 no 4 Decamville Trucks regrouped 8. In front Assembles by Sheet Fume Zu.	sheet 52 DC

CONFIDENTIAL.

WAR DIARY.

of

Lieut. Col..C.M.AINSLIE D.S.O. Commanding

30th Divisional Train.

March 1st 1918 to March 31st 1918.

Army Form C. 2118.

WAR DIARY
or
INTELLIGENCE SUMMARY.
(Erase heading not required.)

Instructions regarding War Diaries and Intelligence Summaries are contained in F. S. Regs., Part II. and the Staff Manual respectively. Title pages will be prepared in manuscript.

Place	Date 1918	Hour	Summary of Events and Information	Remarks and references to Appendices
PITHON	MARCH 1st		Attended railhead & visited refilling points. March 29 3 40th Pet. Rly Refilling Points to AURIGNY-Frises. 2nd 2½ Pean reported for duty from Base.	
	2nd		Attended railhead. Interview 33 Div. C.S.O. re lories to clear load. Sunday. No 2 Lys. 3½ hrs.	
	3rd		Written D.A. Q.M.G. Railhead changed to HAM. New Temp. F. Reserve Supply Depot HAM. Initial rations to issue 5th Feb.	
	4th		Attended the movement of Tren. to group. F. PRICE also ? where in Zone until return of group. Lt. Knapman D.S.O.	
	5th		Attended Divl. H.Qrs. and Railhead changed to VILLERS ST. CHRISTOPHE. Visited J.R.P's	
	6th		Attended Divl H. Qr. Railhead & Dumps	
	7th		Attended Divl. H.Q. & Railhead & Dumps also D.D.S.O.T.	
	8th		Attended Divl. H.Q. Railhead & Dumps	
	9th		Attended Divl. H.Q. Railhead & Dumps. Landed over command of their to MAJOR L. KNAPMAN, D.S.O.	

A.5834 Wt. W4973/M687 750,000 8/16 D. D. & L. Ltd. Forms/C.2118/13.

Army Form C. 2118.

WAR DIARY
or
INTELLIGENCE SUMMARY.
(Erase heading not required.)

Instructions regarding War Diaries and Intelligence Summaries are contained in F.S. Regs., Part II. and the Staff Manual respectively. Title pages will be prepared in manuscript.

Place	Date	Hour	Summary of Events and Information	Remarks and references to Appendices
PITHON	March 10/3/18		Attended Raft Hd. & Visited Div. Troops & Brigade Refilling Points. Inspected No 1 Co Transport Lines. Made necessary arrangements for Transport of Manure to Team Garden Regt. Inspected Farm work in outlying Blocks on which Prs. of P. have been working as detailed in So Sir No H/4073 - 2/3/18. Interview with Div H.Q.	
	11		Interview with Div H.Q.'s, Inspected No 3 Co Transport Lines & made arrangements for payment of Cemetery & Tankage. Inspected No 1 Co H.Q. Horses. Attached the French Farm work at DURY & arranged for repair of same. Inspected work on French Farm Plots.	
	12		Interview Div Hd Qrs. Interview with Corp. & Army Agri. Advisors & French Agricultural officers regarding a level of Land at DOUCHY in several Forage groupings for Transport Animals. Arrangements made with Mayor of DOUCHY for some 50 to 100 acres of land on 20% of crop Basis & Rent. Inspected Transport Lines No 2 & Estrées at EPDEVILLE & No 4 Coy VILLE VILLETTE	
	13th		Interview with Div Hd Qrs. Inspected No 1 Co Transport Lines & Garden Party. Visited Refilling Points. Marked out Div Farm Plots for Forage growing at DOUCHY. Arranged for hire of Transport & implements for same.	
	14th		Interview with Div Hd Qrs. Visited DOUCHY Farm Plots, 24 H.O. working. Six Ploughs. Visited No 1 Co Garden Plots - Visited & Inspected Horses working on French Farm Plots at St SURPLICE, DURY, AUBIGNY, PITHON, VILLERS, ST GAURISTORNE, & DOUCHY.	

A.S834. Wt.W4973 M687. 750,000 8/16 D. D. & L. Ltd. Forms/C.2118/13.

Army Form C. 2118.

WAR DIARY
or
INTELLIGENCE SUMMARY.
(Erase heading not required.)

Instructions regarding War Diaries and Intelligence Summaries are contained in F.S. Regs., Part II. and the Staff Manual respectively. Title pages will be prepared in manuscript.

Place	Date 1918	Hour	Summary of Events and Information	Remarks and references to Appendices
PITHON	MARCH 15th		Visited Ploughing Party. Interview with Sir H.O.S. Visited Trans. Farm Plots. Seven ploughs working with teams of four H.D. in each. Inspected tractor in piggery for French Farmer. Made necessary arrangements for same if "Poppy" begins to 21st. 89th + 90th Brigades. Warning notes sent to Nos. 2, 3, 4 Coy re action to be taken in event of Main Battle Stations Wire.	
	16th		Interview with Sir H—89 Bde. Visited Nos. 2, 3, + 4 Coy Trans. + arranged meet at Transport for Brigade Baggage of the 2 Bdes to be attached to 89 Bde at HUBISNY + of No 4 Coy to No 1 Co. at VILLERS St CHRISTOPHE with further notice. Visited CO's of Agricultural officers wire of Jerusalem etc route of Inspected work in progress at Farm Blocks DOUCHY also Farm garden Plots. Pernoy. — Officers mess of Horses at No 1 Co. Lorries 22 LWDs Sir H. Ellery 241 Horses for other units including 14 H.Q. Sir Transp.	
	17th		Interview with Sir H.O.S. Visited No 1 + 3 Coys. Visited Farm Parties on Farms Villers St CHRISTOPHE — Trossattan Scheme at DOUCHY. Made arrangements to take over + cultivate garden Plots at DOUCHY + VILLERS St CHRISTOPHE.	
	18th		Interview with Sir H. Ost + Ordnance. Made arrangement for 10 Infantrymen to work in garden Plots DOUCHY + 10 for some work daily at VILLERS St CHRISTOPHE. Inspected Farm took on French + Douai Farms. Started ploughing with French Tractor on Douai Farm. Visited Nos 1 + 3 Coys + Corps agricultural officer.	
	19th		Attended Conference at Div HQrs. re posting of all H.S.E. Transport within the Corps. Visited Nos 3 + No 1 Coy of Train. Inspected work on Remel + all Garden Plots. Made arrangements with Corps + officers of garden Plots towards Adam Helps Corps Farm Scheme in reference to feed for cows ploughed at DOUCHY.	

Army Form C. 2118.

WAR DIARY
or
INTELLIGENCE SUMMARY.
(Erase heading not required.)

Place	Date 1918	Hour	Summary of Events and Information	Remarks and references to Appendices
PITHON	MARCH 20		Interview with Div. A/Q as. Arranged for Baggage Wagons to report at once to 2/1st Brigade Units. Worked Nos. 8 & 1 Bays. — Withdrawn all H.O. return on Corps except those accompanying men. 1st Corps orders — Authority asked for to withdraw all baggage wagons from Corps Cecial & H.O. Horses in hand to from front positions. Arrived over to Sir Col Arnold 85.O. orders received from him.	
ERCHEU.	21		Owing to attack by enemy Div Hd Qrs to Tren Mte 9:5 moved to ERCHEU. Worked 2 men to V. LETTE for return of troops. 2 mls. - VILLETTE. Div. Supple Tren Erchev. VILLERS ST CHRISTOPHE to Div Erchev. Div Supplies from NESLE by horse transport. Refill points with Supple Buverchy Bde Amm Erchev. Side up worked to Erchev & oil to Buverchy.	
ROIEGLISE	23		From Tren Hd Qrs retired with Div Hd Qrs to ROIEGLISE & Tren to MARGNY AUX (ERISE Supplies drawn was 11 Forecast NESLE withheld which was indicated by R.S.O. R.T.O. at Nesle. Volume of supplies were thrown round at 6 P.M. from various dumps by railhead, as exploded from being left to worry to dumped in MARGNY Supplies drawn for ROYE depot at 11 a.m. by S.S. Galleymore & Lorries dumped at MARGNY.	
HANGEST	25		Drew supplies from ROYE depot by Horse Transport at 2-am & dumped at MARGNY all B[?]C. Tren H.Q. moved to drew 11th B.C. supplied 2000 rations for ROIEGLISE. A/AMP Deumped all Baggage Wagons under I/c Capt WEBB	

A 5834 Wt. W.4973/M687 750,000 8/16 D. D. & L. Ltd. Forms/C.2118/138

Army Form C. 2118.

WAR DIARY
or
INTELLIGENCE SUMMARY.
(Erase heading not required.)

Instructions regarding War Diaries and Intelligence Summaries are contained in F. S. Regs., Part II. and the Staff Manual respectively. Title pages will be prepared in manuscript.

Place	Date 1918	Hour	Summary of Events and Information	Remarks and references to Appendices
HANGEST	MARCH 25 continued		D/KEEBLE left for base 4 + Dept. ABBEVILLE. 12 men wounded & horses killed by bombs en route & seven more wounded at BOVES.	
BRACHES	26		Train at 9 am moved to BRACHES. No 1 & MONTDIDIER 2,3,0 & 4 Coys to BRACHES. Supplies drawn from La Boissiere withdrew & reached at BRACHES from Tpt Rbts. Supplies drawn for Coys & Groups 2 3 & 4 Coys at. At 11. P.M. marched	
AILLY SUR NOYE	27		AILLY SUR NOYE. Train at 9 am marched to AILLY SUR NOYE at 7 am. Drew supplies from LONGEAU railhead No 1 by present to CONTIGNY. Drew supplies from HARGICOURT Dept. No 1 by again moved in afternoon to MAILLY	
ESTREES	28		Railhead SALEUX. Infantry Point DOMARTIN. At Groups drew from HARGICOURT. Detrained at MAILLY at 2.30 & by night to HAILLES. Train H9 Gp. moved to ESTREES. SUR NOYE. Capt Jackson admitted Hospital. Nos 2,3,4 Coys moved to GRATTEPANCHE at 2 am. & No 2 Coy	
	29		moved to REDMIENCOURT at 4 P.M. Tpt Rbts amalgamated with 1 Confirmed Up. 3 Composite Rations No 3 & 4 Coys obtained at Base Horse Tpt. Depot. Railhead SALEUX	

Army Form C. 2118.

WAR DIARY
or
INTELLIGENCE SUMMARY.
(Erase heading not required.)

Place	Date	Hour	Summary of Events and Information	Remarks and references to Appendices
EST REES	1918 30 March		Railhead SALEUX & trucked at REMIENCOURT. No 3 D & Coy move to AILLY SUR SOMME en route to ABBEVILLE. No 2 by horse drawn transport. 1st line transport to PISSY. Tm Hd Qts moved to ST VALERIE SUR SOMME.	
ST VALERIE	31		Railhead SALEUX. No 2 by rail moved to ABBEVILLE district with 1st line Tpt. No 3D & 4 by rail move more Tpt Depots, Boys'p Wagons reported held by D.W. under St Kulla. No 1 by remaining with units (mops) in forward area. Twenty Therabin cell units received their supplies daily & many other units who find mechy transpt difficult but which be shewn in spirt War Diary. Casualties 2 O.R. wounded 6 Horses killed (g. HD 3 2 riders	

[signature] H/3/
Capt 30th Div Train

CONFIDENTIAL.

WAR DIARY.

OF

LIEUTENANT. COLONEL. C.M. AINSLIE D.S.O.

Commanding 30th Divnl. Train.

April 1st 1918.   -   April 30th 1918.

Army Form C. 2118.

WAR DIARY
or
INTELLIGENCE SUMMARY.
(Erase heading not required.)

Instructions regarding War Diaries and Intelligence Summaries are contained in F.S. Regs., Part II. and the Staff Manual respectively. Title pages will be prepared in manuscript.

Place	Date	Hour	Summary of Events and Information	Remarks and references to Appendices
ST VALERY	1918 1st Sept		Attached to Tirs of Works belonging to 4th Division less Nos 3, 2, 320, 352 Div. No 2 Coy moved to VAUDRICOURT. No 3 Coy to MONS. Nos 4 Coy to RIBANVILLE. Reached St VALERY.	Sheet ABBEVILLE
	2nd		Visited Bde Coys Interim Dv HQ Q=	
	3rd		Made supply & Transport arrangement for move of 4 Inf Bdes to new areas at PROVEN.	
PROVEN	4th		Two Cos Coy moved to PROVEN. No 3 Coy to A113.89. Transport Surplus Ratios disposed of as follows. 3 to 305 D.A.C. 1 to Frenc Horse Transport Depot. 5 retained in Town to replace those lost to Italian Labour Corps. Ruitheau PESELHOEK. No 2 & 4 Coy moved to A11 at 6.9.	Sheet 28 Belgium
	5		Interim 171 Div Tren. Tour with Con and Chiens to ELVERSINGHE	
	6		Interim Dv HQ Q=	
	7		Inspected Nall Coy to new lines. Odinary routine work. Selected refilling points.	
			Rain. HQ Coy moved to ELVERDINGHE. Attended meeting to supply	
ELVERDINGHE	8th		Interim Dv HQ Q= Visited new southhead REIGERSBURG. Visited	
	9		Bde Coy Lines	

Army Form C. 2118.

WAR DIARY
or
INTELLIGENCE SUMMARY.
(Erase heading not required.)

Instructions regarding War Diaries and Intelligence Summaries are contained in F. S. Regs., Part II. and the Staff Manual respectively. Title pages will be prepared in manuscript.

Place	Date 1918	Hour	Summary of Events and Information	Remarks and references to Appendices
ELVERDINGHE	May 10th		S.S.D. Visited 2nd Army. re drawing Hay supply hard to 14 Regts. on supply Col. Arranged clearance of Pack Train by Horse Transport from 11th onwards.	
	11		Cleared Railhead by Horse Transport. Forage for REIGERSBURG. Groceries etc from PESELHOEK. Drawing of 1 day's hard in supply Column to be held in reserve.	
	12		Interview with A.T.E. Officer re Railhead by H.T. HAY for REIGERSBURG. Remainder of Pack from PESELHOEK.	
ST SIXTY	13 14 15		Train H.Q. P.H. moved to St SIXTY. New by H.T. Railway workshop unit. New supplies for arty. front for example 15th — a riging down Pack. Instructed No 3 & 4 by arty. attached to IX Corps	
	16		Attended Railhead. Arty front shew by horse. No 2 by mules with 94th Bde to BOESCHEPE area. Supply Transport wagons sent 16 miles off the Rly	
	17		Owing to hostile shelling PESELHOEK Railhead abandoned & Pack train moved to when cleared for 90th & 21 600 yards by Horse Transport. Double refill for all units	

Army Form C. 2118.

WAR DIARY
or
INTELLIGENCE SUMMARY.
(Erase heading not required.)

Instructions regarding War Diaries and Intelligence Summaries are contained in F. S. Regs., Part II. and the Staff Manual respectively. Title pages will be prepared in manuscript.

Place	Date 1918	Hour	Summary of Events and Information	Remarks and references to Appendices
St Sixty	18 April		No 2 Coy moved From to Shelters ABEELE – STEENVOORDE. Rd.	Shells
			" 3 " moved to G.11.d.5.4. Sheet 23. No 4 Coy billeted	2) 528
	19		to L.21.C.P.S. Sheet 27. Field Supplies from Roubaix (PROVEN) Lorry Pr all ranks. Adv transferred to XVII Corps. Roads refill & all ranks per horses.	
Andon ROUSEBOOM	20		Turn Hd Qrs moved to G.11.d.04. No 3 Coy wk 9th Rd Hd Qrs Staples. Transport of 21st & 50 Rde with Mob Vet moved to ELDERZEELE.	
	21		Hd Qr Coy moved to G.22.a.39, BUSSEBOOM. No 2 & 6 G.17.C.57. Sheet 23 Attended railhead PROVEN	
	22		S.S.O. interview No 3 Coy. S.O.R. transfer of horse supplies.	
	23		Interview Div Vet Qr. Inspected No. 1. 2. 3 & 4 Coy horse lines.	
	24		" 9 " " Field conference respect to LIEDENZEELE.	
			arranged transfer station.	
St SIXTE	25		Turn Hd Qr. moved to St. SIXTE. No 1 Coy to 28.20.4 No 2. 3 4 Coy Shelters moved to St. SIXTE. Interview Div Vet Qr.	

Army Form C. 2118.

WAR DIARY
or
INTELLIGENCE SUMMARY.
(Erase heading not required.)

Place	Date	Hour	Summary of Events and Information	Remarks and references to Appendices
ST SIXTE	April 26		No 2 Coy & 4 Coy moved to DIRTY BUCKET CAMP. attended PROVEN Roulers Sheet 28 Div HQ.	
	27		Sent transport wagons of 21st & 89th Inf Bdes to No 3 Coy Train at LEDERZEELE. Visited M.Loy. Cleared provisions for RENINGHELST. No 2 & 4 Coy drawing to supply moves to F 25 x 33. Supply refilling point - moved to Lt Jenter BIEZEN Sheet 27	
	28		Visited No 3 Coy at LEDERZEELE to war Head 6th Inter attended Q. Sent Supply Wagons of 200 & 201 Field Coy R.E. & 112 S. Company provisions to No 4 Coy 49th Div Train drew supplies to 90th Bde supply train WATTEN. Remainder of Div Train PROVEN	
	29		Drew supplies to Div Bns 95th Bde from ROUSBRUGGE Interview advanced Q.	
	30		attended inter Head 200 & 201 Field Coy R.E. returned to Div to 49 Div. Interview S.S.O. 21st Bdes & Sundry over DGT 21st Bdes Rations to 21st Div for returning to Lumbres & Bury Casualties	

1 O.R. UDowdal
H. Horne Fitchett ??
Capt ??
Camp 30th Div Tn

LIST OF UNITS FED OF OTHER FORMATIONS BY 30th DIVISION.

During operations
21/28 March 1918.

Unit.	Men.	Horses.	Unit.	Men.	Horses.
No.2 Traffic Control.	60	56	130 Hvy.Bty.RGA.	120	119
21st Entrenching Bn.	826		Can.Vety.Sect.	6	12
23rd " "	840		2nd Traffic Con.	12	
21st " "	826	53	"A"Spec.Coy.RE.	147	
Can.Mob.Vety.Section.	18	24	214 Siege Bty. RGA	180	
No.2 Traffic Control.	61	56	267 " " "	150	
23rd Entrenching Bn.	90		Det.29⁰ Bde RFA.	12	4
Rly.Ord.Officer.AILLY.	10		French Troops.	4000	
11th Labour Coy.	71	5	Stragglers.	350	
7th D.C.L.I. Det.	32				
2nd Can.Rly.Troops.	1100				
18th Corps Troops Con.	14				
R.O.D.R.E. No.5 Section	120				
23rd Entrenching Bn.	650	48			
19th Corps School.	100	4			
Hqrs.20th D.A.C.	50	40			
54th L.R.O.C.	22		Total:- 11,081 Men.		
130 Siege Bty.R.G.A.	120	132	1,047 Horses.		
"Y" 18th T.M.B.	22				
"F" Bty.A.A.	24				
"D"307 Bde R.F.A.	370	200			
331 Bde R.F.A.	400	200			
16th Bde R.H.A.		40			
" " " " Hqrs.	74	50			
709 Labour Coy.	203	4			

CONFIDENTIAL.

WAR DIARY.

OF

LIEUTENANT.COLONEL.C.M.AINSLIE D.S.O.

Commanding 30th Divisional Train.

Period: May.1st 1918 - May 31st 1918.

Army Form C. 2118.

WAR DIARY
or
INTELLIGENCE SUMMARY.
(Erase heading not required.)

Instructions regarding War Diaries and Intelligence Summaries are contained in F. S. Regs., Part II. and the Staff Manual respectively. Title pages will be prepared in manuscript.

Place	Date 1918	Hour	Summary of Events and Information	Remarks and references to Appendices
BROXEELE	MAY 1st		Train Hd Qrs moved to BROXEELE. Supplies arranged. 130th AT Bde formed from 39th & 21st Wks Btns from 1st 49 Div Train & detachment of No 4 Coy to 49th Train.	
	2		No 2 Coy move to LEDERZEELE. Railhead Rouxbrugge. M.4 by mule to K.17.6.7.2. Sheet 27. Interim Div HQ Qr=	
	3		Railhead 87 Divl. Res. arty. Visited No 1 & 4 Coys in present area.	
	4		Railhead WATTEN. New formation by Horse Transport. Railhead Nos 3 & 2 Coys. Interim Div HQ Qr=	
	5		148 RFA. 12th & Aux Md Gun & 1 Sect D.A.C. to 1st Division. made arrangements to transfer feeding of above for tomorrow. 1st Division. Railhead WATTEN.	
	6		Interim at 30th M T Coy. Visited refilling point. Railhead STOMER?	
	7		Interim Divl Sgd Qrs. Delivery motive work.	
	8		attended Railhead & refilling.	
	9		Made arrangements for S/o to meet 33rd American Division.	

Army Form C. 2118.

WAR DIARY
or
INTELLIGENCE SUMMARY.
(Erase heading not required.)

Place	Date	Hour	Summary of Events and Information	Remarks and references to Appendices
BROXEELE	MAY 10		S.S.O. Major Price. - Lt Keith left to report 35 American Div at E.U. Lt Kubli to take over all to arrange supply & transport duties. Lt Kubli to take over all transport from 66th Div. 2nd Lt Bell to issue to American units on arrival. S.S.O. interviewed Reserve Army at CRÉCY. 2nd Lt Ware left for CUCQ to arrange cars for concentration of 1st line Transport at 30th Div.	
	11		No. 4 by moved to LEDERZEELE between with No. 6 by. Inchester Inres. S.S.O. interviewed 35 American Quartermaster & arranged when to hold morning at WOINCOURT Southward made arrangements for 1st line Transport by road to CUCQ & for troops entraining for there.	
	12		No 2 by moved to CUCQ. S.S.O. met troops (American) arriving in E.U. area.	
	13		No 4 by moved to CUCQ	
EU	14		No 3 by entrained for BOURAINCOURT. & Train not 97 to EU	
	15		Fixed refilling points for 35th Div. Interview with 35 American Div.	
	16			

Army Form C. 2118.

WAR DIARY
or
INTELLIGENCE SUMMARY.
(Erase heading not required.)

Place	Date 1918	Hour	Summary of Events and Information	Remarks and references to Appendices
EV	May 17		attended HOINECOURT withdrawal & refilling	
	18		attended daily issue. Transport to 35 American Div. ISth't arrival. to date for ration strength 9045.	
	19		Interviews Div Mt Offr & inspected No 3 by.	
	20		attended withdrawal with S.S.O. Visited H.Q. 66 Div. & 22nd BEDFORD Regt - re their move -	
	21		Lieutenant 83rd M.T. Cpy	
	22		attended withdrawal & refilling	
	23		arranged transfer of No 25 & by's arriving on 25th from CVCP	
	24		Met No 25 & by's at RVE & sent to EV even No 4 by arrived FRIAUCOURT & No 2 by BOUVAINCOURT.	
	25		attended withdrawal & refilling. Made arrangements to meet feeding & supplying transport to the 53rd American Div.	
	26		Sent Capt MITCHELL to act as S.S.O. for 33rd American Div.	
	27		to withdraw Major Price from 35 American Div.	

Army Form C. 2118.

WAR DIARY
or
INTELLIGENCE SUMMARY.
(Erase heading not required.)

Place	Date	Hour	Summary of Events and Information	Remarks and references to Appendices
ED	July 28		No 2 Coy moved to OISEMONT. Under Capt REDMAN to attd form Coy for transport for 33 American Batt. accompanied D.A.Q.M.G. to OISEMONT to make arrangements for feeding 33rd American Bn on their arrival. Fd Kits that had arrived	
	29		No 2 Coy forming Coy at RAMBURES. Inspected supply & Interviewed with Capt Mitchell adj. S.S.O. & 33rd American Bn.	
	30		Interview with 33rd American Bn. Lieutenant Shaw Res Cart arrived	
	31		Detailed Fishers for an Res Camp. OC Coy to 33rd American Bn. Special supply trains for 33rd(57) Bn. Inspecting billets at RAMBURES	
			Casualties by enemy NIL	

Col Comdt H.Q.
Comdg 3rd Bn Div Train

CONFIDENTIAL.

WAR DIARY.

OF

LIEUTENANT. COLONEL. C.H. AINSLIE D.S.O.

COMMANDING 30TH DIVISIONAL TRAIN A.S.C.

Period: June 1st 1918 to 30th June 1918.

Army Form C. 2118.

WAR DIARY
or
INTELLIGENCE SUMMARY.
(Erase heading not required.)

Instructions regarding War Diaries and Intelligence Summaries are contained in F. S. Regs., Part II. and the Staff Manual respectively. Title pages will be prepared in manuscript.

Place	Date	Hour	Summary of Events and Information	Remarks and references to Appendices
FU	June 1918 1st		19 Gorters & Waterant reported to Transport CoY. Pr. visit to 33rd Amerin Divn Infantry HdQrs. Interview 33rd Amerin Genl. D. & ADS.	
	2		Orders to Watercart reported. Visited Railhead & party of 35th & 33rd Amerin Divns. Visited O.P.S. Wagon pr. No 33 & 44 Am 2 Coy. Pr Infantry Attached to 33 Amerin Div.	
	3		Pr Work with detached Pr M Foot Pr Tr. Interview — 35 Amerin Divn. Detached without visited Playing out & CoY. Interview 33rd Amerin Dn. & asso. No 233 & Tr. Visited 33rd Amerin Divn Attacked Railhead WOINCOURT Interview Ar Ad. Q.	
	4			
	5		Found reports pm 33rd (2) Div. at ALLERY BIENCOURT HUPPY FIUCOURT. Attended fatherness Railhead Changed to MARTAINVILLE. Pr 33rd Amerin Div attended Railhead Visited Post & checked upon	
	6		& Tr. to Amerin Div. Interview with accounts & to CoY.	

A7092). Wt. W1a839/M1294. 750,000. 1/17. D. D & L., Ltd. Forms/C2118/14.

Army Form C. 2118.

WAR DIARY
or
INTELLIGENCE SUMMARY.
(Erase heading not required.)

Instructions regarding War Diaries and Intelligence Summaries are contained in F. S. Regs., Part II. and the Staff Manual respectively. Title pages will be prepared in manuscript.

Place	Date	Hour	Summary of Events and Information	Remarks and references to Appendices
E U	7th		Unit parties to entraining station of 35(a)Div to recover 1st train to 2.5. trains & return them to Rouen. Intercom Div Hd Qrs	
	8		Move 1st line TPT to 11 Inf Batts 36(a)Div. S.S.O. supervised move at Railhead to America Div in Infantrie attached southward. Visited 33 America Div. Made supply arrangements for rest of 33(a)Div.	
	9		Intercom actg SSO 33(a)Div. attended southward & supply trains.	
	10		Railhead changed to GAMACHES. No 2 Coy moved to WOINCOURT to form TPT Pool.	
	11		No 2 Coy moved to BEAUCHAMP with TPT Pool. Intercom Div Hd Qrs. 6th to 35 (a) Div.	
	12		attended southward & supplying Tr 30 Div to 33 (a) Div).	
	13		Visited No 2, 3 & 4 Coys. Intercom Div Hd Qrs.	
	14		Attended southward & experienced move of TPT to 33rd American Div. Capt HW Morgan reported for duty from Base.	
	15		Attended supplying & visited southwards 1st.	
	16		26 G.S.Wagon reported from A.H.T. Depot ABBEVILLE to 30&33 Div. Tr. Reconstitution of Div Intercom with DC 66 & SW Train & Rwhwy offr 33rdAmerican Div.	
	17			

Army Form C. 2118.

WAR DIARY
or
INTELLIGENCE SUMMARY.
(Erase heading not required.)

Instructions regarding War Diaries and Intelligence Summaries are contained in F.S. Regs., Part II. and the Staff Manual respectively. Title pages will be prepared in manuscript.

Place	Date	Hour	Summary of Events and Information	Remarks and references to Appendices
EU	June 18		Made billeting & Tpt. arrangements for move of Div to RUE area. Interview BGMS Q'rs	
	19		Visited 2, 3 & 4 bys & attended mailhead	
	20		Tn. Hd Qrs moved to RUE 2.0.26.5 NOYELLES No 3 & 5 to HAMEL No 6 by to FROYELLES. 5th by still Pont de RUE & ARMY. Checked new mailhead at RUE	
	21		Formal Inspection No 1 Sec NOYELLES & Sikhs dinner D.Q. Buffs pay parade & moved them to Bn? Visited B/B.T Southern & Arrangements of Tpt Transpn Bus Axemen Pon ABBEVILLE etc & Mail Transpn	
	22			
	23		Div H.D. moved to CO Tooqate & attached Wheeler T & 3 Bn & Interview D.D.M.T. Q. attended mailhead	
	24		A.T.P. Miller returned to duty from Base.	
	25		Interview with A.H.T. Depot ABBEVILLE in many transport for Sec Sup B.A.C. & two wagons for Pioneers.	
	26		Found bus refilling Point in new area & road. Supply & Tpt arrangements	

Army Form C. 2118.

WAR DIARY
or
INTELLIGENCE SUMMARY.
(Erase heading not required.)

Place	Date	Hour	Summary of Events and Information	Remarks and references to Appendices
EPERLECQUES	27		From Nos 6 & 5 moved to EPERLECQUES, Nos 2 & 4 to GRAND PETITE No 3 by SERQUES & No 4 by to BLAUDED MAISON. Railhead to WATTEN	
	28		Inspected Lines & all Rifle brs attended Rainpeed	
	29		Vested hrs attended nightly intelligence Report Feb 6/3	
	30		attended meetings & reports. NOE Sc Div G. & F attached A/Q/A	
			Course held by S/M Kyser to Net	

J.L. Christie Capt
Cmg 336 M.T. Coy

Confidential

War Diary

of

Lieutenant Colonel C. M. Ainslie D.S.O.

Commdg. 30th Divn'l Train.

Period:- July 1st to 31st 1918.

Army Form C. 2118.

WAR DIARY
or
INTELLIGENCE SUMMARY.
(Erase heading not required.)

Instructions regarding War Diaries and Intelligence Summaries are contained in F. S. Regs., Part II. and the Staff Manual respectively. Title pages will be prepared in manuscript.

Place	Date	Hour	Summary of Events and Information	Remarks and references to Appendices
EPERLEQUE	1918 July 1st		Attended withdrawal & resupplying conference Des H.Q. 2nd	
	2nd		Visited refreshment posts - Stan Breakfast returns 2800 for H.Q. division	
	3		Felison - Did not go - attended medical	
	4		Boulogne - Reverend School - CALAIS with S/Sgt Sr. & drawing stores to complete division	
	5		2 Lt MILLER & SMITH to strength & posted to 3/5 DIV Train — attended medical	
	6		Attended medical & visiting posts	
	7		Handed over to Capt. Mickleson army strong places & Rich. list. Bde cmy moved to new area	
	8		Capt. Mickleson attended withdrawal & refreshing	
CASSEL	9		Train Rot Q. moved to CASSEL. No 2 by to EECKE. No 3 by St SYLVESTRE No 4 by to OEXELAERE	
	10		Capt. Mickleson attended withdrawal refreshing	
	11		Capt. Mickleson Interview Div MT O S	
	12		OC Train interviewed & A & Q took over Div supply transport. withdrawal changed to BAVINCHOVE.	
	13		Visited No 3 & No 4 by & refreshing posts, interview DADMS & OC	
	14		Attended withdrawal & resupplying conference Div HQ Q	

Army Form C. 2118.

WAR DIARY
or
INTELLIGENCE SUMMARY.
(Erase heading not required.)

Instructions regarding War Diaries and Intelligence Summaries are contained in F. S. Regs., Part II. and the Staff Manual respectively. Title pages will be prepared in manuscript.

Place	Date July	Hour	Summary of Events and Information	Remarks and references to Appendices
CASSEL	15		Inspected by Major Winter W/O	
	16		Coy joined Div. Class. Inspected by Hose Transport	
	17		2nd i/c Instructed by G.O.C. Div. attended inspection	
			11- Rh 173 63 2 Specialists	
	18		Inspection Div 15th B? attached stretcher	
	19		attended infantry Class	
	20		Horse Stand Off. Horse Lines	
	21		attended military & infantry	
	22		Winning matches with Lines out Off.	
	23		" "	
	24		" "	
	25		attended infantry & machines	
			" " Lieutenant H. Holt & Less Hughes	
	26		Bathe WDM-	
	27		attended Lectures 7th March by 19.5 Sn-groving & Carry	
	28		the Surgeon	
	29		Route WDM	
	30		Inspected by 2nd. 3 74 Lys by J U.C. Brown	
	31		"	

Confidential

War Diary

of.

Lt. Col. C.M. Ainslie D.S.O.

Comdg 30th Divisional Train

Period Aug 1st to Aug 31st 1918.

WAR DIARY
or
INTELLIGENCE SUMMARY.
(Erase heading not required.)

Army Form C. 2118.

Place	Date	Hour	Summary of Events and Information	Remarks and references to Appendices
CASSEL	[blank] 1		Standard railhead. Interview X Corps re move of D.A.F.A. Brigade	
	2		Interview Sir H.Q. O.F.A. F.A. & G.H.Q. Staff Division	
	3		Attended railhead & refilling	
	4		Interview Div M.O. re extended railhead	
	5		Inspected Corps 9 Lorries. Inspected Motor Transport A.T.& B.4.E. Regt 14th	
	6		Stationary motor W.M.	
	7		Inspected 704 Coy. Horse supply & Transport attempts to move if not into the line	
	8		Inspected No.2 & 3 Coys. Coal Barges, Horses & Issues	
	9		Interview Sir H.Q. & G.S. Inspected M.I.Coy	
	10		Moved from H.Q. & G.S. to TERDEGHEM	
TERDEGHEM	11		to 2F 14A & 6. Interview with DC 35-Div Train & SSB & no.4 Coy.	
	12		Attended Review by the Generals, the King	
	13		No.1 Coy moved to P.12 a Central attended Roadway Depoty Interview Sir H.Q. O.F. Inspected No.1 Coy Lorries Trains	

Army Form C. 2118.

WAR DIARY
or
INTELLIGENCE SUMMARY.
(Erase heading not required.)

Instructions regarding War Diaries and Intelligence Summaries are contained in F. S. Regs., Part II. and the Staff Manual respectively. Title pages will be prepared in manuscript.

Place	Date 14/18	Hour	Summary of Events and Information	Remarks and references to Appendices
FERDEGHEM	14		Attended without to visited Inf Bde hqrs.	
	15		Inspected 17th Line Transport & 21st Rifle Bgde.	
	16		Interview Br. Mr. G. Made transport arrangements to move 20 Feb. took party in view of Battle.	
	17		Attended Bricklust & refreshing hut at 9 p.m.	
	18		Ordinary routine work	
	19		Interview Br. Mr. G. Made arrangement to hMM de ma haut. Interview Col. transfer to Regt. & 25th Inf.	
	20		Attended without & refilling	
	21		Interview Br. M. G. Ordinary routine work	
	22		Attended without & refilling	
	23		Completed from weekly re/Supply Col. & to WMM Divn.	
	24		Inspected horses & cars of No. 273 Coy.	
	25		Routine DSVH attended without to refill.	
	26		" "	
	27		" "	
	28		Handed over command of Train to Major KNAPMAN DSO	

Army Form C. 2118.

WAR DIARY
or
INTELLIGENCE SUMMARY.
(Erase heading not required.)

Instructions regarding War Diaries and Intelligence Summaries are contained in F. S. Regs., Part II. and the Staff Manual respectively. Title pages will be prepared in manuscript.

Place	Date	Hour	Summary of Events and Information	Remarks and references to Appendices
TERDESBAN	29ᵗʰ		Orders re: who the NA DS. Visited No 2, 3 + 4 Sup Replenishing Points	
	30ᵗʰ		Inspection Res Col B.U. Horse Lines	
			Interview Res Col B.U. arrangements moved for Entr. transport for Operations	
			Offrs for transport of Supp Supp which was	
			Informed Sir H.E. Dn Brass arrangements for move of all Trans & to	
31			HONE BOSCH. 9+ Central thro' 11 & S.A.C. regulating point	
			Moved to Cape area — Made all possible dispositions	
			made arrangements re M Transport to distribute Supplies	
			New Replenish. Points from receiving Depot	
			Moved Trans H.Q. to (D) DEWAERSVELDE	

CONFIDENTIAL.

WAR DIARY

of

Lt.Col.C.M.AINSLIE D.S.O.
Comdg.30th.Divisional Train.

Period.   September 1st. to September 30th.1918.

Army Form C. 2118.

WAR DIARY
or
INTELLIGENCE SUMMARY.
(Erase heading not required.)

Place	Date 1918	Hour	Summary of Events and Information	Remarks and references to Appendices
GODEWAERSVELDE	Sept 1st		Inspected all Train Company Transport Lines & Refilling Points. Interviewed S.C.M.O. Rouilled all Transport in in good order. R.E. Train H.Q. 23 MM. C-GODEWAER (A)	
	2		Interview S.C.M. H.Q. 2nd Div. Re-mounted roads in Regard cable cups to LOCRE. Saluted Dump at GOESE EDE W.R.A.	
	3		Interview S.C.M. H.Q. 2nd Div. All Train Companies moved to BOESEGHEM and were employed refilling Depots on railhead. Reconnoitred road from GODEWAERSVELDE, BERTHEN [illegible] to ROODSKET. Roads all passable All Brigade + Divn transport moved to ROODSKET. Some transport moving towards Cassel. Will require to be put in order.	
	4		Interview S.C.M. H.Q. 2nd Div. Visited all Train Companies, inspected Transport Lines & Refilling Points	
	5		Interview S.C.M. H.Q. 2nd Div. Visited 1 Kns Transport Corps also Ammunition & M.G. + 148 Brigade H.Q.rs.	
	6		Interview S.C.M. H.Q. 2nd Div. Visited all Train Companies small memory attempts by H.T. from GODEWAERSVELDE Rail Head to 7 Inft + Bay for drawing supplies dragged from R.A. Inftry Brigade to Advd area. All Brigade Horses from R.A. Inftry Bernecked road to Advd area. Major Horse from R.A. Inftry.	
	7		Interview S.C.M. H.Q. Athenaeu Railhead. Visited all Train Coys. Train drew supplies from GODEWAERSVELDE by H.T. at 8.30 P.M. By Way sent out for ammunition 9.0 PM, for Brigade.	

Army Form C. 2118.

WAR DIARY
or
INTELLIGENCE SUMMARY.
(Erase heading not required.)

Instructions regarding War Diaries and Intelligence Summaries are contained in F. S. Regs., Part II. and the Staff Manual respectively. Title pages will be prepared in manuscript.

Place	Date	Hour	Summary of Events and Information	Remarks and references to Appendices
GODEWAERSVELDE	Sept 18a	9a	Interview Sir Ha Qrs. Visited all Train Engs & Repelling Punk.	
	"	9a	do do do Inspected Train Engs Horse Lines & Pilents	
	"	10a	do do do Visited Rest. Mt. & all Train Engs	
	"	11a	do do do Visited all Train Engs & all Repelling Punks	
	"	11a	Div Ha Qrs. Office work. Handed over to Lieut Colonel AINSLIE. D.S.O	
	"	12	on his return from further days leave	
	"	12p	Lost Wr arrangemts from 9p. Maje T Moromer D.S.O Later	
			Intocsper Div HQ OB	
	13		Inspected no 1 & 2 bys attended Parkerd	
	14		attended repelly & inspected no 3 bys.	
	15		Interview Div Adj Qr Office & Rents work	
	16		do	
	17		do	
	18		Interview & 36th Div Tram & Col. Mr attached work 75st 81st 92nd bns. Or 36th D.D. Major	

Army Form C. 2118.

WAR DIARY
or
INTELLIGENCE SUMMARY.
(Erase heading not required.)

Instructions regarding War Diaries and Intelligence Summaries are contained in F. S. Regs., Part II. and the Staff Manual respectively. Title pages will be prepared in manuscript.

Place	Date	Hour	Summary of Events and Information	Remarks and references to Appendices
GODEWAERS VELDT	Sept 19		Mission Div HQ 9th Echelon rte for water tower. Inspected new infantry points on exchange of front zone	
	20		To Div HQ coal dump for 365 Div Tren attended cinema	
	21		Interview with D Corps M.T. Off memory night work	
MONT DES CATS	22		Moved Train M Q & CRS to MONT DES CATS. attended overhead Inter Div HQ 9th Inspected Log Pares	
	23			
	24		attended infantry	
	25		" " Roadhead	
	26		Mail Supply & TSL arrangements for L day attack. JDDSOT 2nd army inspected Train Coys.	
	27		Baggage Wagon sent to all units FULLUR Div HQ 9th new supplies to ests front by M.T. " " "	
	28		moved Coys No.1 Coy to M26.c.3.6. No.2 to R17.B.9.6. No.3 Coy to M8.c. No.5 & to R 14.a 20. Refill Points.	Ref: 2,023
	29		Railhead changed to BUDERDOM. lorry by M.T.	
	30		Observation Coy Shell Fire 1 O.R Wounded	

The Churches GOD Army 30m Lt. Tun

Confidential

War Diary

of

Lieut: Col. C. M. Ainslie D.S.O.

Commanding

30th Divisional Train.

Period:- Oct. 1st to 31st Oct. 1918.

Army Form C.-2118.

WAR DIARY
or
INTELLIGENCE SUMMARY.
(Erase heading not required.)

Instructions regarding War Diaries and Intelligence Summaries are contained in F. S. Regs., Part II. and the Staff Manual respectively. Title pages will be prepared in manuscript.

Place	Date	Hour	Summary of Events and Information	Remarks and references to Appendices
MONT DES CATES	1		No 2,3,4 Coy moved to WYTSCHAETE. No.1, & 5 BAYLEUL HMLS. Railroad P1 in Coy at KENINGHELST	Sket -ch
LOCRE	2		attended withdrawl	
	3		attended withdrawl & rifle. Visited No1, 2 & 5 Cy — 2nd by attended to Izyhylt-sahdi Byffles driven off by men of 6th Brigade F.14.29 d.75. Locre stand out ce Rd Verilish Div ATTK Pos	
	4		ordinary work	
	5		attended withdrawl & rifle	
	6		Interior Ec. No 9 Coy Inspected by Genl. Interior Ec. No. 6th	
	7		No 2, 3, 4 Coy moved to N.13 d.9.5 — N.13 b N.14 a.5.d J.W. moving to change of & N.14 a.5.d J.W. moving to change of & Funeral area. 23.9gt.	
	8		attended withdrawl & rifle. Transport Wagon Lines 2.20.d.8.7	
	9		Inspected Coys & new Lines & ... 139 a F 1346	
	10		Interior Ec. No Gas resets see Ap 9 appendix route	

Army Form C. 2118.

WAR DIARY
or
INTELLIGENCE SUMMARY.
(Erase heading not required.)

Instructions regarding War Diaries and Intelligence Summaries are contained in F. S. Regs., Part II. and the Staff Manual respectively. Title pages will be prepared in manuscript.

Place	Date 15/18	Hour	Summary of Events and Information	Remarks and references to Appendices
LOCRE	Oct 11		Sent out Batty. wagons to work for Divn. Telegram B11719.	
	12		Attended Routhead & refill.	
	13		Delivery contin: work	
	14		Failure. Sen b.q. to lift reserved ammo	
	15		Attended railhead to receive 7 wagons 9 D.D.	
	16		Instructions for H.Q. to 2nd move of D.D.	
WYTSCHAETE	17 10		Twn. 7 C.g.o moved to WYTSCHAETE.	
			" Q.23 central. Sheet 28.	
RONCQ	19		Then H.Q. moved to RONCQ No.3 by to RECKEM.	
CROISE	20		" " " CROISE No. 1 by to M.27.13.14. No.3 & 4 by S-t	
			ROLLEGHEM. Interm. Divn H.Q. Received orders 25 H.E. AH.18.AR	
ADREKE	21		Then H.Q. moved to AELBEKE. Conference as to Greates. y	
	22		Feed of refugee civilians	Sheet 29
			No. 2 by moved to RUDDERVOORDE. No. 3 by T/14 d 9.5 Kur 29	
			No. 4 by to T. 5 c. 80 Evacuated 60 civilians to HALLUIN T	
			Issued item with 3 days supplies	
	23		Interm. Divn H.Q. 9th Trust Reg't Brgd 9th New Zealand Inf. Bgde	
			H.Q. Army Established with 9th Inf. Bgde	

Army Form C. 2118.

WAR DIARY
or
INTELLIGENCE SUMMARY.
(Erase heading not required.)

Place	Date 1918	Hour	Summary of Events and Information	Remarks and references to Appendices
AELBEKE	Oct 24		Attended Conference & inspected Waterworks. Kept supplies & stores & strong escort passing up to the Lines. Rustmed heavy rain all day lead to difficulties from surfaced supplies were sent to Division Dumps. The casualties	Sheet 29
	25		Established & troops in the area.	
	26		Visited all corps & supply	
	27		Interviewed G.1 Q. for fresh returns to be made	
	28		" " routes near G.1	
	29		Ordinary routine work.	
	30		Railhead changed to MENIN. Attended conference & inspected supply arranged that supplies from Railhead to Dumps & Rear either in Buffs lights Coal or Ten wagon Teams or advanced to small dumps.	
	31		Interviewed A.D.M.S. re ordering rations and casualties & Sintotrive Nil	

F.S. Maughan Lt Col
Comdg 30th Div Train

CONFIDENTIAL.

WAR DIARY.

OF

Lt.COL.C.M.AINSLIE.D.S.O.

COMMANDING

30th.DIVISIONAL TRAIN.

PERIOD.   1st.NOVEMBER TO 30th.NOVEMBER.1918.

Army Form C. 2118.

WAR DIARY
or
INTELLIGENCE SUMMARY.
(Erase heading not required.)

Place	Date	Hour	Summary of Events and Information	Remarks and references to Appendices
AELBEKE	1.11.18		Lulu visited Div. Headquarters re portable pumps. Sent out baggage wagons & 70h Sup Coue + 2/3 Reg Pers. Visited dumps.	
"	2.11.18		Lulu visited Div Headquarters - moved ho/ M P5 29/ N.33.C.1.1. No 3 M P to RUDDERVOORDE, NO 4 M N.29.C.9.9	
"	3.11.18		Moved GOODMANS Refilling Point to N.29.C.8.1. RUDDERVOORDE. Lulu visited Div. H.P. + STEVENS S.R.P	
ROLLEGHEM.	4.11.18		Train H.P. moved to ROLLEGHEM. 29/ F.2.a. Ordinary Routine.	
"	5.11.18		Ordinary Routine.	
AELBERE	6.11.18		Changes in Div Area. Train H.P. moved to AELBERE No 2 M moved to N.20.b.4.4. No 3 M mored to M.22 Ant Supply refilling Points moved as follows- STEVENS AELBERE CURRIES N.29.C.8.1.	
"	7.11.18		Ordinary Routine	
"	8.11.18		Lulu visited Div H.P. - re drawing from Railhead by M.T. - all baggage wagons returned to Sup - No 1 M moved to N.8 Central.	

Army Form C. 2118.

WAR DIARY
or
INTELLIGENCE SUMMARY.
(Erase heading not required.)

Instructions regarding War Diaries and Intelligence Summaries are contained in F. S. Regs., Part II. and the Staff Manual respectively. Title pages will be prepared in manuscript.

Place	Date	Hour	Summary of Events and Information	Remarks and references to Appendices
ALBERE	9.11.18	—	Railhead COURTRAI – Stew by H.T. – Stores receipt for arrival of Bn – Baggage & stores reported to Units. Moved 26/ Any H to N.20.d. 4.4. + No 3 Hy at N.29.b. R.2.	
HEESTERT	10.11.18		Railhead cleared by M.T. Train H.P. nursed to HEESTERT. 29/ P.25. – No1 Bn moved to 29/ V.7.t. 4.4 No2 Bn V.12. L.8.7. 20.3 Hy to V.8.t. 9.5 + 204 Hy to MOEN. Supply dumps in BOSSUYT – AUTRYVE Road (29 V.13, 5, 2, 2.) lulu v.n.s – Bn H.Q. in change Captn G Delving returning a Return of Arm. Nonce type Maulin by H.T.	
"	11.11.18		Owing to cessation of hostilities many experiments for B.A.C. wagons (44) to taken place at Ansk H.T. Bn. – Superintendent D.C. 30: D.A.C. Superintend by BG.S.	
"	12.11.18		Lulu viewed Bn Headquarters Railhead. SWEVEGHEM. adjoined Ruoly & No WATIPONT & superintendent changing of wagons. Cert affixed to act no Purchasing Officer 27. 7. D. G.6.	
"	13.11.18		Lulu viewed Bn Headquarters – Arranged Main Supply of transport until 15. Main Bys to moves over River	

Army Form C. 2118.

WAR DIARY
or
INTELLIGENCE SUMMARY.
(Erase heading not required.)

Instructions regarding War Diaries and Intelligence Summaries are contained in F.S. Regs., Part II. and the Staff Manual respectively. Title pages will be prepared in manuscript.

Place	Date	Hour	Summary of Events and Information	Remarks and references to Appendices
HEESTERT.	14.11.18	On 16."? inst	Subs viewed Headquarters. Visited WATRIPONT & arrangevoid Champ B Vehicles Horse supply & trains Parks arrangements for Divisional units to area S. COURTRAI.	
	15.11.18		No 3 by moved to ST ANNE. Supplies for 90th Bde dumped at ST ANNE for ensuing day. 89th Bde continued drawing Iron Rations from dumps from Supplies for 21st Bde for consumption 17. dumped at BELLEGHEM. Delivered Hard rations.	
MOUSCRON	16.11.18		No 4 Coy moved to BELLINGHE H area. Train H.Q. moved to MOUSCRON. 90th Bde Group elected MOUSCRON Railhead by M.T.	
	17.11.18		No 1 Coy Train moved to MOUSCRON. No 2 Coy moved to LUINGHE area – 21st Bde Group closed Railhead by M.T.	
	18.11.18		Inspected Div H.Q. Supplies Coys. Reducing Routine Work.	

Army Form C. 2118.

WAR DIARY
or
INTELLIGENCE SUMMARY.
(Erase heading not required.)

Instructions regarding War Diaries and Intelligence Summaries are contained in F. S. Regs., Part II. and the Staff Manual respectively. Title pages will be prepared in manuscript.

Place	Date	Hour	Summary of Events and Information	Remarks and references to Appendices
	19.11.18		Moved HQ 2 by Train to N. 24. Central. Visited Div'l Headquarters. Attended Conference (Railhead. Transferred Stabled Car to 9th Div. (East S. Washington.) Interviewed Div. H.Q. drawing Routine work	
	20.11.18			
	21.11.18		Ordinary Routine work.	
	22.11.18		"	
	23.11.18		"	
	24.11.18		Interviewed Div HQ regarding the Div'l moves to BLARINGHEM area. Much supply & Tpt arrangements	
	25.11.18		Ordinary Routine work.	
	26.11.18		Attended Railhead & S.R.B's	
	27.11.18		Baggage wagons for 89th Inf Bde joined units - Supplies for Bde cleared by train to LINSELLES	
	28.11.18		HQ 2 bn moved to LINSELLES. Inspected them. Interviewed Div H.Q. Joined 21 Bde Supplies to LINSELLES	

Army Form C. 2118.

WAR DIARY
or
INTELLIGENCE SUMMARY.
(Erase heading not required.)

Place	Date	Hour	Summary of Events and Information	Remarks and references to Appendices
HOUSCRON	29.11.18		No 2 Coy moved to ARMENTIERE. No 4 Coy moved to LINGELLES - Supplies for 90th Bde Issued to LINGELLES. Attended Railhead - Entrained as Usg.	
"	30.11.18		Railhead changed to ST ANDRE. No 2 Coy moved to ESTAIRES - No 4 Coy to ARMENTIERES area. No 3 Coy to LINGELLES.	

Casualties
Horses Nil
MEN   Nil

[signature]
Lt. Col.
OMDG. 30 DIVISIONAL TRAIN

CONFIDENTIAL.

WAR DIARY.

O F

LIEUTENANT COLONEL C.M.AINSLIE D.S.O.,

COMMANDING 30th DIVISIONAL TRAIN R. A. S. C.

PERIOD: 1st December 1918.
          31st   "   1918.

Army Form C. 2118.

WAR DIARY
or
INTELLIGENCE SUMMARY.
(Erase heading not required.)

Instructions regarding War Diaries and Intelligence
Summaries are contained in F. S. Regs., Part II.
and the Staff Manual respectively. Title pages
will be prepared in manuscript.

Place	Date	Hour	Summary of Events and Information	Remarks and references to Appendices
EBLINGHEM	1.12.18		Train H.Q. moved to EBLINGHEM. No 2 Coy to ST VENANT. No 4 Coy to ESTAIRE. No 3 Coy to ARMENTIERES area	
	2.12.18		Railhead AIRE. No 2 Coy to LYNDE – No 4 Coy to ST VENANT – No 3 Coy to ESTAIRE. No 1 Coy (Exhibty) Recce to ARMENTIERES area – Attended Railhead. Interviewed Bri'l H.Q.	
	3.12.18		No 4 Coy proceeded to BANDRINGHEM. No 3 Coy to ST VENANT. + No 1 Coy to AIRE.	
	4.12.18		AIRE Railhead cleared by M.T. with exception of 89" Bde who cleared by L.T. – No 3 Coy to BOESEGHEM.	
	5.12.18		July. 89" Bde + 21" Bde cleared Railhead by M.T. Put all Units one day's rice in supplies owing to had accommodation of R. Ponts. Attempt being made to inspect No 1, 3 + 4 Coy. – Coal Mines Rescue Duncans – Interviewed	
	6.12.18		Railhead cleared by M.T. for all Units – Interviewed Bri'l H.Q. – Supplies to L.M.	
	7.12.18		Inspected 1, 2, 3 + 4 Coys. Interviewed Bri H.Q.	

Army Form C. 2118.

WAR DIARY
or
INTELLIGENCE SUMMARY.
(Erase heading not required.)

Instructions regarding War Diaries and Intelligence Summaries are contained in F. S. Regs., Part II. and the Staff Manual respectively. Title pages will be prepared in manuscript.

Place	Date	Hour	Summary of Events and Information	Remarks and references to Appendices
	8.12.18		Ordinary Routine work.	
	9.12.18		Visited R. Head. Bde. Coys & Dumps.	
	10.12.18		Inspected M.T.04 Coy. Interviewed Brig. H.Q.	
	11.12.18		Inspected No 2 Coy. Visited Southead	
	12.12.18		No 2 Coy moved from LYNDE to SERCUS. Visited No 1 Coy	
	13.12.18		and rail head. Interviewed Div. H.Q. visited No 3.04 Coys.	
	14.12.18		General routine work.	
	15.12.18		Visited R. Head & 15th Coys	
	16.12.18		Interviewed Administrators	
	17.12.18		Attended Rail Head & Supply Refilling Points	
			Later visited Div. H.Q.	
	18.12.18		Ordinary Routine work.	
	19.12.18		Handed over command of Train to Major J. Price on proceeding on leave	
	20.12.18		Interviewed Sw Keneplanhio, inspected dumps	
			Visited Railhead	

Army Form C. 2118.

WAR DIARY
or
INTELLIGENCE SUMMARY.
(Erase heading not required.)

Instructions regarding War Diaries and Intelligence Summaries are contained in F. S. Regs., Part II. and the Staff Manual respectively. Title pages will be prepared in manuscript.

Place	Date	Hour	Summary of Events and Information	Remarks and references to Appendices
EBLINGHEM	21.12.18		Handed over command of the train to Capt P L Bamford owing to illness of Major Chapman. Capt B. Marsh assumed duties as S.S.O.	
	22.12.18		Interview with H.Q. Inspected Coy O. ordinary routine work	
	23.12.18		Ordinary Routine work	
	24.12.18		"	
	25.12.18		"	
	26.12.18		"	
	27.12.18		Our train departed for CHISLEDON area. Interviewed with H.Q. relating to speedier move.	
	28.12.18		Ordinary Routine work	
	29.12.18		Interviewed our L.H.Q. regarding supply & Tpt arrangements for train of 201 & 202 Field Coy R.E. & the Bath: S.M.B. — Received all H. Coy & G.R. points	
	30.12.18		Ordinary routine work — Attended Court Martial of 52 RICHARDSON.	
	31.12.18		Received Railhead. Ordinary Routine	

4/J.S.E. 30 am Train Capt

WAR   DIARY

of

Lieut.Col.C.M.AINSLIE. D.S.O.

Commanding 30th.Divisional Train.

For the month of January.1919.

WAR DIARY
or
INTELLIGENCE SUMMARY.

Army Form C. 2118.

Place	Date	Hour	Summary of Events and Information	Remarks and references to Appendices
BRALINGHEM	1.1.19		Interviewed Div. H.Q. re arrange for supplies transport for Units to hostel areas. Railhead closing by M.T. for 90th & 21st Brigades. Baggage & supplies for units to Train trips area & return to Train trips	
	2.1.19		Supplies for Units moving forward. COYECQUE & DELETTE & MOULLE - LEULINGHEM - attached Railhead + R.P's	
	3.1.19		Units drawing supplies from AIRE RAILHEAD for 90th & 21st Inf. Bdes. Baggage going to 88th? B.de drawn Units. Inspected Units attended Railhead	
	4.1.19		Handed over command to CAPT. CLEU Awaiting S.S.O.	
	5.1.19		Interviewed Div. H.Q. re Inspect No. 1, 2, 3 & 4 A.S.C.	

Army Form C. 2118.

WAR DIARY
or
INTELLIGENCE SUMMARY.

(Erase heading not required.)

Instructions regarding War Diaries and Intelligence Summaries are contained in F. S. Regs., Part II. and the Staff Manual respectively. Title pages will be prepared in manuscript.

Place	Date	Hour	Summary of Events and Information	Remarks and references to Appendices
EBBLINGHEM	6.1.19		Ordinary Routine Work. — No 1 Coy teams inspected by Coy Comdt.	
	7.1.19		Divisional Div H.Q. — Reviewed Photos by sections inspected in rest pound	
	8.1.19		Visited Railhead. Ordinary Routine Work	
	9.1.19		No 2, 3 & 4 Coy teams inspected by O/C Coys. Visited H.Q.	
	10.1.19		Ordinary Routine Work.	
	11.1.19		Major Supply + TpT arrangements for unit to visit H.Q. K-DEVRES.	
	12.1.19		Inspected No 1, 2, 3 & 4 Coy - arranged lectures for men in AIRE	
	13.1.19		Ordinary Routine Work	
	14.1.19		2 Lieut E. WARE proceeded to No 2 Br. Group HAZE-BROUCK for examination Ontario. — No 4 Coy moved to STEENBECQUE.	

WAR DIARY
or
INTELLIGENCE SUMMARY.
(Erase heading not required.)

Army Form C. 2118.

Place	Date	Hour	Summary of Events and Information	Remarks and references to Appendices
BLARINGHEM	15.1.19		Train H.Q. moved to BLARINGHEM — lent — heind H.Q. 30 & Div Artillery —	
	16.1.19		Visited Div'l H.Q. — Oc divisery Ruritio Troops	
	17.1.19.		No 2 Coy moved to THIENNES. Visited Gribeauval Army — discussed demogratisation with D.A. & Q.M.G. — interviewed R.A.S.C. —	
	18.1.19		One Pivotal man removed — B. 2 Bn. Camps. Interviewed R.A HAZEBROUCK for demobilisation. Arranged Tpt. for move of remaining men from Indivisional D.A.D.S & T. Tpt. went in — from Corps shop. — issued with P.Q. to trainings on Up demobile detachment of trainings on Up at LA GORGE.	
	19.1.19		Lieut Taylor t. I.O.R. returned to duty. M. Camps in Corps area — onwarded expedient "10 Y" made arrangements for expedient "10 Y" lorries to Corps collecting camps — this invoiced HQ RA — Arranged with O.S. for Fifth Army to supply suitable Officer residie for demonstration office —	

Place	Date	Hour	Summary of Events and Information	Remarks and references to Appendices
BLARINGHEM	20.1.19		Despatched 107 "Y" hones & XIX Corps Collecting Camp Arques — C3 out & 110 replacements & Eye Horses — Delivered R.1.H.Q — Re-mounted LA GORGUE — Arranged with Adj. to replace horse surplusam — Interviewed H.Q. R.S.? — Arranged with Corps	
	21.1.19		Staff auxilier to examine remounts. Visited No 1, 2, 3 & 4 Coys — Visited M.T. Detachment & observed remounts appearing fairly fit & others remain in view of & S.-T. division on de-supply demands of supply division of air Trans.	
	22.1.19		Discussed with A.Q.M.G. Phage re moving of Detachment to LA GORGUE. Arranged with S.J. Fifth Army to send up Capt Pennink & Army Vet.Q as him. officer with clerk. Inter-viewed R.A.H.Q.	
	23.1.19		Capt B. MEANIN & 2 Supply details proceeded to BAILLEUL to open Railhead & D.S.O.	

Army Form C. 2118.

WAR DIARY
or
INTELLIGENCE SUMMARY.
(Erase heading not required.)

Instructions regarding War Diaries and Intelligence Summaries are contained in F. S. Regs., Part II. and the Staff Manual respectively. Title pages will be prepared in manuscript.

Place	Date	Hour	Summary of Events and Information	Remarks and references to Appendices
	23.1.19		Type written R.A.H.Q. — Received 5 allotments for demobilisation & supply details to proceed on 24.1.19.	
	24.1.19		5 supply details proceeded to No 2 B.R.V.O.R for purposes of proceeding through for demobilisation. Lieut A.S. RYDER reported for duty from HAVRE.	
	25.1.19		No 2 x 4 Arg Train moved to LAGORGUE — Interviews R.A. H.Q.	
	26.1.19		Visited No 2 x 4 Arg Train at LA GORGUE. Telephone & H.Q. + T. re demobilisation — Supplies No 1 Arg Train D.A.S. + T. Syth.	
	27.1.19		Visited No 2 + 4 Arg Train at LA GORGUE — Arg visited site re demobilisation —	
	28.1.19		Interviewed Div H.Q. — Ordinary Routine	
	29.1.19		Ordinary Routine	

Army Form C. 2118.

WAR DIARY
or
INTELLIGENCE SUMMARY.
(Erase heading not required.)

Instructions regarding War Diaries and Intelligence Summaries are contained in F. S. Regs., Part II. and the Staff Manual respectively. Title pages will be prepared in manuscript.

Place	Date	Hour	Summary of Events and Information	Remarks and references to Appendices
BLARINGHEM	30.1.19		Individual trip H.Q. R.F. — Delivery Rendezvous work	
	31.1.19		— do —	

M. Carter Lt.Col
COMDG. 30 DIVISIONAL TRAIN.

W A R D I A R Y. of LIEUT.COLONEL C.M.AINSLIE D.S.O.

Commanding 30th Divisional Train.

FEBRUARY 1919.

Army Form C. 2118.

WAR DIARY
or
INTELLIGENCE SUMMARY.
(Erase heading not required.)

Instructions regarding War Diaries and Intelligence Summaries are contained in F. S. Regs., Part II. and the Staff Manual respectively. Title pages will be prepared in manuscript.

Place	Date	Hour	Summary of Events and Information	Remarks and references to Appendices
BLARINGHEM	1.2.19		Ordinary Routine work	
	2.2.19		"	
	3.2.19		Inspected No 2 & 4 by at LA GORGUE	
	4.2.19		Inspected No 1 by — Interviewed R.T. H.Q.	
	5.2.19		Interviewed R.T. H.Q. Ordinary Routine work	
	6.2.19		Ordinary Routine work	
	7.2.19		"	
	8.2.19		Interviewed R.T.H.Q.	
	9.2.19		Ordinary Routine work	
	10.2.19.		"	
	11-2-19		"	
	12-2-19		"	
	13-2-19		"	
	14-2-19		"	Interviewed R.A.H.Q
	15-2-19		"	Interviewed R.A.H.Q at LA GORGUE
				Interviewed R.T.H.Q. Ordinary Routine work

WAR DIARY
or
INTELLIGENCE SUMMARY
(Erase heading not required.)

Army Form C. 2118.

Place	Date	Hour	Summary of Events and Information	Remarks and references to Appendices
~~No 2 Coy~~ B LADINGHEM	16.2.19		Ordinary Routine work	
	17.2.19		Supervised A.O.M & XIX Corps XX a further detachment of Hagures for salvage work.	
	18.2.19		Ordinary Routine work	
	19.2.19		Arranged for a detachment of ~~regmt~~ reserves at LA LOVIE Chateau for work under 2nd Lieut Birth. RME. 52 Return fort	
	20.2.19		34 O.R. Sappers & 1 L.G.S man 2nd Lieut Birth RME proceeded to LALOVIE via STEENVOORDE	
	21.2.19		Sc No 3 by reported 5.52 return from proxp - LA LOVIE Junrd with PADRE Chaple R A Usep. - interviewed ou step & promising womans J Farm Suspected No 1 by. & no 1 best 200 2 n.m. for at LA GORGUE	
	22.2.19		Visited R.S.O. AIRE. Ordinary Routine Work.	
	23.2.19		Visited Artillery H.Q. Leopected No 3 by Train at LA LOVIE.	
	24.2.19			
	25.2.19		Ordinary Routine work	

Army Form C. 2118.

WAR DIARY
or
INTELLIGENCE SUMMARY.
(Erase heading not required.)

Instructions regarding War Diaries and Intelligence Summaries are contained in F. S. Regs., Part II. and the Staff Manual respectively. Title pages will be prepared in manuscript.

Place	Date	Hour	Summary of Events and Information	Remarks and references to Appendices
BLARINGHEM	26.2.19		Delivering Routine Work	
	27.2.19		"	
	28.2.19		"	

28/2/19

LT. COL.
COMDG. 20 DIVISIONAL TRAIN.

WAR DIARY.

OF LIEUT.COL.G.M.AINSLIE D.S.O.

COMMANDING 30th DIVISIONAL TRAIN.

MARCH 1919.

Army Form C. 2118.

WAR DIARY
or
INTELLIGENCE SUMMARY.
(Erase heading not required.)

Instructions regarding War Diaries and Intelligence Summaries are contained in F. S. Regs., Part II. and the Staff Manual respectively. Title pages will be prepared in manuscript.

Place	Date	Hour	Summary of Events and Information	Remarks and references to Appendices
BLARINGHEM	1.3.19		Individual Rep R.A. — Headquarters Remains at LaLovie	
	2.3.19		"	
	3.3.19		"	
	4.3.19		Visited No 3 hy Train at LaLovie	
	5.3.19		Ord. ... 2orten W.M.	
	6.3.19		Proceeded No 167 L. AIRE	
	7.3.19		No 2 & 4 Gys at LaBague	
	8.3.19		Ordinary Routine Work	
	9.3.15		Inspected No 3 by at LaLovie	
	10.3.15		Made arrangements for Nos 1 No 3 & 4 Gys to NEUFCHATEL	
	11.3.19		Ordinary work	
	12.3.19		" Escheme Nos 2,5,4 Gys at "	
	13.3.19		Nos 3 & 4 Gys Inspected at AIRE en route to NEUFCHATEL	
	14.3.19		" DUVEWAPDIN "	
	15.3.19		G.S.O. proceeded to NEUFCHATEL to make further arrangements for 3 & 4 Gys. Impressed horse to NEUFCHATEL. No 2&10 Rep to Hinges	
	16.3.19		Visited Nos 3 & 4 Gys at NEUFCHATEL	

Army Form C. 2118.

WAR DIARY
or
INTELLIGENCE SUMMARY.
(Erase heading not required.)

Instructions regarding War Diaries and Intelligence Summaries are contained in F. S. Regs., Part II. and the Staff Manual respectively. Title pages will be prepared in manuscript.

Place	Date	Hour	Summary of Events and Information	Remarks and references to Appendices
BLARINGHEM	17.3.19		Visited Post No. 1 & 2 at CONDETTE	
	18.3.19		Ordinary work	
	19.3.19		Interviewed Air Coy re telephone & phone	
	20.3.19		Ordinary work	
	21.3.19		Visited No 2 Coy at LA GORGUE	
	22.3.19		Inspected No 1 Coy at AIRE	
	23.3.19		Ordinary work	
	24.3.19		2nd Coy marched to AIRE	
	25.3.19		(Titan) to go inspect to CONDETTE	
	26.3.19		Inform Spin HQ re ordinary parte work	
	27.3.19		"	
	28.3.19		"	
	29.3.19		Attached No 33 4 Coys left MRE	
	30.3.19		" No 1 & 2 Coys left MRE	

H. M. Warden Lt Col
Comdg 33rd Div Train

Headquarters,
 30th Division.

———————

              Herewith WAR DIARY of Major L.KNAPMAN D.S.O.,D.C.M.
A/Commanding 30th Divisional Train for the month of April 1919.
Kindly acknowledge receipt.

                                          [signature]
                                              Major,
4/5/19.   A/O.C.30th Divisional Train.

WAR DIARY or INTELLIGENCE SUMMARY

Army Form C. 2118

Place	Date	Hour	Summary of Events and Information	Remarks and references to Appendices
CONDETTE	1.4.19		Inspected M lines Tpt 89th Bde with A.D.V.S. Interviewed Brig A-Q	
	2.4.19		Ordinary Routine vet hos by word from AIRE. Staying OUVE-MAROEUIL	
	3.4.19		Interviewed Head vet'n. ho 2 by Arrived ho 10 Vet Hosp. NEUFCHATEL Arranged to inspect 90th Bde M lines on 5th inst.	
	4.4.19		Ordinary routine work	
	5.4.19		Inspected 90th Bde M lines Transport Arranged to send wagons to Lipsels M. CRE 98th Fld Amb. and 20th by R.E. to CADRE	
	6.4.19		Visited ho 1 by AIRE - Arranged with Adm H.T personnel temporarily attached	
	7.4.19		Interviewed Brig H.Q. ordinary routine	
	8.4.19		Total Off. Ranks & O.R. passed on leave Started from ours to May 2 rms O.B.E.	

Army Form C. 2118.

WAR DIARY
or
INTELLIGENCE SUMMARY.
(Erase heading not required.)

Instructions regarding War Diaries and Intelligence Summaries are contained in F. S. Regs., Part II. and the Staff Manual respectively. Title pages will be prepared in manuscript.

Place	Date	Hour	Summary of Events and Information	Remarks and references to Appendices
CONDETTE	9.4.19		Interviewed Div H.Q — Arranged for a force to be taken over change of H.Q by train for instructional purposes	
	10.4.19		G.O.C. 30 Div. inspected train	
	11.4.19.		Ordinary Routine work. Likes record Div H.Q	
	12.4.19.		Inspected 2.3 & 4 by Train. Arranged with H.Q. 65 Brig No 1 by Train divisional Cars "A" to attack new railway waggons to No 3 cops of NEUFCHATEL. Interviewed Div H.Q. Inspected No 2.30 H.Q —	
	13.4.19.			
	14.4.19		Interviewed Div H.Q. Arranged to inspect No 2, 3 & 4 by Train No 1010 for troop to lay Horlandois Dep.H Containeers Camp 3	

Army Form C. 2118.

WAR DIARY
or
INTELLIGENCE SUMMARY.
(Erase heading not required.)

Instructions regarding War Diaries and Intelligence Summaries are contained in F. S. Regs., Part II. and the Staff Manual respectively. Title pages will be prepared in manuscript.

Place	Date	Hour	Summary of Events and Information	Remarks and references to Appendices
CONDÉTTE	14.4.19		Greet DADVS re Mov of Horses &c	
	15.4.19		Interviewed GS HQ. & Army Routine work	
	16.4.19		Interviewed GS HQ. Received the proposal of settling two HQ. Interviewed D.A.D.T. Boulogne re de- mobilisation —	
	17.4.19		Visit to No1 AVE worn led & inspected site where their new arrangements for transit is See by arrangement of P.o & inspection being view. HQ. 10.D. north Em 6 wagons. Luncheon at Horses — Lunch in the trasfrenis & D A D T	
	18.4.19		Interviewed GS HQ. arranged to inspect Boulogne.	
	19.4.19		Interviewed GS HQ. arranged 2.15 "8th" conjon to sew. Mr letter, D.A.D.V.S. & Head Workmen W. I. line Companies	

WAR DIARY
or
INTELLIGENCE SUMMARY.

(Erase heading not required.)

Army Form C. 2118.

Place	Date	Hour	Summary of Events and Information	Remarks and references to Appendices
CONDETTE	20.4.19		Returned to Headquarters.	
	21.4.19		Inspected 1 line transport held. S. a. R. S.	
	22.4.19		Interviewed O.C. b.F. re accountancy. Interviewed O.C. 17.G. Conf. re DANNES	
	23.4.19		Inspected 21 line cab D.A.D.L.S	
	24.4.19		Interviewed O.C. Headquarters. Visited 10/hy A.S.C.	
	25.4.19		At conference on O.C. S.T. Boulogne wharf. Interviewed D.A.D.	
	26.4.19		Interviewed O.C. base horses.	
	27.4.19		Interviewed O.C. H.q. Conveying Boulogne wharf	

Army Form C. 2118.

WAR DIARY
or
INTELLIGENCE SUMMARY.
(Erase heading not required.)

Instructions regarding War Diaries and Intelligence Summaries are contained in F. S. Regs., Part II. and the Staff Manual respectively. Title pages will be prepared in manuscript.

Place	Date	Hour	Summary of Events and Information	Remarks and references to Appendices
CORDETTE	28.4.19		Relief carried out by 2/5th R.F. Battn.	
	29.4.19		" Held by 2, 5th by.	
	30.4.19		" of B.E.D.F. Vanstopel	

30.4.19.

Knyforien
Major
O/C 30th Res Brn.

Headquarters,
30th Division.

          Herewith War Diary of Lieut.Colonel C.M.AINSLIE
D.S.O. for the month of May 1918.
          Kindly acknowledge receipt. to OC No 4 Coy. Train

                                            Lieut.Colonel.
27/5/18.   Commanding 30th Divisional Train.

CR1288

WAR DIARY OF

LIEUT. COLONEL C. M. AINSLIE D.S.O.

FOR THE MONTH OF MAY 1919.

Army Form C. 2118.

WAR DIARY
or
INTELLIGENCE SUMMARY.
(Erase heading not required.)

Instructions regarding War Diaries and Intelligence Summaries are contained in F. S. Regs., Part II. and the Staff Manual respectively. Title pages will be prepared in manuscript.

Place	Date	Hour	Summary of Events and Information	Remarks and references to Appendices
CONDETTE	1 May/19		Interviews with Dir. Hos. G. Inspected No 2, 3 & 4 Boy	
	2. "		Visited No 1 Coy AIRE. " " " to I.A.D.T. Boulogne	
	3. "		Inspected Lines + Billets of No 3 Coy at St OMER. Interviewed with DADT BOULOGNE	
	4. "		Routine Office work.	
	5. "		Interview with the D.D.T. Re Cush Bureau + Coy Bureau. Obtained forms referred to by G.O.C. Troops to draw to D.A.D.T. Proceeded Casne Road + Lent + Aux Bois Boulogne.	
	6. "		Interview with DDT M.D. - Discussed re men for S.Coy to ST OMER for breakfast business. Returned p.m. + to HQ.	
	7. "		Interview cont'd DD M.D. Return re No 1 + No 2. to A.B. to Batte. Left for breakfast 9 a.m. Proceeded to care + G. M.E.R. Visited No 2 + No 3 + No 3 Coy more to St OMER Buglers + WO. Replied to Nº 1 & Nº 3 Co. are + Nº 3 Coy more to St OMER Arranged + Nº 1 Coy Arranged for Engineer personnel by S. Coy. Inspected Lines + Off. + WOs Cess H.T. Sect of A.B.E.W.T.	

Army Form C. 2118.

WAR DIARY
or
INTELLIGENCE SUMMARY.
(Erase heading not required.)

Instructions regarding War Diaries and Intelligence Summaries are contained in F.S. Regs., Part II. and the Staff Manual respectively. Title pages will be prepared in manuscript.

Place	Date	Hour	Summary of Events and Information	Remarks and references to Appendices
LOMBETTE	Aug 8/19		Interview with DDMS & first visited No 7 Br Units. No 3 B.S.R reported for duty at ST OMER. Horse ambulance commenced training by Lt Col Kerr's ADS	
"	9			
"	10		Inspected No 2 & 4 Coys at DANNES.	
"	11		" No. 3 Coy at St. Omer.	
"	12		" " 1 Coy at AIRE.	
			Interview Div H.Q. 9. re break up of Train M. 9s	
	13		Interview with D.A.D.T. Northern re No 1 Cy Train up Spr — Calne Strength	
	14		ordinary routine work.	
	15		Visited No 2 & 4 Coys. Afternoon D A.D.T. Dr. Wg's	
	16		ordinary routine work	
	17		visited No 3 Cy at ST OMER	
	18		" " 1 " AIRE	

Army Form C. 2118.

WAR DIARY
or
INTELLIGENCE SUMMARY.
(Erase heading not required.)

Instructions regarding War Diaries and Intelligence Summaries are contained in F. S. Regs., Part II. and the Staff Manual respectively. Title pages will be prepared in manuscript.

Place	Date	Hour	Summary of Events and Information	Remarks and references to Appendices
CONDETTE	MAY 19		Taken over from M₄ 68 ᵗ No 4 Coy.	
	20		Routine work	
	21		Arranged transport Draft of 9 OR's + 345 OR's to Infantry Base Depots + received orders to send Acting S/Sergeant Parkhouse + Pioneer Pte Arens of Authority 18916 BP Base D.d.g.g. Ahd 7ᵗʰ Inst	
	22		Inoculated party assembled & proceeded to the 26 Coy Inf.	
	23		Interview Sr Mʲᵈ Gᵒ Inspector No. 23 + Coy Inf the last time. Checked stores-Physical Education	
	24		Inspection No. 3 by Gʲ Officer	
	25		" 1 "	
	26		Closed all records + despatched same	
	27		departed to report to Units at 1500 offices Authority G.H.Q.	

90/ASC/23036 dated 7.5.19
[signature] H/Lt Col
OiC 305 Div Train